Charming Charlbury,
its Nine Hamlets
and Chipping Norton

John Kibble and his wife, Florence, photographed about 1950

Charming Charlbury,

its Nine Hamlets and Chipping Norton

John Kibble

Including:

Charlbury and its Nine Hamlets

and

Charming Charlbury

The Wychwood Press

A royalty on each copy sold is paid to the Victoria History of Oxfordshire Appeal

The advertisements in this book are reproduced from the originals in *Charlbury and its Nine Hamlets* (1927), *Wychwood Forest and its Border Places* (1928) and *Charming Charlbury* (1930)

ISBN   1 902279 05 0

Charlbury and its Nine Hamlets, first published 1927
Charming Charlbury, first published 1930
This edition first published 1999 by
The Wychwood Press
An imprint of Jon Carpenter Publishing
2 The Spendlove Centre, Charlbury OX7 3PQ
Printed in Bristol by J W Arrowsmith Ltd
Cover printed by KMS Litho, Hook Norton

Charlbury and its Nine Hamlets

Chadlington, Chilson, Coate, Fawler, Finstock,
Pudlicote, Shorthampton, Tappewell, and Walcot,
with Spelsbury

Contents

Introduction

Some years ago the late Miss Pumphry said to me, 'Have you ever put down in writing the things of interest you know about this district? You take my advice, get a manuscript book and write it down.' I have always found it wise to listen to a good woman's advice, even if, alas, I have failed in carrying it out, but in this case I did get a book and tried to put in black and white such as I knew.

'A history of Charlbury', some have said to me, and at once my unfitness for such a work presented itself.

I believe many advantages beyond what have fallen to the share of some of my fellows have come my way, kind friends with information and knowledge, some with vast learning, access to books here and at Oxford, objects of interest I have seen, and some that I possess, and I owe much to my late father, his knowledge and information, the things he told me, facts, incidents, ideas, what he had seen, and what others had told him. I think what helped to make him the man he was, beyond school and the field, and nature, was that my grandfather received weekly through the post *Jackson's Oxford Journal*. I do not believe anyone else had it in Finstock in those days, also there were some books in the house, especially a big vast dictionary, and these sources of information to a boy with an alert mind meant very much in our obscure village as Finstock was then when books were scarce and expensive.

To all who have given me information and help I give my best thanks, and trust they will feel they have helped to gather up and store what perhaps in some cases would have been lost as the years roll on.

Once I had the privilege to be present years ago in the strangers' gallery in the House of Commons on a rather notable occasion, and as I listened to the speeches one thing struck me and remains, that was the constant reference made to 'the man in the cottage'. It was so very pleasant to know that the thought of the folk in humble life was in their minds and on their lips as they debated the momentous affairs of our great nation.

I have written for the cottage people who would like to know something of the place in which they live. Information may be, and is, available to those who are able to consult authorities at Oxford and elsewhere, but not easy for the man in the street. Long ago for instance men of research and learning could say, 'Yes, Fawler once had a Church and a Monastery,' but who amongst working people could get to know anything about these interesting facts? I believe the thoughts and feelings of so called rustic minds are worthy of regard and attention, the poet Gray has well put in his Elegy:—

> 'Let not ambition mock their useful toil,
> Their homely joys and destiny obscure;
> Nor grandeur hear with a disdainful smile
> The short and simple annals of the poor."

The records or 'Cartularies of Eynsham Abbey' printed by the Oxford Historical Society in 1907 are a mine of information and these quote earlier charters.

In a parish, as in a kingdom, a few names stand out, and are recorded, and through them and their doings we get glimpses of those that were about them. Looking over records of olden days we see they were men like ourselves, walking the paths we walk, working with our tools, thinking our thoughts; now and then we see them standing as we have done looking into the great deeps of life. Why? When? How? Clamouring for an answer.

Peer or peasant, we are one in our naked souls, though the years and fortune divide us. The story of our brothers interests us —

> 'Ever their phantoms arise before us,
> Our loftier brothers but one in blood,
> At bed and table they lord it over us,
> With looks of beauty, and words of love.'

One kind friend said 'Avoid the personal note', but country bred people know that in a parish we are all more or less like one big family, and when we gather in peace about the fire some winter's night and one tells a story of an adventure or an experience, all thoughts of the individual disappear, we are all in it. So with these slight records of our wonderful manor we all share who belong to it, and if others like to come in and join our circle we will not bid them nay, but they will be gentle in their judgments as we unbend and tell our tale.

Skeletons? Yes, we have them, but not for parade or curious eyes. They are in the cupboard and the key is turned.

Charlbury

Charlbury has been spelt in various ways:—

1197-1208. Churlebiry.

1238. Cherlebiry.

1274-9. Cherlebir.

1539. Chorlebury.

In a Finstock document dated 1701 it is spelt Charlebury. The name is said to signify the hill, stronghold, or town of free men.

EARLY DAYS

Many people think that when the Romans came to this land they found a race of pre-historic savages utterly ignorant of any sort of civilisation, but recent thought and research show that this was not the case.

In our parish and neighbourhood objects exist, and relics have been found, showing that for long ages men of intellect, resource, and skill were here.

Tools and weapons of the Stone Age of a high order of workmanship constantly turn up. Specimens of craftsmanship in bronze, also the numerous earthworks as Grims Dyke, testify to the same fact.

To erect Enstone Hoar Stone and place the top stone in position, about 9 feet by 8 feet by 3 feet in thickness, was no undertaking for savages!

There was a gold coinage. Tin was mined in Cornwall and a thousand years B.C. was exported. They were able to put 4,000 chariots in the field against Rome, so they must have had roads as well as a government.

Thinking of early days in this land Druidism is in our mind and from remote times this was our religion, Julius Caesar 55 B.C. found the Druids in great power and glory, showing that they had been leading in religious and other matters for many years. They are thought to have settled here from a land far away and some say to-day that they were the lost tribes of Israel.

There were Priests, Bards, Judges and Teachers. Their learning and doctrines were not put into writing but were taught in verse, and a pupil had some 20,000 verses he might learn to get a full course of instruction, which lasted in some cases for twenty years. The schools were in the depths of the forest, so Wychwood possibly had its academy.

Worship was expressed in four different ways:—

1. Songs of Praise.
2. Prayers and Supplications.
3. Offerings and Sacrifices.
4. Augury and Divination.

But after all they had some knowledge of God, and to these men, used to prayer and worship and with a firm belief in the immortality of the soul, the story of Jesus and the Cross would come to their hungry hearts; and in our land, and let us hope in our parish, there were those who rejoiced in a Saviour's love.

Some think that St. Paul in his journeyings came to our shores, and there is a story that Joseph of Arimathea came to Glastonbury and a lad who came in the ship that was come to fetch British tin from the Cornish mines was none other than the youthful Christ. It is pleasant, even if these are but tales, to know that the story of our Redemption, for certain, was in very early times proclaimed in these parts.

This part of Oxfordshire seems to have been brought under Roman rule by Aulus Plautius, a famous Roman general, and settlements were made. We were near to Akeman Street, parts of which can be traced at Coombe, Wilcote, Ramsden, etc. Villas were built, as at Northleigh, Stonesfield, and at Fawler, and all over our manor lie in the soil fragments of pottery, and Roman coins turn up in all directions, so there is no doubt Roman influence and civilisation played a big part here during the centuries we were a part of the Roman Empire.

When the Roman legions were recalled and the Anglo-Saxons over-ran the land bitter persecution set in, and our forefathers seem to have had a cruel time of it. After A.D. 582, when the desperate Britons met the invaders near Bristol, and the heathen triumphed, the depleted British tribes were reduced to the position of serfs in many parts.

The Saxon king, Penda, was no friend to Christianity, he seems to have been a champion of Paganism. His objection was, the Christians failed to live according to their teaching. He was slain in battle against Oswy. 'Paganism', says Dr Hodgkin, 'never again found a defender in arms'. His son Penda being, says Bede, 'an excellent youth, and most worthy of that title and person of king, he was by his father elevated to the throne of that nation and came to Oswy, King of the Northumbrians, requesting to have his daughter Elfleda given him to wife; but could not obtain his desires unless he would embrace the faith of Christ and be baptised, with the nation which he governed.' We were in that kingdom.

'When he heard the preaching', says Bede, 'of the truth, the promise of the heavenly kingdom, and the hope of the resurrection and future immortality, he declared that he would willingly become a Christian even though he should be refused the virgin'. He was baptised by Bishop Finian with all his earls and servants that came with him, at a village called 'At the Wall', and bringing four evangelists with him he returned home with great joy A.D. 653. The priests he brought were Cedd, and Adda, Betti, and Diuma, the last of whom was a Scot. These men were willingly listened to in these parts and many of all classes, rich and poor, were baptised daily. Diuma was made bishop of the Middle Angles, as also of the Mercians, where he died, the record says, 'in the county called Feppingum', and in a list of Saxon burying places, we read that 'St. Diuma rests in a place that is called Charlbury'. Cedda, or Chad, as treated later on, has his name yet in remembrance amongst us in the name Chadlington. He died A.D. 672.

Oxfordshire had its share in the troubles that rent the land as Dane and Saxon fought; and war, fire and pillage must have made life hard and difficult, and King Harold being slain, 1066, the crown fell to William the Conqueror, and the Normans came.

The first Bishop appointed by William was Remigius de Feschamp to the see of Dorchester, this was transferred in 1072 to Lincoln and the Cathedral there was built. He appears to have been one of the Commissioners to make the Domesday Book, and as Charlbury is not mentioned in that we were most likely returned with Banbury, to which our parish then belonged. But as such places as London, Worcester, and others were not included in that remarkable work it is not so much of a disgrace for us to have been left out. At least we have survived it.

Bishop Remigius died in 1092 and the next year William Rufus gave the see to his Chancellor, Robert Bloet, and in his day we get to know something more definite about our manor.

In 1094 or 95 Robert Bloet, Bishop of Lincoln, exchanged Charlbury to the Abbey of Eynsham for lands elsewhere. Fawler and Finstock had already been given to two of his knights. Part of Finstock belonged to the king. It was called Tappewell and was held from him by the sergeantry of guarding the wood gate when the King was at Woodstock. Robert Bloet whilst riding with the King at Woodstock in 1123 fell from his horse and died the next day. His bowels were buried at Eynsham and his body at Lincoln.

King Henry was at Cornbury in 1105 and on Christmas Day 1109 he grants a Charter which speaks of Charlbury 'whole and quiet as Bishop Robert held it, in its woods, and its meadows, and its fields, and its streams.' This charming description of our Manor is plain proof that here was not all forest, but recognised pasture land and tilled fields. Masons at this time were building the seven mile wall round Woodstock Park. Surnames came into use. The making of woollen cloth was introduced to the land, weights and measures were established, the King's arm giving the length of the yard.

Charlbury has been spoken of as 'a large and complicated parish with nine hamlets, and extending into two hundreds.'

The division of territory into hundreds is of very ancient origin, and is mentioned by Tacitus. In England the divisions are so without rule or order that it is impossible to know the principles upon which they were formed. A hundred parishes, some have thought, but this cannot be proved. Mr. A. Ballard in his book 'The Doomsday Survey' does not attempt an explanation.

Charlbury, Finstock, and Fawler were in the hundred of Banbury, whilst 'Tappewell' was in Dorchester hundred. The Bishops were allowed to attach any scattered properties. This explains why isolated places are in hundreds some distance away.

WAGES AND PRICES

All farm hands in the 13th century were paid in kind. About 1211 a farm hand was allowed 36 to 40 bushels of corn for a year, this for his bread, and beer.

In 1252 a good horse was worth 10s.; in 1288 a duck was worth a penny; in 1237 wheat made 3s. 4d. per quarter, barley 2s., oats 1s.; in 1288 an ox cost 6s. 8d., a cow 5s., a sheep 1s.; in 1309 eggs were nine a penny, a pair of shoes 4d.; in 1314 eggs were 24 a penny.

In 1288 a cart and two horses impressed by the King was paid for at 10d. a day.

In 1315-16 ale went up in price and cost twopence to fourpence per gallon.

In 1310 there were 66 tenants in Charlbury.

Eynsham Abbey Registers

We enter now on a period when definite information is to be had about our Manor from the Cartularies or Registers of Eynsham Abbey, which were written on parchment and are yet preserved. In them items and names occur which relate to our parish, bailiffs' names, amounts collected, etc. Many places of greater importance have no such details such as we can gather from these old records.

ABBEY ACCOUNTS

Names and items from the Eynsham Abbey accounts:

In 1254 the tithes of Fawler and Finstock were valued at 30s., and yet in 1291 the whole of the tithe received from Charlbury was estimated to be worth only 40s.

Fawler paid rental in 1310, £4 16s. 0d.; Finstock in 1399 paid about £4 10s. 0d.

The bailiff of Charlbury in 1354 was John Wrench (a good name for a rent collector). He entertained the servants of the Bishop of Lincoln who made visitation to our Manor, and the expenses are charged.

September 29th, 1355, John Cubbal makes his return to the Abbey. He was the Reeve of Charlbury. The Reeve collected the dues for the Lord of the Manor, heard complaints for the parishes under his care and reported to the Lord. He was one who held a plough holding. The rest of the villeins put him into the post of Reeve, and for this he was exempt from service to the Manor and got a fee of perhaps 20s. per annum as pay. The Beadle was his assistant.

John Carpenter held office in 1365.

In 1373 John Cubbylle (with another spelling to his name) collected assize rents of Charlbury and assarts of Spellsbury.

John Baldock returns accounts of Cote, Chadlington, Fawler, and Finstock, 1394.

William Poneray, 1391.

William Baugh, 1409.

William Poneray, Beadle in 1412, returns profits of the courts and woods.

James of Ramsden was Abbot at this time. He held the distinguished position from 1414–1431.

He is charged in 1419 fourpence for repairs to Charlbury Bridge which was bound to be done.

What bridge was this? Was it a timber one at the bottom of Dyer's Hill? There was no bridge but a ford and stepping stones before the present bridge was erected, about 1800, but there may have been, probably was, a wooden structure earlier.

William Weller, Beadle and woodward, 1431.

The woods of Charlbury were divided into seven parts, one portion being cut once in seven years. In 1363 it was estimated the value of produce would be worth £15 6s. 8d. Expenses each year to fence the copse were 1¼d. or 1½d. the rod.

Robert Alkerton, head forester, had a fee in 1426 and 2s. was paid to Nicholas Jeffes. The name of the piece of wood cut in 1363 was 'Vasemerequarterter', and the same name, or word, was used in 1412, so it looks as though our fore fathers could spell and use some tongue-twisters about even such common things as the name of a copse.

The number of bushels of corn received as tithes in 1431 are recorded, and I think the barn here at Pound Hill was the Reeve's barn, where it was stored, the original name in the deeds being Reeve's barn, and the wall at the upper end of the buildings now used as a stable, is one of the most ancient bits of masonry of its class in the parish. It is 2ft. 10in. in thickness, and walls for ordinary buildings have not been built anything at all so thick as that for ages. The name occurs in the field name, 'Reeves Close'.

Richard Asshe, collector of rents in Charlbury, the Vil of Coote, the Vil of Fawler and the Vil of Finstock, including a rent of *Three barbed arrows* from the tenants of Charlbury for an acre of land called 'Pleyying Place' for the year ending June 24th, 1448. This is a quaint rent for what is now called The Playing Close.

John Grey, beadle and woodward, 1448.

William Downesley, bailiff of the manor in charge of the demesne. He also accounts for the tithe corn received from Charlbury and Fawler, 1448.

William Bekyngham, farmer of the tithe corn at Pudlicote in 1448.

Thems Sercheden, ditto at Walcot.

During the 15th and 16th centuries monks and landowners found it best not to farm their own lands but to let them out to resident yeomen and squires. Thomas Sheparde, collector 1539 of Charlbury and its hamlets.

John Maynard, ditto, 1419.

John Martin in 1422.

William Drinkwater 1442.

Thomas Pauley in 1457.

In 1310 there were 66 tenants in Charlbury, and Villa de Cootes was leased to John Edwards for £2 a year.

Shorthampton is first mentioned in the Abbey accounts in 1298.

In 1269 Charlbury is described as follows:—

The Demesne is 3 hides, value £3. Vill and holds 32 virgates, and the rent and service of each are worth 5s. Two mills worth 50s. Rent of freeholders, 10s. 4d.

In 1270 the Bishop confirmed to Eynsham Abbey its tithe in Charlbury, by which it appears that the Rector of Charlbury only had his glebe to depend on in Charlbury Manor, and the tithes of Finstock and Fawler. He seems to have had the tithes of Chadlington, Shorthampton and Walcot.

In 1293 when the Rectory became vacant the Bishop ordained a Vicarage. His grant asserted that the offerings at Charlbury and Shorthampton were £12 and the tithe of hay £6, Chadlington tithe £5 6s. 8d. and £2; also he was to have 65 acres of glebe in Charlbury tithe free.

The Manor Courts used to be held in the house near to the east gate of the churchyard, but it is thought that the house to the south-west of the church now known as the Priory was the original Manor House. It has an interesting pointed doorway of very early date. A portion of this house is seen in the sketch of the Church Tower.

The Church, Charlbury

The Church of St. Mary is finely situated on the brow of the hill rising from the Evenlode valley, and visitors coming by rail or Forest Lane way must be impressed with its situation and appearance.

Our Anglo-Saxon ancestors did not at first bury their dead in towns, but on hill sides, upon open plains, or by the wayside. Before 606 this was the usual practice, so we can fancy when St. Diuma died here in 656 no doubt there were those about him with sad yet loving hearts who thought as they selected a burial place for him, 'This is just the spot, near yet well above the stream, and open to God's great heaven he has taught us to seek,' and devout and loving hands carried him to his burial. Later, near to that spot a timber church would be erected, most likely the dwellings of the people were over the hill near to the springs of water and out of the cold, piercing winds that doubtless then, as now, swept down from the North Pole, carrying off all tender weakly ones.

When the Norman came with his skill in hewing stone and building walls, a more permanent structure was begun, some of which can be seen in the square edged pillars and arch near the pulpit within the church. Here is the work of men who knew the Conqueror and William Rufus, whilst a little later the other two arches with carved capitals similar in design to some at Rochester were built; those on the opposite or south side of the aisle were built in the 13th century, as were the three arches, one of which is the chancel arch, also the arch over what is now the organ chamber.

There are some bits of carving belonging to the period, roses on one capital, and the three-lobed leaf which is such a noticeable feature of the style on another, a figure at foot of the arch label in the aisle has been disfigured at some time. It is holding a paten, or an alms dish, edgewise (to show it is empty), an idea to bear in mind when it came round to the worshippers.

There are some good corbel heads in the south aisle under the roof, cut by one who was skilled in the work. These have characteristic headgear, the chaperone being on one quaint head. At the east end of this aisle in the south corner jutting out from the wall, now covered with boarding, is what was formerly perhaps part of an altar. The niche in the wall above with corbel for a statue, and not in the centre, perhaps contained a picture or some shrine; central, over the altar, and in the south wall is a recess or locker where the utensils, wine, etc., could be placed.

In the wide aisle eastward from this is evidence of another altar; in that in the south wall is a fine piscina and cupboard with stone shelf, with arch and moulding similar in idea as the south main entrance doorway. The tower arch was for many years blocked up. The quaint wooden stairs to the ringing loft is an interesting bit of old craftsmanship in wood.

The north, or Finstock, aisle is roomy and seems bare, but at the west end a now closed-up doorway and signs of a stairway to the roof give food for thought, also a lancet window of nice proportions is in its original position, I think, and on the outside just over it can be seen in the wall where the high-pitched lean-to roof which covered the rather narrow former north aisle was placed.

In the west face of the tower a very good perpendicular doorway has been inserted, but is not now used.

In days past at a baptism, all the doors in a church were set open and the Evil One was supposed to go out by the north door, hence the term, 'Devil's door', outside which were buried unbaptised persons, suicides, and other folk about whom there seemed to be no hope. Seldom are there any tombs to be seen on that side of the church. Our north door was lost when alterations were made to this aisle, as there have been at two periods.

At some places where there is a north and south door, at a burial the body is brought in at the south door, and taken out at the north. Our Lord is expected to appear in the east, and the way of Christian burial is to put the feet that way, so as a parish clerk said to me, 'they will be just ready to stand up to meet Him'. There is a saying *re* the east wind, 'The wind of the dead men's feet'. The eastern portion of the churchyard is the place of honour, next the south, next west, last of all the north, from an old belief that in this order the dead will rise. A curious instance of this is in an epitaph on a stone at Epworth:—

'And that I might longer undisturbed abide,
I choosed to be laid on the northern side'.

The tower, built in the 13th century, surmounted by a perpendicular belfry and battlement, has been a sight of beauty and strength these many years, and has no sign of weakness; strong and unbending through all the storms that have beat upon it, gladdening the soul of the beholder, so it stands, still fulfilling the purpose for which it was built, telling of rest and forgiveness, heaven and home.

The chancel window is of the decorated period, filled with painted glass in memory of the late Rev. C. F. C. West.

The window in the adjoining aisle is somewhat similar. It has the memorial glass to the men who fell in the Great War, whose names are recorded on a tablet in the north wall.

Many stones are in the floor bearing names of former vicars, also Jenkinson, Mavot, Copeland Bateman, Harwood, Allen, Coats, etc.

'A WEEPING CHANCEL'

When Charlbury Church was built the builders expressed thoughts and ideas that speak to-day, to those that hear. The ground plan was a cross; the nave the shaft, the transepts the arms, the chancel the head. Other parts have been added and enlarged as years have passed, but the idea is there.

Our Church has another feature not so common; only to be found, it is said, in very ancient churches; that is the chancel wall turns towards the north, out of straight with the nave. A glance along the sides of the Norman pillars to the chancel gives this at once, or take your stand underneath the tower and look straight up the centre to the point of the chancel window, and it is not in the centre of the other arches. Outside it looks as though some later builders have brought the wall over, and made it 'hang', as the masons say, trying, no doubt, to bring the wall plate of the roof more on the square.

This turning towards the north is the same at Peterborough Cathedral, and is what is called a 'weeping chancel', because, so it is said, the head of the dying Saviour fell slowly over on to his shoulder towards the north, as the light went from His eyes, and as from His lips fell the words, 'Into Thy hands I commend my spirit'.

A very quaint box for freewill offerings is near the porch entrance. It was made by forming a cavity in the top of a post and covering it with an iron lid with three locks.

Another piece of church furniture was a barrel organ. That has gone, but the handle was given me by an old man who had preserved it.

Charlbury beadle's staff is in my possession. It is 5ft. 2in. in length, a neatly turned top with faded lettering surmounts it, and the foot is shod with a ferrule and a quite formidable iron spike. If this is the long stick I have been told one of my kin used to keep the lads in order with during service time not many cracks with it would be needed, especially when wielded by a stonemason, to make it a dreaded wand of rule and order.

The records state:—

'The Abbey to keep the chancel in repair and to start the Church with books, etc.

'The Vicar to pay something on the fourth Sunday in Lent to the Bishop for the Chrism with which the font was consecrated on Easter eve.'

What became of the old font? The old font at Woodstock was in someone's garden and has been returned to the church. Is ours in some cattle yard, or what became of it?

If a re-dedication of the Church was necessary, unless it was the fault of the Vicar, the Abbey was to bear the expense. In 1364 a tailor who took sanctuary in the Church was assaulted there and left half dead. Eynsham Abbey no doubt had to bear the expense of re-consecration of the Church, blood having been shed within the building.

Pulpits were not considered essential in days past. Few churches had them, and sermons were delivered from the altar steps. Not till 1603 was it ordered that the churchwardens or quest men provide 'a comely and decent pulpit'. Probably the one discarded when the present one was erected was of that period. The steps of a pulpit must be four in number because all its teaching rests upon the four gospels.

The last sermon the Rev. S. H. Russell preached he sat in a chair on the chancel steps, as he found himself too unwell to ascend the pulpit stairs.

Vicars of Charlbury

1234 Walter de St. Edmundi.

1264 Bartholomew de Newenton.

1292 Philip de Barton, resigned 1295.

1296 Richard de Benewick. Charlbury made a Vicarage, Eynsham Abbey holding the Rectory. The Black Death.

1364 John Hastings (went to Uffington), exchanged with Robert Frankelem 1364 (from Uffington).

1389 Thomas, Vicar of Charlbury.

1526 Edwardus Derby.

1539 Thomas, Chaplain of Charlbury.

1557 William Sale.

1578 Hugo Lloyd.

1593 Ralph Hutchinson (translator).

1606 Rowland Searchfield (became Bishop of Bristol, 1618–19).

1612 James Clanford.

1654 Thomas Downer (probably ejected).

1672 William Brown.

1681 Thomas Fulke.

1683 William Coles (ejected as a non-juror).

1688 John Brain.

1697 Dr. John Bradburn.

1726 Thomas Heywood, held the living 20 years.

1746 Dr. James Luck, 25 years

1771 Dr. William Seward, 19 years.

1790 Dr. John Cobb, 38 years.

1828 Dr. Thomas Silver, 25 years.

1853 W. W. Stoddart, 4 years

1857 S. H. Russell, 17 years

1874 C. F. C. West, 25 years.

1898 A. C. Smith, 5 years,

1903 J. D. Payne, who kindly supplied me with the above list of Vicars.

In 1526 a tax was paid by the Lincoln Diocese. Chadlington clergyman was Richard Mere; Spelsbury, Robert Chard.

On the wall near the pulpit in Charlbury Church is a tablet with the arms of St. John's College above it, bearing the following inscription:—

A.D. 1611—A.D. 1911.
In Memory of Dr. Ralph Hutchinson, president of St. John's
College, Oxford, Vicar of Charlbury A.D. 1593 to 1606, a
Translator of the Authorised Version of the English Bible.
This tablet was erected by the Vicar and people of Charlbury,
A.D. 1911.

An effigy of him is in St. John's College Chapel, Oxford.

It has been said that all possible pains were taken to secure the services of the best possible men as translators. Fifty were chosen, but it appears forty seven did the work. Dr. Hutchinson belonged to the sixth company, who had the Epistles as their part of the work, and after 18 months' work at translating he died January 16th, 1606.

He was a close friend of Bishop Andrews, whose schoolfellow he had been. He received King James at the gate of St. John's College in August, 1605.

He finished his long life engaged on a grand work angels might have loved to do, about which it has been said: 'The translators did not lose sight of the all-important fact that the English Bible must be a book not merely for trained scholars and theologians, but also for the common people and ordinary men'.

Our present Vicar's book, *The English Bible*, is splendid. It should be in every library. All should read it.

Dr. Rowland Searchfield, born 1565, entered Merchant Taylors School 1575, Fellow of St. John's College, Oxford, July, 1582, aged 17; B.A. October, 1586;

M.A., June, 1590; B.D. 1597; D.D. 1608. In his theses he held that 'heretics should be compelled to conform outwardly'. Appointed Proctor 1596; licensed to preach 1596. In 1601 he became Vicar of Evenly, Northampton, and Rector of Birthrop, Glos. In 1606 Vicar of Charlbury and on March 18th, 1618-19, he was elected Bishop of Bristol. He died October 11th, 1622, and was buried in the Cathedral.

His wife, Anne, by whom he had one or more sons, was the daughter of Dr. Ralph and Mary Hutchinson.

The stone over his grave was subsequently removed to make room for the communion table.

Charlbury Parish Registers show plainly the disturbance and upheaval the Civil War made in the land. Thomas Downer was probably ejected in 1644, as after April 28th there are but few entries for about 15 years. He lived on here, as the burial of his daughter Elizabeth is recorded, 1654, the words 'late Vicar' following the entry.

About six baptisms a year are recorded instead of 24, and for the first eight years no marriages are entered. Civil marriages before a Justice of the Peace in dwelling houses were made legal, the banns being cried at the top of the street on market days. More remarkable is it that more burials are not entered. Instead of the average 15 a year there are but 15 in 15 years. One entry of some dark deed reads: 'Edmond Harris, murthered. Buried Mar. 11, 1649'. From 1653 till 1657 births only and not baptisms were by order to be recorded.

William Coles, a non-juror ejected in 1689 lived on here till his death in 1735. He was buried in the chancel, near to the organ. It is said of him that he was 'a man of saintly life whose example was remembered by the people of Charlbury for many years'. He resided here for 52 years.

Under the shade of the old yew tree are the memorials of many Finstock people, the names 'Langford' and 'Busby' occur, and near by is the memorial of the Rev. S. H. Russell, B.D. During his last illness the hymn

'The King of Love my Shepherd is,
Whose goodness faileth never'

was sung daily at his bedside, and at his funeral it was sung at the graveside, there being present members of all the various Christian bodies in the town, all met on common ground, and to the memory of him they had all learned to respect. On the following Sunday his friend, J. A. Hessey, D.C.L., preached a funeral sermon from 'Made great lamentation over him'.—Acts viii., 2.

The Rev. C. F. C. West, B.D., rests near, who for 22 years most heartily strove to care for all his parishioners with kindness and equity, making no difference, treating all alike.

Once when in his study with him he said 'Can you tell me why the unconsecrated portion of the Cemetery is not buried in more than it is?' and at once I replied, 'Your friendly bearing towards Nonconformists is to be thanked for that,' and with a smile he said, 'I do not see why one should not be friendly.'

A tablet in the porch records that the porch was restored by Rev. A. C. Smith in 1898.

The Church — II

The Great Pillage, 1547

The cleansing of the churches, as it has been called, made changes in our Church. Money was wanted to carry on war with France and the Scotch, so commissioners were appointed to see what lands and valuables could be had from the churches. Images and lights were no longer needed, and in face of much opposition this was carried out. Sir Thomas Bridges was one of those for our district.

The altars were removed, the little figure with the alms dish and the little chap near by in our nave lost their faces, the canopy over the arch in the south aisle was cut away. This work is generally laid at the door of Oliver Cromwell, but this was in 1547, and he was not then born. There are no plate or valuables recorded from our three churches. Objects were hidden away to save them in some cases. Did the image from our Church niche go like this? Report says, 'In Coate field is buried a silver image'.

Edward Pease and Wm. Wynlove bought the land at Chadlington set apart to find funds for the Church altar light, so it is probable our lands as also Shorthampton went into the same hands.

Charlbury Church had 'Stocke in cattall 3 kyne and 28 shepe' to keep 3 lamps lyghts Roode and Sepulere.'

Charlbury had 49 howseling people, lands for an obit (anniversary service) and lyght value 9s. yearly. Chadlington 84 howseling people lands for lyghts 2s. 9d.

Howseling people means people who were qualified to take the Sacrament, the Eucharist. 'Howsel', bread of communion.

Spelsbury 53 returned. Land from which 7s. was distributed to the poor — it went to help the war funds.

The Armada

A coin I have of Philip II of Spain dated 1577 connects us up with November 29th, 1588, when everyone was summoned to attend on that day at the parish church by command of Her Majesty to render thanks to God. This day was observed by being 'wholly spent in fasting, prayer, and giving of thanks,' says the historian. Not many days before beacon fires had carried the tidings first, as they burnt up on one hill after another, that the terrible Armada had arrived. Now, the winds and the storm had broken, shattered, crippled and well-nigh destroyed it, and men felt that deliverance had come from the hand of the Lord. No doubt as Hugo Lloyd, our Vicar, led the worship, all Protestants with heartfelt gratitude joined in the solemn service of praise that England was spared from the mightiest effort of armed force ever put forth by Popish power against Protestantism.

THE GALLERIES

To the left hand of the Church porch in the wall of the south aisle can be seen where was the doorway that led to the galleries. The sinners in the nave, the *blue*, and the *oak* in the south aisle, with free seats, they were connected by a kind of suspension bridge. This was all removed in 1857, as were the pews about which Rev. Geo. J. Davies writes: 'Every pew could be distinguished by its height, size, shape or colour.' Some were of carved oak, some had curtains for comfort and privacy. They must have looked very different to the uniform seats in use to-day. The carved oak screen had gone in Dr. Silver's time. The Royal Arms and wall texts were not allowed to remain.

THE BELLS

Our slight description would not be anything like complete without the bells. They make their tuneful presence known to saint and sinner, and *do* bring some message to us all.

Bells filled a larger place in our forefathers' lives than they do in ours. They came into use in the 5th century. Trumpets and sometimes a 'clapper' was used as a call to Church before then.

In Saxon times if a churl possessed five hundred acres of land and had a church with a bell tower on it he could be a Thane. This helps to account for churches being built so near to each other as in our district.

The curfew law that at the ringing of a bell at 8 p.m. all fires and candles were to be put out and all to go to bed helped to make bells more common.

Bells were often cast near to the town where they were to be hung. I wonder if Ab. Rudhall made ours in the church or churchyard, or somewhere near. Wherever it was done, he made a good job of it, and his work proves that he was a master in the art of bell founding. On a bell at Badgworth, Gloucester, is this inscription:

'Badgworth ringers they were mad,
Because Rigbe made me bad.
But Abe Rudhall you may see
Hath made me better than Rigbe.'

Abel must have been pretty sure of himself to have cast that on a bell about his own work, and that of another founder. Our bells are inscribed thus:

No. 1. 'Peace and good neighbourhood.'

No. 2. 'Prosperity to this town.'

No. 3. 'God preserve the Church of England.'

No. 4. 'Abr. Rudhall of Gloucester cast us all, 1716.'

No. 5. 'Prosperity to all our benefactors.'

No. 6 (tenor, 16 cwts.). 'Wm. Ryman, Thos. Cooke, John Rogers, Edmund Brain, Churchwardens.'

They still ring on, as Abel made them. Neither one has had to be re-cast, only re-hung.

The custom of ringing a bell on coming out of church maintains here, and whatever the original meaning I have heard it called 'the dishing-up bell'.

The 'Pancake Bell', as it is called, is rung on Shrove Tuesday.

Many years ago a stranger came here and fastening the bell ropes down to the floor he played tunes on the bells by striking the ropes with his fists.

'When thou dost hear a Toll, or Knell,
Then think upon *thy* passing bell.'

The remains of a bell cot were on the wall between the nave and chancel, the 'Scaring bell', Sancte-bell — it had various names — used to be rung on the elevation of the Host, when the words 'Sanctus, Sanctus, Sanctus, Deus Sabaoth' were pronounced. Though the use superstitious to Protestants had gone, it was an interesting relic as long as the old stones remained.

THE CHURCH PLATE

The Church plate consists of:

A silver flagon and baptismal font, the gift of Henry, Earl Rochester.

A massive alms dish given by Sir Robert Jenkinson.

A silver chalice and paten, the gift of Sarah Canning, dated 1716.

A silver paten inscribed 'Wm. Coles Vicar, John Hastings, Thomas Holloway, Ch. Wardens. 1683.'

A silver chalice was given by Wm. Coles in 1716.

THE BRIDGES MEMORIAL

In the Pudlicote aisle on the east side of the south door is a brass let into a stone surround of quaint design, to the memory of Joan, wife of Sir Thomas Bridges, with the Bridges and Sydenham arms carved on shields.

The original brass having disappeared many years ago, a new one with a copy of the original inscription has been placed in position by the present Lord of the Manor. The Vicar has kindly furnished me with the following translation:

'Immediately beneath this stone lies buried Johanna, late wife of Thomas Bridges, Knight, Steward of the most excellent and worshipful Henry VIII. — By the grace of God King of England, France and Ireland, defender of the Faith and on earth supreme head of the Church of England and Ireland — and guardian of the hundred of Chadlington and of the manor of the aforesaid Lord the King of Shipton Spelsbury and Langley and also of his manor and towns of Burford and Minster Lovell in the same county of Oxford, and also master of the Forests and guardian of the deer of our Lord the King in the Forest of Wychwood and his parks of Langley and Cornbury. Elder sister and co-heiress of John Sidenham of Orchard in the County of Somerset, Knight — who died on 17 April 1541 and in the 33rd year of our Lord the King — On whose soul may God have mercy.'

There is a black slab in the floor beneath the above wall tablet with an empty matrix showing the characteristic dress and hat worn by ladies of that period. Also in the floor as paving stones are parts of an altar tomb (from, I think, the same kind of stone as Lady Bridges' slab) that have quarter foil and other panels upon them.

Sir Thomas Bridges was present at the burning of Cranmer at Oxford, and he was one of the judges at the trial of the martyr Robert Testwood, the musician, who got into sad trouble by knocking a bit off the nose of an image with a key he had in his hand as he exhorted some pilgrims to worship God, the living God only (he found them kissing this Alabaster figure), telling them the figure could not help itself and how, then, could it help them? 'For God's sake,' he said, 'be no more deceived.' This gave great offence, and he was burnt at the stake praying God to receive his spirit.

Our Parish Registers record the burial of Thomas Bridges, Knight, and Rowland Arnold, Gentleman, both on 11th December, 1559. It is remarkable that there is no memorial to Sir Thomas Bridges.

Mural tablets are on the walls to Elizabeth Viscountess dowager Hereford, who was born March 26th, 1678, married May 1st, 1690, died November 17th, 1742; also of her grandson, Lord George Henry Somerset.

A tablet records the death at Genoa of Rev. Wm. Wellwood Stoddart, B.D., Vicar, November 15th, 1856, aged 46 years.

Tablets to the Jenkinsons are near the chancel window. That on the north wall has a little group of singing cherubs beneath it.

Frank Allen's name reminds us that his consecrated spirit was needed for higher service, to which he was called on April 5th, 1913.

A brass to Midshipman C. P. Delmege, R.N., lost his life in action September 22nd, 1914, aged 16.

Also a brass to Arthur John Payne, R.N., drowned doing his duty, October 13th, 1904.

And a very nice little panel to the memory of Major General Robinson, C.B., of Bengal, died 1922.

A window near to the Bridges brass is filled with glass to the memory of Lady Whinney, and to her son John, who fell in the Great War.

In the Churchyard an ivy covered tomb with railings is in memory of William Harris, Gentleman, a mercer of London. The verse has been recorded, though not now to be deciphered, on the tomb:

> 'In hostile arms from Normandy
>   Our ancestors descend
> With William King of England,
>   His rights help to defend.
> Some of us since have into
>   Foreign nations strayed,
> But God within or near this place
>   Our heads in peace hath laid.'

Mr. Harris left 10s. per annum to keep his tomb in repair. What has become of this money no man knoweth.

Eynsham Abbey

Our long connection as a manor with the Abbey at Eynsham may raise the question, what kind of monastery was it and what rule were we under for so long a period, from about 1094 till 1559?

The Abbey was founded in 1005, and Alfric the first Abbot is famous to this day as a translator of the Scriptures and as an author. Some of his work is extant. On reading the Scriptures he says, 'Whoever would be one with God must often pray and read the Holy Scriptures, for when we pray we speak to God, and when we read the Bible God speaks to us.' His letters addressed to members of his flock, prominent land owners, are very faithful. To one he writes, 'Thou lovest drunkenness,' to another, 'When I was with thee thou wouldst fain have persuaded me to drink for pleasure more than was my custom. But know, beloved, that he who forceth another to drink more than he can bear shall answer for both, if any harm come thereof.' It seems evident that as a Christian, a temperance reformer, and a patriot, he was a remarkable man.

In their best days monasteries were places where men could do work they could not very well do elsewhere, the love of letters and learning was kept alive in days of ignorance and strife. Were they not training college, Bible society and Missionary centre all in one, and the treasures penned and adorned by loving hands are of wondrous interest to-day. Eynsham Abbey was of the Benedictine order.

In a monastery the church was prominent, generally in plan, like a cross. The large dining hall, called a refectory, was provided with a desk from which something could be read during dinner, this informed the mind and kept frivolous talk in check. Everyone assembled in the chapter house each morning. All business was done there, disputes settled, accusations heard, punishments (often corporal) were publicly administered. Addresses were given there. The dormitory was the public sleeping place, where they slept in their day clothes. The cloisters were often very beautiful, their arches opening out to lawns or gardens. The infirmary had its chapel. The parlour was for conversation, when silence was enjoined in other parts. The almony was so placed that those who came daily for help could be easily served. The library and scriptorium were stored with manuscripts, and there were written those wonderful specimens of penmanship and illuminating that have come down to us. The song school speaks for itself. In the mint coins and abbey pieces were struck. The cells were not commonly used, except in cases of severe discipline. The granges were the farms with which monasteries were endowed. To each man his work, was the rule, but if any brother got proud of his skill, say at penmanship, he was taken from that and, say, made a swine herd.

At the conquest, 1066, the monks fled and the place was deserted, and in Henry I time it was ruinous and had to be re-started, and eventually a beautiful building was in existence.

Wealth and fame came to the Abbey; it had acquired a relic, the arm of a saint, and miracles were said to have been wrought by it. Money came and went, ease and superstition spoilt and wrought havoc there. In January, 1433, the Bishop issued a commission to enquire concerning the mode of life at Eynsham, where report says religion had been cast aside. After a visit and giving injunctions which he heard were not carried out, any who deserved it were to be removed from office. An arrangement was made for the payment of the Abbey's debts. Thomas the Abbot was shortly after found to be guilty of gross immorality, and he was summoned to show cause why he should not suffer the penalties for the crimes of which he was guilty.

The Abbey Jewels were found to be in pawn, and they were to be redeemed.

This was a sad state of affairs, gambling had been indulged in by the monks. The glory had departed.

There is a list of the twenty-eight Abbots, the first was a man of distinction and worth. Thomas, mentioned in this slight sketch, had a sad stain upon his character; and the last, Anthony Kitchen, with his prior, sub-prior, and thirteen monks, subscribed to the King's supremacy, and surrendered the Abbey in 1539 upon the promise of an allowance of £135 6s. 8d. per annum. Abbot Kitchin was soon promoted to the Bishopric of Llandaff. It is curious to note that Anthony Kitchin was the only bishop who, when Queen Mary's terrible reign ended and Elizabeth became Queen, would take the oath of allegiance to her; all the other bishops refused to do this, and so were deprived of all position in the Church and the Realm. Kitchen remained alone, till several bishops who had been deprived in Mary's reign were restored, and these consecrated others to fill the vacant sees. The consecration of Dr. Parker, which took place at this time, has been disputed by Romanists, but whatever view is taken of this matter it is of interest to us to know that our Anthony Kitchin was the one link that kept the chain from breaking, so it appears. But there seems to be great difficulty as to the facts re Parker's consecration, and we must leave that and go on with our story.

The Manor was purchased by Sir Thomas White, and conveyed to St. John's College, Oxford, which he founded 1555. It passed into the hands of Lord Churchill of Cornbury, but the College retains the advowson of the Vicarage.

The Quakers

Anne Downer, daughter of Rev. Thomas Downer, Vicar of Charlbury, was born here June 14th, 1624, and at Drayton in the Clay, Leicestershire, in July the same year was born George Fox, the son of Christopher Fox, a weaver, called by his neighbours Righteous Christie. The one became the founder of the people called Quakers, the other probably the first woman preacher.

Through the reading of *The Way to the Kingdom*, by George Fox, it appears Anne Downer with a few others met together for meditation and worship. Fox taught that there was a direct divine revelation 'inward light' given to every man. Spiritual insight was needed to use and understand the Scriptures. The sacraments, baptism and the Lord's Supper were not essential. That there was no need for ritual, or form, or ordained ministry, that women should be free to preach, that war was not in agreement with Christianity, and that taking an oath was contrary to Christ's teaching. Their views brought the Quakers into colli- sion with both Church and Puritan, and they had rough times as they went from place to place, they found many adversaries. Prisons were full of Quakers, many died in them. Scholarly men disputed with them, good men failed to understand them, but they increased in numbers rapidly. Anne Downer found herself in the House of Correction, sent there by the magistrates for the part she had taken. Later on George Fox sent for her to go to assist him and write shorthand for him, she could do this well, he says, and she walked from London to Launceston to do this, with real Oxfordshire spirit, which when it sees where duty or danger calls goes straight on; may thy spirit never die, brave, dauntless Anne.

Later in the year 1656 she returned to Charlbury and preached at Chadlington, where many were convinced. I can fancy how she walked down the road here on her way, a few feet from where I write.

She married Robert Greenwell, who died in Newgate Prison in 1664. Six years later she married George Whitehead, a Quaker of note, who interviewed Royalty again and again on behalf of Friends, gaining thereby the release of many who were in prison for conscience sake, John Bunyan amongst them. George says, 'The Lord was pleased to show me that it would be convenient and well for me to marry an honest, faithful approved Friend of London, and accordingly that faithful, ancient servant of the Lord and His people, Anne Greenwell, whose maiden name was Anne Downer, and after consideration and seeking the Lord for full satisfaction and resolution and also having the appro- bation to several ancient faithful brethren I made known my mind unto her which, upon due consideration, was by her accepted.'

The marriage was a happy one, though she was much older than her husband. Seventeen years was she a true helpmate, encouraging her husband in his service and sufferings. She said to him these last words, 'Do not trouble yourself or make any great ado about me, but, my dear, go to bed, go to rest, and if I should speak no more words to thee, thou knowest the everlasting love of God.' About 3 o'clock the next morning she quietly passed away, 27th, 5 month, 1686.

At Chadlington Francis Strength and William Coles were convinced under her preaching, and at Coles's house here in Watt's Lake next to the wool ware- house, friends met, and Thomas Taylor coming, many were convinced, who 'being broken off from the world's way of worship met often together to wait upon the Lord.' A meeting house was built, an old minute reads, 19th 2nd 1681, 'Agreed yt there shd be a M. H. at Charlbury.'

The present meeting house was built on a site given by Robert Spendlove (who built the Corner House) in 1779. Edward Burrow and Francis Hougill visited the meeting here.

Elizabeth Gregg had a Friends school for girls, and another for boys by Mary Palmer and her husband, later she was joined by Mary Lamb. Mr. Richard Cadbury, of cocoa fame, as Mr. Newman, of Leominster, being scholars.

I heard when I was a lad that the Quakers did not want anyone to join them unless they were very well off, that is, had money. This was the idea it appears in those days. They were debarred from much in which they might have taken part, and gave themselves to commercial enterprise and philanthropic objects, and I think were exclusive, hence the opinion I heard when a boy.

The slaves ever found the Quaker a friend, after John Wolman's seed had borne fruit amongst them. Having no creed and believing in freedom, some things seem hard to reconcile even to this day. Wm. Penn's *The Sunday Foundation Shaken* printed in 1669, and some of the addresses one has heard at the meeting house, seem far distant from each other in other ways than years, but the elements, the mystic and the evangelical, have produced a society that has been a power for mercy and righteousness in the earth, there is no doubt.

In our town education and temperance owe much to Quaker influence. The British Schools were chiefly founded and supported by Friends. Robert Spendlove gave £100 to start the School, and Temperance was introduced by William Albright about 1836, and had the ardent support of his son, John Albright. He came with Mr. Jesse and Mr. Edward Clifford to Finstock when I was a lad and held a temperance meeting, and it came to the mind of one young lad, whose heart was sore pained as to the evil of intemperance, here is a way out, and he has followed the gleam.

William Albright came here in 1767 to assist William Squire, taking over the business in 1771. His son, William, began work at 13, and presently he had the business. His son, Arthur, settled in Birmingham, and when he commenced business on his own account his mother wrote to him, 'I much desire that thee my dear Arthur, and all my children, may guard against aspiring after great things, there is much more peace in moderate and rather humble desires than grasping after wealth.'

He discovered a way of making phosphorus non-explosive and a Swedish firm sent an order for a considerable quantity, they having found that striking matches made with it retained their power to light on being struck, this had been a difficulty to make matches that would 'keep.' His reply to their order was — 'Gentlemen, Amorous Phosphorus in such quantities as stated in your letter can to the best of my judgment only be used for purposes of war. As I belong to the Society of Friends and disprove of war, I beg respectfully to decline your order.' He promptly heard that not for destruction, but the enlightenment of mankind in the paths of peace, was this required for the making of matches.

He bought 'The Royal Oak' public house here, turning it into a Temperance Hotel. He built the Town Hall and Club and Institute Room and gave the site for the Y.M.C.A. Hall. The town water works was one of his schemes, he bearing most of the original cost.

The *Oxford Chronicle* August 17, 1900, records the proving of his will, by which he left £500 to the Royal Oak Temperance Hotel, Charlbury.

John Albright, born 18 days before the battle of Waterloo, lived to a good old age in the town, and for fifty years lived in the house he built as a residence. A curious thing happened during the building. The plan was lying (open I suppose) and a whirlwind took it up and carried it away into the sky it seemed, it was found in a cornfield at Taston shortly after. Wonder if that plan is yet in existence?

Mr. Albright followed the light as he saw it, and I am glad to record the following. Many years ago he gave me an order asking for an idea as to the cost, which was sent to him, when to my surprise he came and said, 'Thy price is not enough, I want thee to have living profit, go through the matter again,' which I did, wishing more folk were like friend Albright.

There was not a congregation of Friends in the British Isles that had not received a visit from Mr. John Albright before 1880. He passed away in his ninety-fourth year, 27th January, 1909.

Edmund Sturge the friend of the slave resided here, he had married Lydia Albright. *Punch* had him in its pages. All he could do in the interests of the man in bondage he did.

J. M. Sturge, J.P., spent the declining years of his life here, and I miss him to this day.

Methodism

I cannot find that John Wesley ever visited Charlbury, but he came into the neighbourhood several times. Was Lenten preacher at Coombe in 1737; his first sermon was before that at Southleigh, and several times in his Journals he records visiting Finstock. After his experience, May 24th, 1738, when he had 'assurance' as he says, he swept the land, and not only the services, but his tracts and hymn books were everywhere. He said it was the privilege of an Englishman to speak his naked thoughts, and tracts, such as *A Word to a Smuggler*, *A Word to a Drunkard*, etc., show his stinging, stirring words. Satan raged every time Wesley cut a new pen. Canon Peter Green said, 'Had it not been for Wesley and his men, England would have been a heathen country.' The upper classes were mostly hostile to Methodism, which became the religion of the neglected poor; gifts, talents they had, found expression that could not be found elsewhere, whilst the close study of the Bible, with its wonderful range of contents, educated the mind and gave a dignity to the lives of these people they would otherwise never have known.

The Methodist society here first met in Market Street, at the house of Mr. Grace, a rope spinner, and was a part of the Oxfordshire Circuit consisting of nearly the whole of what is now the Oxford District. Wesley put three men in charge of this wide circuit. They were J. Peascod, Joseph Entwistle and Richard Reece. The two latter lived in Oxford together in a garret, over a shoemaker's shop in New-Inn-Hall Street, which was bedroom, dining room and study to the two men, for which the Oxford Society paid sixpence a week rent.

Richard Reece was a remarkable man, who had been very well brought up and educated. He it was, I think, who opened up Charlbury to Methodism. Twice he was President of the Conference, and in 1823 he preached the first sermon in Charlbury Wesleyan Chapel.

The Society as it extended got to a barn in Fishers Lane, and then a man came to the town who took quite a prominent part as a Methodist, Mr. John Gatfield, who was born here about 1767, and at 12 years of age had been apprenticed as a seaman on board a trading vessel.

After some years he was pressed for the navy, and though he offered fifty guineas and another man for his liberty Captain Nelson (as he then was) said pleasantly: 'He is just the man I want, and therefore I shall not part with him.' On his mother becoming a Methodist a relative tried to get him to use his influence against it, but, said he, 'I thought my mother knew better than I did, therefore I should not interfere.'

On one of his visits home his mother prayed with him and used the words 'a present and everlasting salvation.' Years after, when walking the deck of his ship at midnight, these words flashed into his mind, and he thought 'What does this mean?' Presently he remembered. 'This is what my mother prayed for me.'

On leaving the sea he resided at Freeland, where he heard a Methodist preacher for the first time. Later on, coming to live here, he opened a school that was a boon to the town and neighbourhood. Advertisement from the *Oxford Journal*:

Charlbury, Oxon.

Mr. and Mrs. Gatfield return their sincere thanks to those parents, &c., who have already entrusted their children to their care, and beg leave to inform them, and the public, that their separate Schools for the tuition of children of both sexes, will commence on Mon. Jan. 20th, 1817. The most unremitted exertions in the discharge of their important trusts confided to them may at all times be relied on.

Mr. Gatfield was the principal means of the erection of the Chapel on a site given by Mrs. Bolton, of Finstock, and on his death, according to his wish he was buried beneath his pew within its walls, as recorded on a tablet.

Some items from early accounts are:

'4 bushels malt, 3lbs. hops, £1 13s. 0d.' This was to brew ale to give out to the workmen during the building.

'Postage on a letter from Burford, 7d.'

'Mr. Reece's bill for journey, etc., £4 14s. 0d.'

'Men's seats with backs by arrangement.'

There were no backs to early chapel seats; the earnest business in hand allowed no listless leaning back.

'Mr. Harrison for the Bass Voil for the use of the chapel, £1 6s. 0d.; ditto for strings, 1s. 6d.'

The trustees at the erection were: Thomas Gatfield, Edward Bolton, William Bolton, Fawler; Joseph Early, Wm. Roberts, Burford.

Other names of those who have taken part in the Methodist life of our town are: ★'Allen', 'Baughan,' ★'Baskett,' ★'Biles,' ★'Brooks,' 'Burden,' ★'Butcher,' 'Clary,' ★'Clifford,' 'Cross,' ★'Crockett,' 'Couling,' 'Canning,' ★'Eeles,' ★'Harrison,' 'Heel,' 'Harwood,' 'Hall,' ★'Jarvis,' 'Jones,' 'Kench,' ★'Kerry,' 'Lardner,' 'Mann,' 'Wytham,' and a goodly host whose record is on high.   ★—Local Preachers

The Sunday School has taken a share in dealing with the young life of the town. It appears to have been started in 1822 by two young women named Clary, joined by Edward Lardner, in a cottage, and in 1837 Richard Thos. Heel was secretary and began to keep a minute book.

In 1838 a library was in existence, for the committee agreed to purchase a cupboard for seven shillings, and a new and larger one was ordered to be made by Mr. Baughan.

'Mr. Payne, of Fawler, to be requested to train the children to sing ready for the Anniversary. One hymn to be sung by the children in the morning, two in the afternoon, and two in the evening, with a piece or anthem, a platform to be erected to accommodate the whole of the children.'

Questions were asked re the school at the committee meetings as follows:

Question 1.—Do the scholars make any improvement in learning, behaviour, morality and religion?

Question 2.—Is there any instance of incorrigibleness to report to the committee?

Question 3.—Any charge against any of the teachers, etc., as regards morality, punctuality or discipline?

Question 4.—Any person to be recommended to be received on trial as a teacher?

Question 5.—Any improvement in the internal management of the school to be suggested to the committee ?

On this a good school was maintained, and it seems a pity that the old list of quarterly questions should have been dropped.

In May, 1838, the treat was to be held on the 29th — the day of the Club Feast.

'No cake is to be taken home by the children. Tea only shall be provided, cake without limitation. The children shall not walk to make any exhibition in the town, it being a day of worldly amusement, namely Charlbury Club Feast.'

'Mr. Fairbrother to be invited to take tea with the teachers, as a token of their respect for his kind services in teaching the children to sing, at different times, each teacher to pay threepence to defray the expenses of his or her tea.

'A man to be hired for one and sixpence and his tea, to boil the water and do all that may be required of him.'

In that year D. Clifford and A. Harwood were nominated superintendents of Finstock Sunday School, which was carried on as a branch of the Sunday School here.

The joyful note is struck how that there are several desirous of 'Meeting in Society.'

The fashion of wearing pattens came in for comment and action, in that it was suggested that the girls should take off their pattens at the door, and Messrs. Jesse Clifford, W. Kibble, H. Kerry, J. Harrison and S. Harwood volunteered to stand at the door and see this carried into effect.

In 1839 Finstock school was to take off its pattens at the door, later a visible improvement was noted in the behaviour of the children at Finstock.

For many years Finstock has been a separate school. I note at one treat in the thirties: 'The Finstock children are to be met at the Turnpike.'

The circuit ministers reside at Witney, and are the Rev. G. P. Lester and the Rev. Norman Knock. The chapel is registered for marriages.

A marble tablet near the pulpit is in memory of Mr. Henry Hall, of revered memory, his good wife, Susan, their daughter, Alice, and her son, Rev. Henry Hall Norton, M.A., Wesleyan Minister, who died of wounds in Alexandria after singing 'Rock of Ages' to his fellow patients, January 27, 1916.

PRIMITIVE METHODISM

Primitive Methodism was introduced and was very flourishing, and I have been told that at one time it was almost a question as to whether Charlbury or Witney should be the circuit town. I think differences over strong drink made some dissatisfied at the Wesleyan Chapel and several left and threw in their lot with the Prims. The chapel still bears the name and date of erection, and it seems a pity that a building built with consecrated money should be used even for a laundry. Mr. Eli Larner told me he held a plate at the stone laying and saw a sovereign put into it. Coins of gold were in use in those days.

Charlbury Baptists

The Baptist Chapel at Charlbury occupies a splendid site, and was built in 1853. Mr. George Baughan left £250 towards the building. In 1875 it was united under the pastorate of the Rev. G. B. Richardson with the Baptist Church at Chadlington. There is a Baptistry for immersion within the chapel, but during the pastorate of the late Mr. Matthews public immersions took place in the river here, and many years ago, I have heard, the Strict Baptists baptized in the river Evenlode.

It is not generally known perhaps, but baptism by immersion is not unknown in the Church of England. There is a baptistry under the pews at St. Lawrence Church, Reading; it was used to baptize a family in 1866. There is also a baptistry at Cranbrook in Kent, another at Scarborough, and at other places.

Some Charlbury Baptist Ministers: Rev. John Light, 1866–1876, Rev. G. B. Richardson, 1876–1882, Rev. W. Pontifex, 1882–1886, Rev. W. Kelsey, 1887–1891, Rev. R. Parkin, 1891–1900, Rev. C. Sirett, 1900–1907, Rev. J. H. Matthews, 1907–1915, Rev. A. H. Field, 1915–1916, Rev. J. Warren, 1917–1922, Rev. R. S. Burden, 1922–1923, Rev. A. V. Barber, 1923.

Charlbury charities and gifts

'The Playing Close' has been used as a place for games and gatherings from early times. A rental of three barbed arrows was paid to Eynsham Abbey for it.

Where did our arrow maker have his forge, and what was his name? Some specimens are found; I have some so wide in the barb they would make a wound about three inches across, whilst those used for shooting birds had two points, like a fish's tail. When all the men in the parish were bound to practice shooting at the 'Butts' many arrows were needed.

The Playing Close property passed into the hands of good Thomas Gifford, who left it to the town as follows.

GIFFORD'S CHARITY

Thomas Gifford in 1592 demised to George Tennant and others of Charlbury, Fawler and Finstock, the messuage or tenement situate between the churchyard on the West and widow Rawlin's tenement on the East: Two acres of ground in Church Slade: one other tenement between land called the Burial and the tenement of Thos. Jennings: also a cottage on the East side of Charlbury called the Playing Close, abutting upon a lane called Brown's Lane on the North, except the use of the messuage adjoining to the Churchyard for keeping the Court of the Manor, to the only use, benefit and commodity of all the tenants of Charlbury, Fawler and Finstock, except only that the Playing Close and the cottage thereupon is for the use of Charlbury only for the term of 998 years, yielding unto the lord of the manor 4/- at Lady Day and Michaelmas annually.

By Indenture 19th November, 1733, William Cole assigned the said premises to Sir Robert Banks Jenkinson and others.

By Indenture 2nd May, 1801, Samuel Harris, in whom the premises were then vested, assigned them to George, Duke of Marlborough, and others, except the cottage on the Playing Close, which had been sold to Francis Wyatt.

By Indenture 18th April, 1815, George, Duke of Marl borough, and others assigned the same property to William Albright and others, except the afore-said cottage.

Part of the messuage originally demised by Thomas Gifford near the Churchyard was used and fitted up as the school house of Mrs. Walkers's school. The other part had become the possession of Mr. Malins it is supposed, taken by Fawler and Finstock as their share of the joint interest they had with Charlbury, and exchanged with Mr. Malins.

The tenement described as being between the Burial and Jenning's house seems to have been lost, and the trustees did not even know the site.

The money for which the Playing Close cottage was sold was applied to erect a workhouse.

The parts of the Playing Close let off to tenants brought in £3 per year, but the trustees reserved the right to take possession of these parts whenever they wished to do so.

Upon a part the British School, as it was called, was erected.

THE GRAMMAR SCHOOL

In the year 1687 or about, Anne Walker, of London, spinster, endowed the Grammar School solely for the benefit of the town. She left by her will an estate at Cropredy and other property at Shotteswell, in Warwickshire, to the princi-pals and Fellows of Brasenose College, Oxford, that they should appoint a

Master, who could teach Latin and Greek, and that £40 per annum should be paid to him, appointing as visitors to the school the governors of the said college, who in appointing the Mastership should give preference to a member of their own college. She also founded two exhibitions of £5 per annum to be paid to any two young men who may go from the school to the college. I do not think in the whole history of the school anyone has ever gone to Brasenose College. Mr. George Morris was master from 1855–1902.

THE BRITISH SCHOOL

Robert Spendlove gave £100, other Quakers gave and supported the scheme, and in 1815 the school was built and it continued by the Friends support till 1887, when the School Board came in.

The late Mr. Jesse Clifford was head master for 42 years.

The Infant School was built in 1857, Friends again making it possible. Mrs. Pollard gave £50, other Friends, £50. The Vicar, Rev. S. H. Russell, helped and the farmers did work with their teams.

'POOR BOYS' CLOSE'

A piece of land bearing this name, the rent of which is used to apprentice needy lads, seems to have no history. When left, or by whom, is not known. 'When thou doest thine alms, do not sound a trumpet,' one said long ago.

RECENT GIFTS

The present Lord of the Manor has been generous in gifts to the town, helping with the schools in different ways, and though there has been no 'blowing of trumpets or beating of cymbals' about it, his gifts and help, as also the two gentlemen who have given the part of Nine Acres to the town as a place for recreation, should all have a place in our esteem and gratitude.

The late Harvey Du Cros gave the Jubilee Memorial Fountain, which stands on the Playing Close, which bears on a bronze tablet the inscription — 'This Fountain is erected to commemorate the visit of H. M. Queen Victoria to Charlbury in November, 1886, the provision of a water supply for the town in 1896; the 60th anniversary of the Queen's Accession, June 20th, 1897.'

The stocks, whipping posts and gallows

In 1376 Stocks were desired to be set up in every place. Ours were under the eaves of the Market House, so when it rained the drippings fell on any poor wretches who were confined in them; it must have helped to cool their courage. The late Mr. Jesse Clifford saw them broken by a man who had spent the night in them. The iron straps on top of the posts were to hold the hands of any who were to be whipped or have their ears cut off, or a letter neatly branded with a hot iron for some crime as the Statutes directed should be done, or for whipping at the order of any J.P. 'Stripped naked from the middle upward and openly whipped till his or her body be bloody,' says 'Parish Law.'

In earlier days cutting off the hands and feet was a punishment for theft. For most crimes there was a price set, and even murder could be got over by those who could pay.

For knocking out a tooth the fine was 6/-, breaking a thigh 12/-, but a greater crime than this was destroying a man's beard; 20/- had to be paid for this.

Hanging was the penalty for many crimes, and the fact is kept in mind by the name of the field in our Manor, 'Gallows Piece,' and not so long ago stood there no doubt the grim object.

In an old sketch of Banbury in 1730, the gallows there is plainly to be seen standing in a field near to the town as did ours, and in a charter to that place mention is made of authority to hang Felons, Murderers, and other Malefactors. If a person was caught red-handed he was taken and forthwith executed: if there was a doubt as to his guilt he was sent from our Manor to Banbury Castle, and if within three days no further evidence was forthcoming he was liberated. The Castle was built by Alexander, Bishop of Lincoln, in Henry I time, and Leland says at Banbury there was 'a terrible prison for convict men.' In 1276 it was said that William Basiate, having been arrested for robbery and imprisoned in Banbury Castle, had escaped from the prison and had gone to the Church, and from there by office of Coroner. The law being that anyone guilty of felony taking refuge in the Church or Churchyard he might there before the Coroner, within 40 days, confess his trespass, and on his oath of perpetual banishment go direct to the sea, and leave the realm.

But Robert le Mund and others came, and by order of Philip le Burn the constable finding the said William going toward the sea, did drag him off the King's highway, and cut off his head. Also, the said Philip le Burn it was said, took William Balle and him imprisoned till he gave him three and eightpence to let him go. Philip, the constable, carried things on in high-hand fashion, cut off one man's head and let another have his liberty for 3/8 at Banbury Castle. We hope many from our manor were not put under his charge.

A few extracts from the Parish Laws ruling in our Manor, by breaking of which offenders made themselves liable for punishment, may be of interest.

'The Churchwardens are to see that the Lord's Day be duly observed, for if anyone do any work or business on that day, he forfeits 5/-. If any publicly cry or expose for sale any wares, he shall forfeit the said wares. If any Carter, Wainman, Carman, Drover, Horse courser, Waggoner, Butcher, Higler, or their servants shall travel on the Lord's Day everyone of them for so offending shall forfeit forty shillings. Any person on the Lord's Day who shall use or travel with any boat, shall forfeit five shillings. If any butcher shall kill or sell victuals he forfeits six shillings and eightpence. And if any meet at Bull-baitings, Bear baitings, Interludes, Common Plays, or any other Sport or Pastime whatsoever, every one so offending shall forfeit three shillings and fourpence.

All such forfeitures the Churchwardens are by warrant to levy by Distress or Sale of Goods, and apply to the relief of the poor and where no Distress to be had, to put the offenders in the stocks.

Churchwardens to visit (frequently in time of service and out of it) Alehouses, and any found tippling to pay 3/4, the landlord 10/-, and 5/- for using his trade on Sunday, if in Service time 1/- each for not being at Church, or all to be put into the stocks. Also to be presented at the next visitation.'

The Archdeaconry Papers I have gone through at the Bodleian, and they are singularly free from records of misdoings in our parishes, very few persons were presented, generally the words are 'all is well.' So it appears the old parish laws were well carried out, and the fines, stocks, etc., had a most restraining effect on any who might have been offenders.

A barn at Fawler always went by the name of 'Jail Barn,' and it was said that there was an underground passage from it leading to 'Gallows Piece.' The underground way was no doubt imaginary, but I daresay the overland route had been real enough to poor wretches who had been sternly hurried from imprisonment in the barn to the gallows standing near to Charlbury in days of yore, hence the tale of the passage which always filled my heart when a boy and the lads used to speak of it, with a kind of awe or dread.

The stocks at Finstock were on the green near the Crown Inn, and were removed perhaps 80 years ago.

Charlbury market and fairs

No market or fair could be held in England without a Royal Charter or right of prescription. William the Conqueror gave the first Royal Charter for a fair in this country to the Bishop of Winchester.

In days of old there was much resentment by traders in the towns where the fairs were held, for they had to close their shops, and all trading, buying and selling was done in the fair, sometimes, too, it was held in the Churchyard. It brought together all the riff-raff of the countryside, and drunkenness and immorality and thieving abounded. All London fairs were abolished before 1855. John Bunyan in his immortal 'Progress' gives a fair as he knew it in his day, 'Vanity Fair,' his eye saw things from the Christian standpoint most truly.

It has been said that Stephen granted a market; this I cannot trace, but the Eynsham Records state the date as 1256, Henry III gave the market to be held every Monday and four fairs a year.

The ancient Market House stood at the top of Church Street, timber built with stone slates. It was taken down and carted away about 50 years ago. The shame of it!

Charlbury Market House

An old man told me as lads they used to climb up inside on to the roof timbers, and one night the constable, grandfather of Bishop Barnes, came underneath to hunt them down; he jumped and came right on top of Mr. Kerry's tall hat and drove it down over his ears, poor hat, poor constable.

The fairs were rather a big thing, and an advertisement in the 'Oxford Journal' re the sale of what is now 'Sycamore House,' next the Playing Close, says 'The premises have the privilege of tying one hundred horses round the walls at three fairs yearly, the profit arising from which more than clears all tithes, taxes, and poors' rates.'

If this number of horses were to be found on fair days at that one corner, what about the number at other points of the town.

Crosby's Gazetteer says of Charlbury — 'Here is a weekly market on Friday, which was formerly considerable, though now much decayed. There are annual fairs for horses, cattle, etc., on January 1, the second Friday in Lent, ditto in May and July and October.'

Mr. T. H. Smith can remember as a lad seeing the cattle and corn fair down Market Street, Thames Street and Dyershill, also the horses in Church Street. A number of tradesmen whose names are in a list at the Record Office were in Queen Elizabeth's reign each fined 2d. for 'excessive lucre.' I am sorry men from our manor gave way to profiteering in those far away days. The following heads a long list of Farmers and traders—

> 'At a meeting held 6th October, 1853, it was resolved unanimously that for the better accommodation of Dealers and others who may desire to attend the Weekly Corn Market, the same shall be held from and after the 21st instant every Friday, commencing punctually at 12 o'clock.
>
> R. J. WHIPPY, *Chairman.*'

For a number of years a Stock Sale, generally the first Monday in the month, has been held, when much stock and cattle come under the hammer. Our streets are alive with dealers, drovers, and motor vehicles. Church Street packed with the latter is a sight to see on these days.

Grims Dyke and Ditchley

This important relic of antiquity, as it has been called, can be traced in our parish from Ditchley to the railway in Baywell, where it rises bold and lofty. After all that the wise and learned have said about these dykes (there are some 20 in the land), as to who made them, and when, they hold their secret still. Ours is of interest that it gives the name Ditchley to an estate nearby, and possibly part of our parish went under that name, till Sir Henry Lee, K.G., arrived at the house there at the end of his distinguished career as courtier, etc., and who is reported to have said, 'Here shall my rest be.' It is called 'Lee's Rest' to this day. Here he spent the eventide of his life, and more than once entertained Queen Elizabeth, besides other illustrious visitors.

He died there in 1610-11 and was buried at Quarrendon, Bucks; the monument he had prepared has entirely gone.

In the old hall was a massive oaken table and chair, and stags heads killed in the chase by Royal hunters, as brass plates testify bearing couplets with names and dates. These were removed to the present mansion about 120 years ago.

There is an old deed extant, 1295, Ed. I., relating to Margery de Dycheleye, relic of Radulf, whose daughter became the wife of Jacob de Torstan.

Evelyn describes the house in 1664 as a 'low ancient Timber House with a pretty Bowling Green.'

Thomas Gibbons was the owner before Sir Henry bought it from him in 1580 for £1,600.

Flowers spring up in the turf at Lee's Rest year by year, descendants of those that nodded in the breeze to cheer the old courtier in his old age.

When George Henry, second Earl of Litchfield, was about to build the present mansion at Ditchley, it is said he saw the owner of Heythrop, where is a fine deposit of building stone. 'I want to build a cottage, will you give me some of your excellent stone?' Permission was given, and after stone had been hauled for some time the Heythrop owner thought he would go across and see what sort of cottage was being built; he was surprised, but said, 'You may as well finish it now.'

Lee's Rest was threatened with pillage by a mob from Witney in 1596. Perhaps they thought that the influence of the Lee's might be used in high places to help to redress the wrongs under which the poor were suffering in these difficult days, if Sir Henry's house was threatened.

Some of the Lee family owned, and added to, Lee Place, a very charming residence in Charlbury. There is a famous ceiling there. For many years it was the residence of Capt. J. H. Waller, who improved the place in many ways.

Field names of Charlbury, 1820

The Plot (wood). Coldron Hill. Lambell Hill. Deadlands. Ticknell. Ward's Close. Pintle Hill. Greens. Briar Gap. Long Hedge. Banbury Hill. Stump Ground. Under Coleman's Hedge. Holly Bush. Sallies. In Butts Furlong. Devils Piece. Dustfield. Aubridge. Hoarstone. Hixes Wood. Church Slade. Coate. Hixes Wood Ground. Woodstock Way. Mile Oak Piece. Banbury Bottom. Bar Acre. Hundley. Home Close. The Acre. Rye Furlong. Great Greens. Pest House Piece. Poor Boys' Close. Bobwell Corner. Great Conygree. In Long Furlong. Long Furlong Butts. Doctors Pitts. Banbury Hill. Sidelands. Hundley Sidelands. Town Quarry Piece. Harwood's Acre. Near Hinds Park. Thrift. Woodfield. Winter Slade Bottom. Island. The Ham. Bar Acre. Sheppards Ground. Smock Acre. Aubridge Bottom. Rushy Close. Leassew Hill. French's Ground. Adjoining Rainbow. Twenty Bushel Piece. Ledwell Assarts. Ox Pen Ground. Hunting Bridge Meadows. Pruelts Close. Wigwell. Bullham Corner. Long Furlong. Meadow. Bushy Close. Lower Lays. Wittle Style. Lady Meadow. Sidnam. Moor Platts. Ceaver Piece. Tillason. Hinds Park. Sandford Slade. Gibb's Closes. Marebridge. Fairbrother's Coppice. Coate's Oaks. Lordis Close. Reeve's Close.

Clarks Bottom. Picked Close. Swan Lane Corner. Green Riding Piece. Sturt. Aikin's Piece. Baywell. Ridgeway. Wash Brook Hill. Long Ground. Spires Lake. Church Slade. Osborn's Wall. Brookswell Corner, Rainbow Acre. Opposite Cock Pit. Under Badgers Hedge. Butt's Furlong. Kenrick Acre. Cock Shoot. Volgar Assarts. Fennants Cops. Norman's Grove. Knaves Knoll. Price's Piece. Bleaching Ground. Dixe's Park. Mackerlshire. Eight Leys. Joiner's Close. Hand and Post Piece. Sheep Croft. Castle Head Close. Long Close. Dyers Hill. Brockwell. Shovel Piece. Crowborough. The Straits. Leaseu. Dyers Orchard. Holloway's Close. Low Furze. Crooks at Low Hedge. Ash Close. Lankett. King Meadow. Mear Meadow. Hop Yard. Vetch Hill. Pig Hole. Messy Close Field. Spring Ground.

In 1363 Cherlebery is the way the name is spelt in the Abbey records, and the field names occur 'Makerels-harve,' evidently now 'Mackerlshire,' see above list. The name 'Sedenham' is still in use.

'Puttes lane.'

'Hundeley' lane we all know.

'Dede land' is to-day 'Dead land.'

'Ankus dene.'

'Shepe croft furlong.'

'Mythy land.'

'Holle Broke' is 'Holly Bush.'

Mackerelshire is a field name that is out of the common, but the name Mackerel gives the idea that it was the share belonging to one 'Mackerel.'

Matthew Mackerel was executed in 1537, and if the king's instructions were carried out, Matthew and those who shared his crime were to suffer by 'hanging of them up in trees and by the quartering of them, and the setting of their heads and quarters in every town great and small, and in all such other places as they may be a fearful spectacle to all others hereafter that would practise any like matter,' so reads the king's letter to the Duke of Norfolk, February 22, 1537.

'Devils Piece' is said to have got its terrible name through some youths one Lord's day getting a badger there and treating it most cruelly, and when conscience stricken one or more of the same party passed that way shortly afterwards in the night, the evil one himself was there to terrify and condemn them for their evil deed, or was it to uphold them in their cruel sport?, anyway the Field name stuck. A pleasant story is told about it and its name. The Quaker weaver, William Jones, used to feel it his duty to give one day in harvest to the work of helping to gather in the corn, and one year the farmer to whom he offered his services told him he could go and work his day in 'Devils Piece,' when friend William said, 'I think thee mightest get a more respectable name for thy field.'

THE PESTHOUSE

Our natural position on a spur of the Cotswolds, well upon the sharp pitch, with an abundance of beautiful water, tends for health and long life, but when some fell disease or plague came along as in 1559, when a pestilence raged for 5 months, many were carried off. To isolate persons with small pox and similar complaints, the pest house, as it was called, was provided and kept in repair till recent times. It was in the little sideland field on the left hand going into Banbury bottom, called to-day 'Pest house ground.'

It appears from some M.S.S. I have, that in 1821, Jan. 11, there were 266 inhabited houses, 7 empty and 1 building, whilst the population is given as 718 females and 678 males.

Charlbury names in rhyme

About the year 1876 the following lines appeared, and strange ot say the author is not known. Possibly it was Dr. Clifton, who assisted Dr. Cotterel for a time.

> Fiction is strange, but facts more strangely fall,
> And CHARLBURY NAMES eclipse in strangeness all.
> Pass we then, reader, thro' each lane and street,
> And mark the curiosities we meet.
> Ascending from the railway, first we note
> A Taylor lives who never made a coat.
> In Market Stret what wonders on us pour,
> Behold a Draper there who deals in Flour.
> And at the entry of the street we stop,
> Amazed to find a Baskett keeping shop.
> While, to increase the wonder of our stare,
> A Farmer shaves you, or curtails your hair.
> On t'other hand there doth exist the charmer,
> A Cooper, who by business is a farmer.
> With sweetest smile pervading all his face,
> A Miller offers ribbons, tapes, and lace.
> (That placid smile the consequence, 'tis said,
> Of leaving every fear, at least Aldred).
> And of these prodigies the list to close,
> A Collier stands the Landlord of the Rose (and Crown).
> In Church Street, too, believe me, 'tis no myth.
> A banker, druggist, grocer, is a Smith.
> And Park Street shows – will wonders never cease? –
> A Fox the Charlbury Constable of Police.

(Here parenthetically – don't say fudge –
The man who was our policeman is a Judge).
And if to legal matters we're compelled,
Our Sessions in a brewery is held.
Descend the hill, and, reader, if you choose,
A Parrott will provide you boots and shoes.
(Here I'd remark, that searching Charlbury through,
You'll find a stock of Boots and Sandalls too).
Again ascend, behold, and 'tis most queer,
A Parrott's nest a noted house for beer.
If Hixet-wood you now incline to scan,
A gardener's wife you'll find who is a Mann.
And still a little farther on you'll find
A Gardner lives, who'd nothing of the kind.
Of Charlbury facts a trio more to give,
Dames may be Widdowes while their husbands live.
The Park Street folks need never want for meals,
For Watts Lake now contains a stock of Eeles.
By him no flock to fold or pasture led,
A Shepherd's time is spent in making bread.
The study, Charlbury, of thy fair domain
Affords one pleasure, but 'tis mixed with Paine.
Nought that appears deceitful would I praise,
And yet I must admire your Holloways.
To tell the truth, e'en to the very letter,
Your Paintings and your Parsons might be better.
And how with Mason's work doth it accord,
To drop the trowel, and assume the sword?
Once more the muse gives Pegasus the rein,
Stranger, whoe'er thou art, attend the strain.
As for the climate, strange though it appear,
In Charlbury there is Winter all the year.
But fear of frost dwells not in Charlbury souls,
For Winter never fails to bring us coals.
For total abstinence we do our share,
Of Wells and Brooks have plenty and to spare.
Although the muse in whispered accents tells
There's not much water in some Brooks and Wells.
Tho' Nonconformists swarm on Charlbury ground,
A host of little Churches may be found.

And to Conservatives a joy how great,
Our town can boast that she has Church and State.
As to her children and her numerous friends,
So to her Godson, Charlbury's love extends.
So firm her sympathies, that nought can shake 'em?
Offers her Hands to all – will no one take 'em?
Let sporting gents drop in, as they pass by,
We'll give a Hunt, or for a Salmon try.
But rogues avaunt, with such we've nought to do,
We have our Dores and keep a Bolton, too.
Hast music in thy soul? A visit pay
The White Hart Inn, and thou shall hear a Lay.
Or Fawler's turnpike shall provide thee Ayres
To charm thine ear, or dissipate thy cares.
The feast of reason and the flow of soul
Are thine, do thou but seek the enlivening Bowl.
Though deepest sorrow wrap they soul in night,
Seek but the Enstone road, thou'lt find Albright.
Doth Flora charm thee with her motley train?
Thou'lt Plooards find, nor Sorrell seek in vain.
And if perchance thy steps to Thames Street stray,
Fair Eden blooms with beauties ever gay.
Hast love for aught that tells of scenes of yore?
Behold our Priors and our Castles hoar.
Or doth thine eye for novelty entreat?
Each day a Newman shall they vision greet.
Tired Pegasus would rest his wearied wing,
And haste to quaff the cool Pierian spring.
Falters the Muse, although she fain would tell
Of other Graces that amongst us dwell.
Parting she turns, and with a smile demands
How as a type of life, fair Charlbury stands?
Canst answer, reader? Thus, throughout the Town
Crosses enough thou'lt find: a single Crown.

Waterloo

William Dyke fired the first shot at Waterloo, by accident, which started the battle. For this he was court martialled and sentenced, but reprieved on account of the victory. Was he a connection of our respected family of that name?

Situation and roads, etc.

Charlbury is prettily situated on a corner of Wychwood forest. Comfortable homely accommodation is to be had for man and motor. Capital roads diverge from it, and being on the end of the Cotswolds, hill and dale prevail.

The road to Banbury passes The Hoar Stone, Enstone and Great Tew.

That to Burford past Walcot, Shorthampton, Chilson, Pudlicote and Capp's Lodge with the Dunsden Gibbet Tree still standing.

The road branches about a mile from the town to the left, near to an ancient oak at the roadside, leading through some of the finest parts of the forest, to Leafield.

The Witney road goes past Finstock, and on the heath fine forest views are to be seen, and a splendid prospect reaching far beyond the county is to be had.

The road to Oxford, via Woodstock and Blenheim, passes Lee's Rest.

To Chipping Norton, via Spelsbury and Chadlington, is a delightfully crooked road. No, 'don't straighten and spoil it.' Go slow, and look around.

Footpaths abound, there are stiles to climb; brooks to cross, wade or jump, lanes to explore, and Watery Lane, take it in its various moods and seasons, might almost do as a setting for Bunyan's immortal Allegory; stepping stones, quagmire, and fair going, the setting sun at the far end away in the west to remind one of glory past telling beyond and over the river.

Cornbury Park close to the town is crossed by the Finstock footpath. The whole of this charming park (its 'Beech Avenue' is the finest in Europe) is open to the public in summer on Thursdays. The historic mansion has been the home of the great, the wise, and the famous, for many centuries. Kings, Queens and Princes from earliest times have been entertained there. It is the seat of Vernon James Watney, Esq., M.A., F.S.A., J.P.

The stone from which it was built was quarried in Wychwood forest nearby, which found the stone of which the Guildhall, London, was built, as also much of Blenheim Palace.

The hollow way from the quarries towards Finstock, where much of it was hauled, is in use to-day. That for Blenheim was taken through the Park, over the bridge, and up Gallows Piece road, then an old road, not long obliterated, was struck just opposite the mile stone up to Fawler sheep common, and so on to Blenheim. The stone bridges down Park Lane to Cornbury have not been built so very many years. There was a ford and stepping stones.

Waggons to take goods and passengers with up to eight horses to draw them, used to travel the roads, such as they were. Waggoner Johnson, of Charlbury, used to go to London, and Wards, of Chadlington, had waggons also, and used to take a week to journey to London and back.

Turnpikes

'Tolls for horses or beasts drawing carriages conveying passengers or goods for hire are payable every time of passing.

Tolls for horses or cattle drawing carriages travelling for hire are payable on every new hiring.

Tolls for horses or beasts or cattle drawing any waggon, cart, or similar carriage are payable again the same day if drawing a different laden carriage.'

So reads the lettering on an old board that used to be fastened on the wall at Baywell gate house.

I can remember the gates across the roads and I have some of the old D locks that were used to fasten them. Mr. Ayres was at Baywell gate and Mr. Morse at Dyers Hill gate, near the station. He used to take several gates and farm them out to other men. The locks were some of his stock. The gates were put up at auction, and as will be seen Baywell gate collected a good bit of money during the year. An advertisement in *Jackson's Oxford Journal* for 1811 re Charlbury, Witney, Woodstock, Enstone and Great Tew Turnpike Roads gives:

Notice of a meeting of the Trustees in the Bell Inn, Charlbury, to let by auction to the best bidders the tolls of the above gates, which produced last year over and above the expenses of collecting them:

Witney gate and side gate		£158 0 0
Ditchley ,, ,,		£121 0 0
Baywell ,, ,,		£152 0 0
Dyers Hill ,, ,,		£55 0 0
Brown's Lane gate and side gate and Henley Nap		£85 0 0
Great Tew gate		£52 10 0

And will be put up at these sums respectively and let from the 11th day of May next.

Whoever is the best bidder must at the meeting pay down one month's rent, give security, find sureties, and be approved by the Trustees.

SAMUEL CHURCHILL.

Jan. 29, 1811.   CHARLES LEAKE.

When Charlbury Wesleyan Chapel was built there was paid turnpikes £4 4s. 9d. John Wesley, it is said, paid more turnpikes than any other traveller.

The tolls fell heavily on small business people. They could not journey far on any main road without coming to a gate, and they could not jump it Dick Turpin-like, so there was nothing for it but to pay and then the gate was unlocked. The former keeper at Baywell gate, Wm. Kench, so his Grand-daughter tells me, could tell of a few adventures. He heard a gun fired one day and went in the direction of the noise and there lay a gamekeeper bleeding from a shot wound, dead, and there was the poacher who had done the dastardly deed, who said to Mr. Kench: 'There he lies.' Being the first person to witness this tragic scene he, to his dismay, had to go as witness against the murderer. She tells me it made her grandfather ill, it upset him so.

Preachers were allowed to go through the gates on Sundays to their appointments. Baywell gate house used to have a little place over the door with glass in it to hold a candle on dark nights.

When the road was made past Lee's Rest my great grandfather had the contract for the work.

High sheriffs

The office of sheriff is of great antiquity. The King commits to the sheriff the charge or custody of the county. He is the keeper of the King's peace, both by the common law and by special commission, and as such is the first man in the county.

Three names are submitted to the King for each county and he pricks a hole in the parchment opposite one name for each county. This has been the method since 1340.

In 1521 King Henry VIII. gave the honour and responsibility to John Osbaldiston, of Chadlington, Esquire.

Thomas Gibbons, of Ditchley, Esquire, was High Sheriff under Queen Elizabeth for the year 1569.

Ditchley again finds the man in the person of Sir Henry Lee, Baronet, in 1613.

Pudlicote in 1622 was the home of Sir Rowland Lacey, Esquire, who was the first man in the county.

In 1630 Sir John Lacy, of Pudlicote, is High Sheriff.

Sir Robert Jenkinson, of Walcot, Knight, fills the post in 1643, whilst his son, Robert Jenkinson, Esquire, is High Sheriff in 1649.

In 1681 Fawler is the home of the first man in the county, in that Robert Mayot, Esquire, is that man.

Sir Rowland Lacy, of Pudlicote, Knight, High Sheriff in 1686. There was an inscription in Shipton-under-Wychwood Church:

'Here lyeth the body of S. Rowland Lacy, who espoused Arabella, second daughter of Sir John Fettyplace of Swinbrooke. Who departed this life the 28th September, Anno Dom. MDCXC. Aged 26 years and 3 months.'

Chadlington in 1710 finds Sir William Osbaldiston, Bart., in this important post. He married Catherine, eldest daughter of Viscount Wenman, of Thame, and widow of the Honourable Robt. Bertie. Sir William and Catherine had one son and three daughters, who all pre-deceased him except one daughter, Catherine. He died September 18th, 1736, and was succeeded by his brother Charles, who died April 7th, 1749, and the baronetcy expired.

Rowland Lacy, of Pudlicote, is Sheriff again in 1743.

Robert Fettiplace is at Pudlicote and Sheriff in 1758. He was, I think, about the last to bear this name that was of such long standing and good account in this district.

1766. — Thomas Rollinson (as the name was then spelt), of Chadlington, Esquire, is High Sheriff.

In 1855 Queen Victoria gave the post to a Charlbury man, and it is a pleasure to record the name of a most worthy gentleman, Benjamin John Whippy, of Lee Place, Esquire. The north window in the chancel in Charlbury Church is to his memory. He died April 28th, 1868.

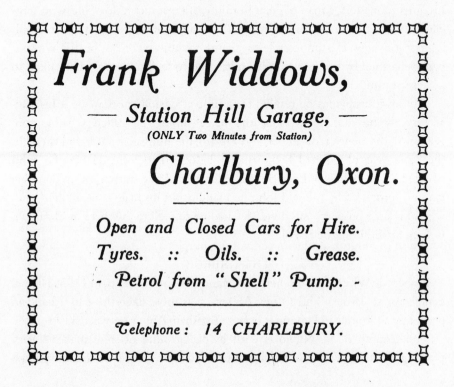

Chadlington

The name is spelt in Domesday, 1086, as 'Cedelintone 2¹/₂ hides, Roger de Welton holds one knights fee of the Fee of John de Nevill.'

In 1216–1307 Chedelinton.

1268 Chadelyntone.

The name is said to mean the hill or tun of Ceadda or Chad. 'A cluster of houses being called in Saxon times a 'tun.'

There is a division of the parish at the Green Lane into Chadlington, East and West, (there being a penny difference in the land tax), and on the south nave of the Church the ancient carver notes this division. There are two little figures with a big barrel or ' tun' between them on one of the spout blocks.

ST. CHAD

St. Chad, or Ceadda, died 2nd March, 672; was a native of Northumbria, and Bede records in his history how he was made bishop over these parts, and left his quiet monastery, a man of great humility, of great rectitude of life, who travelled on foot till almost forced by Archbishop Theodore to use a horse for his longest journeys. It is impossible to read the whole record of his life without being charmed by the man and his spirit, and to feel one would have liked to have seen him.

If in his journeyings he resided for a time at Chadlington, made it his 'tun' as possibly he did, no wonder the place should be called Chadlington. Reginald, the bowyer, or archer, and Siward, the huntsman, had land there. In the 32nd year of Edward I. the manor belonged to John de Handlo, who married Maud, heiress of Lord Burnell. A charter of free warren for his demesne land was procured by the said John de Handlo, but his male issue all died, and, when his large property was divided, Chadlington fell to the share of Elizabeth, wife of Sir Edmund de la Pole.

THE CHURCH

Robert de Whitfield, who held the Manor, was at his death, in 1195, a liberal benefactor to Bruern and Osney Abbeys; it is most likely he had a hand in providing a Church and giving it over to Eynsham Abbey between 1190–1195.

The Church of St. Nicholas with its background of trees makes a very pleasing picture; the various parts group well as seen from the Charlbury road.

It is built chiefly in the Early English and Decorated styles of architecture, and consists of chancel, with vestry and organ chamber; clerestoried nave; aisles; north chapel; south porch, with a narrow western tower that has had a perpendicular belfry and battlement and pinnacles added. A decorated window has been inserted in the western face of the tower.

The arches between the nave and aisles are supported by circular columns, and at the restoration about 1860 the three columns on the south side were removed without taking down the arches which they carry, and re-fixed, new stones being used where necessary.

The men who did this work were John Curtis, John Titcomb and my father, William Kibble; Thomas Smith, a wise and clever mason, being the foreman. It will be of interest to masons and others to know that the centre pillar was fixed with sheet lead to bed the courses instead of mortar, with the result that as soon as the props were slackened, and the weight came on, the stone began to fracture. Lead is not suitable to use to bed soft stone with.

The marks to be seen on the tower inside the Church show where the high-pitched roof went against it before the clerestory was added.

The small opening or squint up above the springing of the chancel arch was so that a sight of the altar in the chancel could be got from a rood loft, and the stones of an arch above the arch opening into the north chapel or transept show that at some time that wall was pierced also. In the south east corner of the north chapel is a piscina with shelf, the shelf being above the tracery head, which I think is rather unusual. A much restored piscina is in the south aisle of similar design near the eastern end. The font is modern. Where is the old one? In some garden rockery? or in use as a pump trough in a farm yard? It would be nice to discover it.

An ancient lock of massive proportions is on the door — original door, I believe — in the north aisle, and is worthy of notice. The key has S-shaped wards and the locksmith used to live at Chadlington. His name was Smith, and he made his keys like that. His son, who was an old man living at Spelsbury some 80 years ago, used to be called 'Lockie Smith,' because of what had been his father's trade.

The corbels inside the nave are quite worth notice; several of the heads outside the church are modern, Church and State at the chancel east window, Queen Victoria and, I expect, the Archbishop of Canterbury.

The north doorway is Perpendicular and the south Transitional, re-built, using much of the old stone. The porch has a very nice Early English arch with a neat moulding round it.

There are mural tablets to the Rawlinson and Osbaldiston families, and there are some inscriptions on the paving stones beneath the tower, but when the tiles were laid the old stones, with many a name engraved, were cast out into the churchyard, where many now lie. One with a long inscription to a lady it must have been a privilege to know, is in the floor of the south porch. Two small Early English windows with wide splays are one in each aisle at the west end.

There was not any floor but beaten marl before the paving stones were put down, there being provision for straw to litter the church. That is kept in mind by the fact that the sum of six shillings per annum is received from the lessee of the great tithes, and is called straw money, being paid in lieu of straw for the use of the church.

Straw, hay, or rushes were luxuries used in great houses. There were no carpets, or but very few, and it is recorded of Becket in Henry II's day, that 'in winter his apartments were every day covered with clean hay and straw, and in summer with green rushes or boughs … those who could not find a place at the table might not soil their clothes by sitting on a dirty floor.' And in more recent times it is recorded of Burford Church 'the floor being covered only with sand and unpaved.' A cottage floor not far away till quite recent years had an earthen floor. Marl, and possibly sand, used to be beaten down firm and hard, and there was the floor. The few pieces of furniture were furnished with legs to lift them above the floor, tables had a rail along, as did chairs and benches, a little above it, so the feet could be put on to keep them dry and comfortable. In churches there were no seats for worshippers. They stood or knelt.

There was no right of burial at Chadlington till, in 1389, Eynsham Abbey and Thomas, the Vicar of Charlbury, consent that they have right of burial, the people of that place binding themselves in return to give two wax candles every Easter to Charlbury Church, one to remain in the chancel at Charlbury, the other for use at Eynsham. They also bound themselves to observe the dedication festival of Charlbury Church by abstaining from work, also the dedication festival of their own church, and by making offerings, as on Christmas Day.

Names of Chadlington people who had to do with this: Margaret Appulby, Ric. Withfield, Roger Badford, Reg. Stacy, Wm. Martyn, John Shepherd.

Burials took place in other than consecrated ground, and remains are found again and again.

Prehistoric cup-shaped graves have been found at the Bratch Quarry, and hand-made pottery and bones at the gravel pits in Catsum Lane.

THE COURT ROLLS, 1441–2

'Chadlington. — Wm. Settle tithingman there sworn and commissioned presents that John Hewes is a common trespasser and has broken the bye law. Fined 6d.; and that Wm. Cowell is rogue and sells rotten meat. Fined 2d.

In 1517 Thos. Wisse is fined 4d. for cutting off the head of a tree.

1523. — Chadlington miller took toll to excess. Fined 2d.

So justice and order was kept in the parish.

In 1517 Chadlington Hundred had the largest area of enclosed land of any hundred in the county.

The stocks were at the cross roads near to where is now the Village Hall, and a big stone used to be on the opposite corner with a hole in it called 'Maypole stone.'

THE GREAT REBELLION

It is yet told how the morning before the famous battle at Edge Hill, troops were drawn up in Chadlington street and given refreshment before going on to take part in the first fight in the Civil War, 1642. Another link with that fateful time is an old Charles sword found hidden in the thatch of the roof of Mr. Cluff's house.

THE GREAT WAR, 1914–1918

There are tablets bearing the names of those who fell, both in the Church and the Baptist and Wesleyan Chapels.

MEN OF RENOWN

In recent times there have been men of note connected with Chadlington.

Lord Raglan, youngest son of the fifth Duke of Beaufort, lived, I think, at Lower Court. He served under the Duke of Wellington through the Peninsular Wars, at the siege of Badajoz was the first to enter the breach, lost his right arm at Waterloo, went from Chadlington to command at the Crimea, when disheartened by failure, the loss of his men, Press criticism at home, he took cholera and died before Sebastapol, 1853.

Sir Henry Creswick Rawlinson was born at Chadlington in 1810, became a soldier and diplomatist, but he will be chiefly remembered for the splendid work he did in taking impressions of the great inscriptions of Darius at Behistun, which gave him a great advantage over other scholars, adding many new words, and altogether he made the work of translating the ancient cuniform writing of the Babylonians more possible than it had previously been.

George Rawlinson, brother to the above, was born at Chadlington in 1812. He became Camden Professor of Ancient History at Oxford, and was the author of several works of interest and note. He wrote the memoirs of his distinguished brother. Died 1898.

Stained glass has in recent years been placed in the north transept windows of the church. Memorials of love and thankfulness.

CHADLINGTON CHARITIES

In 1811 it appears that about 32 acres of land let to William Bagnall (he now rests under a big tomb in the churchyard) were allotted to the trustees in lieu of a yard land and other rights of pasture left or given by one Johane Ferforde, time out of mind, for the maintenance of the chapel of St. Nicholas, and about that time the chapel was re-paved.

There is a plot of ground in the hamlet of Dean called Constable's Close, 26 perches.

In the 14th year of King Charles I, Alice Hemming left a bequest towards a lecture every Lord's Day at Chadlington, and also to the poor for ever. It was from land and property at Orsett, Essex, and at Northumberland Alley, near Aldgate, London.

CHADLINGTON BAPTISTS

The Baptist Chapel, built in 1840, is a very good building with Manse and graveyard.

The Baptist cause in the village seems to have been begun by the Rev. W. Gray, of Chipping Norton, who in 1821 preached in the open air from a waggon, and later on a Mr. Evans fitted up a building for worship, services being conducted by Mr. Gray and his students. Then Mr. Hiorns, a Home Missionary who had charge of a large district, took it in hand, but as he could not visit Chadlington more than once a fortnight Mr. Thomas Eden was invited to labour with him. Other places in the neighbourhood were ministered to by these earnest men, and at a meeting held at Little Tew, June 1864, at the 25th anniversary of Mr. Eden's ministry at Chadlington, Tew and Clevely, he spoke as follows:

'During the first five or six years he laboured in connection with Mr. Hiorns, since entered into his rest, when Milton and Ascott were supplied by them, since that time his labours had been confined to his present sphere. For four years at Chadlington they worshipped in a barn, till the chapel was opened in 1840. During his pastorate he had baptised 147 persons and 20 had been excluded, three only for immoral conduct, the rest having left from growing wiser than their teachers, and desiring stronger meat than we could give them, but he was happy to say they were all walking in the fear of God and he hoped eventually to meet them in Heaven, where they would all be one.'

Before the meeting ended one of the deacons, Mr. Ryman, of Great Tew, in the name of the Church presented Mr. Eden with a purse of £30. Mr. Eden, who had no previous acquaintance with this intended token of affection, rose and briefly thanked them, evidently overcome by his feelings. The meeting was one long to be remembered.

In 1875 the Baptist Church at Chadlington became united with Charlbury and has since continued under a joint pastorate.

The members who had left, referred to by Mr. Eden in his speech at Little Tew, went, I believe, to the Calvinist cause still continued at Milton-under-Wychwood. Those who are curious to know more about the faith of such as meet there should read the XVIIth Article of Religion in the Prayer Book, and Romans, Chap. 8.

The great Baptist preacher, Rev. C. H. Spurgeon, preached at Chadlington.

WESLEYANS

The Wesleyan Methodists have a very good chapel with Sunday school room, and are in the Chipping Norton circuit.

CATHOLICS

The Roman Catholics had a room fitted with an altar in Brook End, but it went to decay and services were discontinued.

KNOLLBURY CAMP

In the fields above Chadlington, on the right hand as you go up the hill from Tite End, is an enclosure called Knollbury Camp.

Rough grass-covered banks rising in places from 15 to 20 feet above the surrounding field enclose a space on the slope of the hill roughly about 100 yards by 150. The side nearest the road is fairly straight, the upper end is a flat sweep. The other side has a bend in it, whilst the lower end has its appearance disturbed by large openings through which cultivation is carried on.

The site is a broad open spur between two hollows, and commands a splendid view of all the countryside right away over the Evenlode valley.

It is remarkable that not far away, just over the hill and nearer Lyneham, there is a circular one — at least what remains of it, a quarry having been dug through a good part of it, spoiling the circle, but fortunately leaving enough to give an idea of its size and importance.

Is the explanation that two friendly tribes agreed to live near to each other and whilst perhaps the original clan of which the other was an offshoot, occupied the earlier camp, ancient then, a new camp was formed to a newer shape?

Inside the camp tents or other shelters could be erected, the flocks and cattle enfolded at night safe from robbers, wolves, and other animals that infested the land. The banks were higher then than they are now, and when topped, as they were, with a strong wooden sharp-pointed railing of small trees must have been a formidable barrier to anyone without, and when one tribe went to war with another the dwelling place became a castle. Before the Romans there were no written records in this land, and these banks with which the hills are dotted were most likely hoary with age then.

The plough and agriculture has destroyed some and parts of others, but banks of loose stones, rubble and earth no one cared to move. Stone walls would have been a quarry and been used in all the buildings nearby, but the banks abide and after all they yet silently hold their secret. Flint and bronze and other antiquities found in and about them give some light, but the story is very incomplete and scrappy.

Flint arrow heads are picked up in the fields, and a very fine long shaped axe or tool came to me from Chadlington field, and a beautiful bronze sickle from further on.

Lascelles Directory says human bones have been found at Knollbury, and that it was thought to be a Roman camp.

There are other banks in the fields in the parish, but on visiting them I could not feel at all persuaded that they were very ancient or of any particular interest.

Fawler

The name has been spelt in different ways—
In 1205 Fauflor.
In 1213–25 Fauelore; Fauflore.
In 1274 Faueflore.
In 1300 Faufelore.
In 1316 FfaueIour.
In 1428 Faulour.
It is said to mean the 'coloured or variegated floor.'

Fawler Monastery and the Church of St John

During the reign of Stephen the Abbey of Eynsham was allowed to absorb a small establishment which belonged to Bloxham, called Phelelie. It was a gathering of Benedictine Monks under a 'prelatus', presumably a prior. It is called the Church of St. John in the Forest of Bloxham, really in Wychwood Forest. There were several brethren, and the position of head of Phelelie was of sufficient dignity to be coveted by a monk of Tewkesbury. Some Benedictine had retired to our lovely district, and there up on the hill somewhere on the outskirts of Fawler parish was joined by others and became their prior. Henry I assigned it as a cell to the Abbey, and the next two owners of the Manor renewed the grant. Finally on the death or removal of the head of the community, the Count of Menlan asked Walter the Abbot of Eynsham to take charge of it. Apparently the monks and their endowments were transferred to Eynsham.

In 1231 a chapel of St. John still existed at the spot, but in 1315 it is known by the name of 'la forsaken ho,' namely, the forsaken hoke or enclosure. What endowments the monastery had it is not easy to discover. No doubt some land in Bloxham worth £3 10s. a year, which Eynsham possessed in 1291, was a part of it, and possibly the tithe at Appleton, Berks., and Naunton, Glos., belonged to Phelelie.

The site of the above monastery it seems impossible to define with any certainty. It is stated to have been situated somewhere on the outskirts of Fawler towards Stonesfield, and as the field names give no clue I think most likely it was on the site of the farm known as Hill Barn. The old stone walls to the farm buildings, and the presence of water, and the name 'Hill' which is not because it is on anything much of a hill, but the first part of the name of the monastery

'Phel' would be pronounced in common-speech as 'Hill.' The situation is part of the high land on which not far away is Stonesfield, an ideal spot in the great forest as it then was, to live at.

Ruddy Wells, never failing water, is not far away.

About 1170 half-a-hide of land in Fawler and Finstock was confirmed to Gilbert Tayland at 6s. rent, his father and grandfather had held the same holding.

In 1279 Nicholas Tailard held one virgate and a half for 6s. 6d.

Four virgates were held by Peter Telmashe; one of the Bishop of Lincoln's knights, Robert de Stokes, also had land at Fawler. Other Fawler names were Robert Danvers, and Thomas Caprum, the place being spelt 'Fauelor.'

In 1349 Jacob le Blunt lived at Fawler.

At Fawler and Finstock land was enclosed during the 14th and 15th centuries, and the value increased.

Iron ore was excavated and extensive brick and red pottery making carried on in the early seventies at Fawler.

THE MILLS, CHARLBURY AND FAWLER

Fawler Mill

The value of the two mills in 1269 was 50s. This would mean that good business was done, as in 1279 the annual value of Iffley Mill was 'one shilling and sixpence.' The mill was the most valuable property in a parish. All were bound to grind at the manor mill.

To make and dig Charlbury mill pond, so pleasant for boating, was, next to Grim's Dyke, the biggest work undertaken in our parish. Fawler was not such a big business.

FAWLER FIELD NAMES

Gallows Piece; Ruddy Wells; Collier's Hill; Hay Grove; Crow Hill; Paddock Hill; Old Road; Big Common; Ladbury Wood Field; Water Sops; Jllins Piece; Sheep Common; Arral; Top Bog Ground; Parson's Piece; Three Oaks; Bottom Big Ground; King's Acre; Holly Bush King Acre; Sar Close; Pump King Acre; Old Field; Bush Stockey; Picked Stockey; Grass Hay Grove; Pebble Stockey; Long Lands; Townsend's Piece; Down-ess; Berry Close; Elms Close; Reed Hill; Bottom Meadow; Mary Hill's Grave; Commons; Barns Weed and Tree; Ashey Close: Little Barns Weed and Tree; Pound Close; Rickyard Ground; Eldern

Lane; Long Stockey; The Grove; Bradley, Grandmother's Acre; Hitchin; Big Meadow; Paddock; Lanket; Num-skulel Spring Ground; Windmill Ground; Blunt's Bush; Well Ground; Little Barn Ground; Round-a-bout Ground; Five Acres; Ironstone Pits; Show Field.

BISHOPS IN BATTLE

It may seem strange to modern minds that Robert de Stokes and Peter Talmashe, of Fawler, knights, were military tenants of the Bishop of Lincoln, but in those stern days bishops took the field again and again in time of war, and the lines were true of many a prelate:

'Princely was his hand in largesse, heavy was his arm to smite,

And his will was loaded iron, like the mace he bore in fight.'

When Queen Philippa marched with an army to repel the Scots in 1346 the Bishop of Durham commanded the first division and the Bishop of Lincoln the third.

It is due to the bishops that as ambassadors and councillors they by their education and training were able to serve the State to advantage when it came to settling differences, though on occasion they did not seem to 'turn the other cheek.'

When the magnificent Anthony de Beck, Bishop of Durham, drew sword against Wallace and the Scots in 1298, previous to the battle he celebrated Mass on the field clad in mail, with a long kite-shaped shield slung over his shoulder, and sword girt at his thigh. The ceremony over, he was ready to charge the enemy, but seeing those who had preceded him, man and horse impaled on the huge Scottish spears, he proposed to wait till the English archers should come up and shoot down the doughty Scots spearmen. But the men-at-arms were eager to close, and Radulf Bassett scornfully advised the Bishop to stick to his Mass while, said Bassett, 'I'll lead the charge.'

This stung the Bishop to the quick, and, sword in hand, he gave the word and led his men furiously to assail the Scots, to be hurled back again and again. I can fancy a grim smile on Bassett's face as he saw how his taunt had goaded the faltering prelate to the terrible fray.

When Radulf came home with his clanking armour and his mighty war horse, with other knights of these parts, I expect they rejoiced to see our quiet neighbourhood and rest and be quiet from their awful trade of war.

Finstock

1154-61.—Finestockes.

1191-1205.—Fines-stockes.

1274-9.—Finestok.

It may mean the stronghold of 'Fin,' or the 'Fin' or 'Fair' town.

Before 1095 Finstock was given to two of Bishop Bloet's knights.

The 'terra de Finstokes' was given to Eynsham Abbey by Rudolphus Bassett between 1154 and 1161, and the gift was confirmed by Reginald St. Walery for a payment of ten marks. It looks as though Basset lost his Finstock property granted him by the usurper Stephen when Henry II came along, it being his custom not to recognise grants his enemies had made, and it was given to his favourite, Reginald St. Walery. It is described as 'terra' and within the bounds of the forest.

The Honour of St. Walery was a vast estate known in the twelfth century and after by that name. It was granted to Guy St. Walery in 1112 and remained in his family for a century.

There was a family of the name Magnus holding property in Finstock by King Stephen's grant before 1154. It is thought they were of the same family who had 13 acres called Tappewell for minding the wood gate for the King. Tappewell cannot be located to-day unless it is Topples.

The Bassett family was one of great rank and position in this neighbourhood for many years. Nicholas Bassett founded Bruern Abbey in 1147, and a Rudolf Basset figures in our next chapter.

ROYAL PETITION

In the year 1349 the men of Finstock and Tappewell sent a petition to the King, and it is interesting to note this and what came of it — it gives food for thought in many ways.

They asserted that they were too highly assessed for fifteenths and wool, and besought the King to provide a remedy. He appointed William de Shareshall (who became Lord Chief Justice the next year), Thomas de Langele and Richard de Williamscote to make a survey and take an inquisition.

They found Charlbury had 22 virgates of land and quantities of chattels, Cote had 13 virgates, and that Fynstock and Tappewell 7 virgates, and that the two latter were too highly assessed at £4 11s. 8d. for fifteenths and 2 sacks 2 stones 1 pound of wool, while Charlbury was assessed at £3 4s. 6d. and 1 sack 11 stones 3lbs. wool; Cote at 27s. 6d., 16 stones 2$\frac{1}{2}$lbs. wool; Fawler at £2 7s. 8d. and 16 stones 4$\frac{1}{2}$lbs. wool.

In consequence of this 'the men of Fynstock were reduced to such misery and want that some having abandoned their houses were compelled to seek their food by their own bodily labours, others to beg from door to door.'

There was a new assessment. Charlbury was raised and the other places made less.

King Edward III listened in 1347 to Queen Philippa's plea for the Calais citizens, and he also listened to Finstock when it was oppressed in 1349.

THE CROSS

In days of yore at cross-roads and other places crosses were erected and there are the remains of many in this neighbourhood. There is not, as far as I know, any word or sign of there having been one at Charlbury, but I think there was one at Finstock. It was thought that some stones on the corner property opposite the Manor Farm orchard were the remains of a cross. There are some long stones to be seen to-day, built into the end of the building that comes to the road, some distance from the ground.

The spot is always spoken of at Finstock as 'the cross.'

It was the general custom formerly to erect crosses at cross-roads as a place self-consecrated, according to the ideas of the time. Suicides and notorious bad characters considered too bad even for burial at the north side of the church were frequently buried near to these, not with the idea of being outcast but in a spirit of charity; that, being excluded from consecrated ground and religious rites of burial, they might be in some place next in sanctity to ground actually consecrated, because the roads made a cross.

Mary Hill's grave, between Fawler and Stonesfield, is well known, as also is that of O'Condoe's here on the Enstone road. He, poor chap, turned out not to be a suicide, as was thought when he was found hanging dead in a house in Sheep Street. Years afterwards some person made a death bed confession that they saw from across the street someone hang O'Condoe and kept the secret. The murderer had gone abroad. There was some feeling at the time or soon after about the burial, and I have heard that men went and dug up his body in the night, and brought it to Charlbury and made a grave and buried him in the churchyard here.

The memorial to the men of Fawler and Finstock who fell in the Great War 1914-1918 is at the 'Cross,' Finstock.

FINSTOCK TOKEN

After the Civil War Edward Gardner, of Finstock, issued a farthing token. Very many were issued about that time by business people to use as small change. This token is recorded in Williamson's revised edition of 'Boyne's Tokens':

O. Edward Gardner — a hart lodged

R. In Finstock, 1666. E.K.G.

I have a very nice specimen. I have not been able to find out what was E. Gardner's business. Though thousands of traders issued these tokens — Northleigh, Shipton and other places had them — I cannot find that one was issued at Charlbury. Surely there must have been several persons here doing business enough to need small change. I am looking for a Charlbury token to turn up.

TAX ON HEARTHS AND WINDOWS

Hearth money, a tax which appears to have been imposed as early as Anglo-Saxon times, was re-imposed after the Restoration. It was very unpopular, and it fell very heavily on the poor. Two shillings per hearth was the amount, and inspectors looked over the house to see how many fireplaces there were. This tax was repealed in 1689.

I have before me a receipt dated 27th day of December, 1785, to show that £3 14s. 6d. was received as window tax for that year and 1783, for the parish of Finstock. The same receipt records the two amounts — £6 6s. 6d. and £6 9s. 6d. — as though this was House Duty for the aforesaid years. An earlier receipt records the payment of Land Tax, £38 3s., and as House and Window Duty £10 0s. 4d. for the year 1773. It used to be quite a common thing to see closed-up windows so as to avoid the tax.

THE CHURCH

The Church of the Holy Trinity was erected in 1841 and is built of local stone with lancet windows, on a site given by Francis Almeric, first Baron Churchill, and consists of nave, chancel and vestry. The western turret has one bell. The chancel and vestry were built in 1906 through the generosity of a gentleman who lives amongst us. In 1877 six stained glass windows were erected by the Rev. A. Redifer in memory of his mother. In the west end are two stained glass windows to commemorate the jubilee of her late Majesty Queen Victoria, June 20th, 1887. The east window is also stained.

The stone pulpit is a memorial to Frances, late Dowager Lady Churchill, died January 7th, 1866. There are brasses to the parents of the late Lady Jane Churchill, also a brass to Francis George, second Baron Churchill, died November 4th, 1886. Also one to the Rev. Alfred Redifer, late Vicar, 1863-1902.

On December 28th, 1900, Jane, Baroness Churchill, was buried at Finstock. She had been Queen Victoria's maid for forty-six years and was one of her closest friends. Queen Victoria paid a visit of condolence to Lady Churchill at

Cornbury on the death of Lord Churchill, December 4th, 1886. At the funeral we were of all ranks. Peer and peasant rubbed shoulders, or almost so, in the crowd. Not only the Royal house of Britain, but overseas were represented.

I saw the wreath the Queen had made herself for her whose loss she mourned, in the hand of the gentleman who bore it for her. She had written a few touching words, with her Royal signature, "Victoria, R.I."

Lady Churchill used to visit the day school at Finstock and call and see my grandmother, and I treasure a book her son, Viscount Churchill, brought me once when he came as a boy with his mother to our house.

In the churchyard is an enclosure with a mausoleum of the Du Cros family.

The epitaph on the first memorial erected in the churchyard is to the memory of a member of a Huguenot family:

'Susannah de Bank, the wife of Edward de Bank
Died 28th March, 1849. Aged 71 years.'

On a tomb:

'Eliza Matilda, wife of Rev. M. A. Farrar, of Cowbridge, Glam.
Died February 26th, 1854. Aged 28.'

VICARS OF FINSTOCK

Rev. A. Redifer, M.A.

Rev. A. Cary-Elwes, M.A., who built the beautiful chancel to the Church.

Rev. Field.

Rev S. G. Wade.

THE WESLEYANS

In 1840 the Wesleyan Chapel was built, seating about 200 people. Being in the 'Bottom,' as it is called, it is fairly central. Previously services had been held in the Manor House at the. Charlbury end of the village, the fine old house with gables and date stone with 1660 upon it, for many years the home of the Bolton family, though it was occupied by Mr. Fairbrother about 1818. The Mr. Bolton who was an associate of John Wesley and at whose house he stayed, as recorded in the famous journals, died at Blandford Park, as Cornbury was called for a time.

Wesley wrote, October, 1775: 'I preached at Finstock. How many days should I spend here if I was to do my own will, not so; I am to do the will of Him that sent me, and to finish His work.' Three years later he wrote: 'How gladly could I spend a few weeks in this delightful solitude, but I must not rest yet. As long as God gives me strength to labour I am to use it.' The following day he wrote at Witney: 'Since Nancy B. has been detained here the work of God has greatly revived. Mysterious providence that one capable of being so extremely useful should be thus shut up in a corner.' She was sister to Mr. Bolton, of Finstock;

the Bolton family at Witney were victuallers and blanket weavers. Nancy was one of Wesley's correspondents, and several letters he sent to her have been published, but I can insert one that has not been publicly printed. She became Mrs. Conybeare, and I have failed to trace much of her later history. I hope she had a good husband, and died in peace. She died about 1822.

Epworth,
June 22, 1780.

My Dear Nancy,

Your letters are always welcome to me, but none more welcome than your last. It gives me much pleasure to hear, both that God has delivered you from torturing pain, and that He has established your soul in His pure Love and given you abiding witness of it. I doubt you have met many in the Oxford Circuit whom you can converse with on that subject. I believe the two that have ye same de [paper torn] experience are Hannah Ball (of High Wycombe) and Patty Chapman. I wish you could converse with them, either by Writing or Speaking. I think each might be profited by the other. I have been a little uneasy since I saw you, for fear you should want anything. If you conceal any difficulty you are under from me, you do not use me as your Friend. Would not you give me all the pleasure you can? I cannot tell you how unspeakably near you are to,

My dear Nancy,
Yours most affectionately,
J. Wesley

Once after Mr. Wesley had preached at Finstock it is told that he thanked the audience for their good attention. One can pleasantly fancy the wonderful man standing in the corner of the farmhouse kitchen and delivering his discourse to the village folk and a few friends from Fawler and perhaps Charlbury, and so we shared in the great evangel it was given him to proclaim to this land. The religious influences set going continue to this day and are throbbing in the pulse of the world. Lives otherwise drab and grey became tinged with a glory alike to that about the eternal throne. Men trod the clods of Finstock sharing the joys the angels know. 'My God I know, I know I feel Thee mine' was their experience, and 'O let me commend my Saviour to you' their attitude to those about them.

Finstock men and women could truly say:—

We are His, and we will praise Him.
Love has won us, laud His name,
Raise the song Redemption's finished,
Lift the voice in glad acclaim.

We have now begun the measure,
  Never more our song shall cease;
We shall sing His praise for ever
  In the home of joy and peace.

In that Land beyond the river
  We shall see Him face to face,
Love Him, serve Him, aye for ever,
  Saved and gathered by His grace.'

Class tickets given and received at Finstock are treasured and kept, as well they may be, as mementoes of the days of glad triumphant experience.

THE FOREST

Wychwood is one of the few forests about which particulars are given in the Domesday book. The love of William for the tall stag needs no mention. The tenants of the manor could cut timber for the repair of dwelling houses, and for fences and firewood. These rights have gone, but the carpenter at Minster Lovell, John Lock, who was working in his shop at 80 years of age, told me that in his father's time if they wanted a small tree for any purpose they had only to speak to the keeper about it, and they went into the forest and helped themselves.

I have in my possession the middle part of an 'Inspeximus of the forest of Wichewood,' dated 11 July, 7 Eliz., 1565; many names appear of places in conjunction with the forest. Where are the two ends of this old document? It is indented.

In the State Papers (Chas. II.) there is a copy of a warrant, dated July 13, 1664, 'To Col. Rich. Legg ranger of Wichwood Forests to take away all setting dogs, guns, etc., *within ten miles* compass.'

No account of Finstock would be anything like complete, especially of days gone past, without mention being made of the Forest. The name Whychwood being seldom used in common conversation.

When the Forest was enclosed it was a sad blow to many who lived on its borders, for some of them got a great part of their living out of the Forest. Burdens of wood for firing, fallen branches, and furze were brought and sold to those who could buy. In spring wild birds' eggs helped to make many a nice pudding. I knew an old man very well when I was a lad who in earlier life used to go on Sunday morning round Topples and collect wild birds' eggs for his wife to put into the pudding for dinner.

In the season nuts were gathered and sold for the extraction of nut oil, others were saved for sale. I have one of the old measures, turned out of wood, a cup turned in both ends, holding a penny worth at one end, half-penny worth at the other.

Some developed the trading instinct and went to markets and fairs with a basket; one man — a nice old chap I knew very well, everybody called him 'Uncle Ned' — was exceedingly skilful in making black sweets, 'Lollies.' They were tip-top, and never stuck together no matter what the weather; he was well known all over the countryside.

Some had 'Common Rights,' and could turn out cattle. I saw the Finstock branding iron at my uncle's, he was the last marksman for the parish, and had kept the iron that he had used to mark the Finstock cattle with before they were turned out. When the enclosures were made and these people lost their right of pasture they had some tiny plots awarded them as compensation, and they were of such land and several of them so situated as to be of very little value. I have heard my father say very plain things about the injustice done to these people, but there was no hope for it, 'take your worthless bit of land or nothing,' seems to have been the rule.

The famous Forest Fair got so unwieldy, and wickedness so rampant, that Lord Churchill did a wise thing when, in the face of much opposition, he refused to allow it to be held.

A nice old man I remember said when he was a lad he was sent at nightfall some where and he had to go through part of the forest. A headless man on horseback was, so it was said, to be seen there. As he went on his way lo, he could see a horseman coming, and thinking 'here he is' he dropped on his knees in the bracken by the side of the path and putting his hands together he began saying aloud the Lord's Prayer. The horseman rode up and, no doubt greatly wondering what it could mean, said, 'Good night, my lad.' The prayer ended abruptly, and dropping his hands, he said, 'O, thank you, sir.'

DEER, POACHERS AND ROBBERS

Deer would stray out of the forest in bad weather and if a certain plant was growing in the cottage gardens they would leap the fences in search of it. One way of trapping them was to put a fork in the ground tines upwards at the spot where they would leap and impale them on it. A deer once caught provided food in plenty for the family, and some to spare for neighbours. The gipsy could make a hole in the ground and bury what he could not eat and make his camp fire over it and sit around, and make his pegs, and ask the time if the keepers came along as cheerily as could be, but other means had to be found by house dwellers, and I have heard of lively, busy times when word went round, The keepers are coming to search!' Venison carried out right amongst the standing corn, slung up into trees, and the leaden roof of one church near the Forest could tell a tale of what had been hoisted over the parapet by strong hands, to rest safely on the consecrated roof, till the course was clear.

Witney seems to have been the market for the sale of deer, and in the night from the forest borders, deer were carried by footpaths to that place, where were tasty palates waiting to be tickled by that which starving, daring men ventured to bring them.

I knew a dear old woman quite well — slept in her house for a long time — who, when she was a girl, had to give evidence re the shooting of a keeper. She told in all sincerity what she knew and on her evidence two innocent men were hanged. Another man confessed on his death bed that he saw the keeper pushing through some bushes head down, and he, deceived by the darkness into thinking it was a deer, fired, and found that the slug he had intended for a deer had, to his horror, killed a man. How he could keep his guilty secret I cannot think. My old friend never wished to harm these poor fellows, only they had gone out into the night and she knew it and said so. People said it troubled her. That I do not know. Perhaps it did — her black eyes used to flash like fire when she looked at one.

Houses had to be carefully bolted and securely fastened in the hungry years when desperate men did desperate things even to get bread. Guns were taken upstairs and kept loaded. The stairs door at The Crown Inn was short at the top. Standing on the landing above you could see into the passage. This was done so that if a robber got in he could be shot over the top of the door.

One night Mr. Goodman, hearing a noise, ran downstairs and catching up the fork used to put the furze on the fire, ran out into the other part of the house just in time to see a man with blackened face scrambling out of a window. He had knocked down a steelyard weight into a tin tray, hence the noise. He made off. The next day when a man went into the village shop the woman who kept it noticed black about his head and said to him, 'What a lot of black you have round your face!'

Many years ago the College Farm, Chadlington, was broken into and a robbery effected. The robber got away with his booty, but owing, I expect, to being disturbed, left his hat, and this clue was used in quite an original way and resulted in his capture. A man could be told by his hat in those days. I knew a man who wore the same straw hat in the hot weather for twenty years or more. The Chadlington robber's hat was taken to Chipping Norton market and put up on the top of a stick in the midst of the fair, when someone from Dunstew came along and said at once, 'That is so-and-so's hat from our place.' 'Ah, that it is,' said another, and the game was up. The robber was taken and, I daresay, not very gently dealt with.

The most thrilling story was of Tom, Dick and Harry Dunsden, who were born in an old house at Fullbrook, and 'Mary Dunsden' is on a stone — possibly their mother's gravestone — to be seen to-day near the church porch there.

They were highwaymen and, it seems, did not stop at anything in carrying out their shameful calling. Anything or anybody they would rob, and it was known that warrants for their apprehension were issued when, on Whit Sunday, 1784, Tom and Harry joined a party at Capps Lodge, which was then a public house in the Forest. They remained drinking and gambling till the early hours of Monday morning when Harry, flushed with drink and pride, threw out his chest and said 'Here's Harry Dunsden, and no one dares take him.' At once Mr. Secker, the landlord thought he would try, but Harry drew a pistol and fired. Fortunately for mine host the bullet found its billet amongst the big, bulky coppers contained in his waistcoat pockets, and did no harm. The struggle then became furious. The tapster was shot in the arm, but he hung on until another bullet in the chest put him out of action. Then someone tripped Harry up from behind, and he was on the floor. Meanwhile Tom had been rendered senseless by a blow on the head from the butt of a heavy pistol, and the capture was complete.

They were hanged at Gloucester and then brought to Capps Lodge. The top was cut off an oak tree and a big beam fixed across it, and from the gibbet so made the bodies hung in chains for a time. Then they disappeared, but were found some time later in the slate quarries close at hand, where some of their friends had buried them.

One Charlbury New Year's Fair a dealer rode here on horseback, calling on his way at the Crown Inn, Finstock. Before starting for home at night he put his pocket book, full of notes, into a pocket in the lining of his waistcoat. This book had been seen by someone who was on the look-out w⸱¹ ¹⸱ he was having some refreshment at the Bull Inn before starting for home. W⸱¹ ¹ he got along the road near the milestone he was accosted by these men, pulled from his horse and, I believe, killed. The robbers, however, could not find the pocket book so, taking his hat, a low-crowned boxer, they made off. The horse made its way to Finstock and went to the Crown, where its master had called in the morning. Taking the hat proved to be the clue which led to the arrest and conviction of these men. My grandfather had to go to the trial to give evidence as to the horse coming up to his house at Finstock.

THE SCHOOLS

The schools were built about 1869, I think, and a mistress was in charge — Mrs. Foster, with Miss Caroline Bayliss, as she then was, in charge of the infants' school. I have never forgotten things Miss Bayliss told us in those days, when to me the world was young.

Then came Mr. Robert Butler. I owe him a big debt for what he tried to do, only wish in my case he had had a better scholar, but very pleasant memories linger about the old lessons, for though he had to be stern at times generally the lessons were a pleasure and went off well. How he managed to control the whole school, and yet give individual attention to each one who needed it, I cannot think. And he would go beyond the subjects he had to teach us, and give us information and ideas about many things that I know I should have been very much the poorer to be without. Mrs. Butler also gave us some lessons, and one or two others assisted him.

Mr. Butler out of school hours, gave some of us lessons in drawing *without fee or reward*. This was good of him, and I am in his debt greatly. The Vicar, the Rev. A. Redifer, used to go through a letter I had to write him, as had others, fortnightly.

There was an earlier school for lads in a house next to the school playground, to which my father went before he came to the Grammar School at Charlbury. This was kept by a Mr. Goodman, assisted by his daughter. Nearly opposite, a school for girls was kept in a cottage by Mr. Armstrong.

An earlier school had been kept in the house next to the Crown Inn by a Mrs. Paintin. I have heard from one of her scholars that she used to make them stand underneath a table for punishment where they could not stand upright. Of course this got very uncomfortable, and boys would spit on the floor. When she noticed this she would fetch them out and give them a thrashing. No doubt this was better than standing with bent, aching back — at any rate it was over sooner.

FINSTOCK CHARITIES

'Elizabeth Martin left a rent charge of £2 per annum to the poor of Finstock hamlet.' This is not now given by the present owner of the estate.

'Thomas Martin by will in 1773 left an annual rent charge of £2 to be given to 20 poor labourers or their widows, inhabitants of Finstock.'

'Hannah Neal left half an acre of land in the open field of Ramsden for educating poor children of Finstock.' This piece of land is on the left hand side of the road leading from Ramsden Church to White Oak Green.

The hamlets of Finstock and Fawler possess jointly some tenements called the 'Church Houses.'

Christmas money

This used to be given out at the Manor House at Christmas to poor women. I am sorry to hear this has come to an end and 'Christmas money' is a thing of the past.

Mrs Oliver's gifts

Many years ago a Finstock girl went away to London and married well, and she and her husband came to Finstock to make a residence at the old place where her grandfather had had his smithy The house was enlarged and stabling for ten horses put up, for they rode to hounds — he in his red coat. Whilst the work was done they rented Lee Place, Charlbury

A little before Christmas when they first came she went round the village and took the particulars of all the families and then made preparations so that everyone should have a good time in their own homes at her expense at Christmas. There was a pound of meat for each adult and half a pound for each child; bread, beer and tea, flannel and shawls, thick and warm. I hope she had a good time herself, as I expect she did. 'It is more blessed to give than to receive,' an old book records. She rests under the big marble tomb near the churchyard gate at Finstock. Her gifts were continued for many years.

FINSTOCK, RECENT

The River Evenlode flows between Finstock and Fawler and is crossed by a bridge near Fawler Mill built in the year 1800, the date being on a keystone on the south side. New parapet walls were built in 1878, and it was discovered then that this bridge of two arches was built on an elm wood frame boarded over like a floor, the wood being perfectly sound and good, being always under water. The other water bridge near by was built when the railway was made in 1851, and there can plainly be seen in the meadow on the south side where was the hollow way that led up from the ford towards Finstock before the road was mounted high up as it is now on the embankment and bridges.

Close to Fawler village was the ford leading to Witney, and the late butcher Andrews of that town used to make a practice once every year to drive as in his youth to Charlbury market by the old road, coming to Wilcote, then down Topple Lane to the ford at Fawler and so on to Charlbury. Gates were not then across Topples Lane. It is a public road, and Mr. Andrews did his part to keep it and the ford open.

Gates used to be at the entrance to the field lanes at Finstock, kept up by the parish. A receipt before me reads:

'The Hamlet of Finstock,
            to Thomas Dore
For mending the parish gates and keeping them in repair for one year, 10s. 6d.
Settled the above, the mark X of Thomas Dore.'

Another bill gives details:

'Mending the Rideing Gate, 2s.; Mending the Dark Lane Gate, 2s.; Mending the Field Lane Gate, 1s. 6d.'

The Pound was kept and straying cattle were put into it.

Under the walnut trees in Cornbury Park, on August 12th, 1807, two men fought about some sheep, and the farmer from Fawler killed the other man. Nothing seems to have been said about it. Now if a deer had been killed or stolen there would have been a stir.

An old warrant here is for the arrest and conveyance to Oxford jail of a Finstock man for killing deer in Studley, but as the warrant is yet with the old papers I expect he cleared off and was not caught.

How was it in olden days Finstock men made for London, and Charlbury men for Birmingham, till unpleasant things had blown over?

In the *Gentleman's Magazine*, July 2nd, 1811, it is said: 'This evening Oxford was visited with a storm of thunder, lightning and torrents of rain. A barn at Finstock was set on fire by the electric fluid, which communicated to another barn, and both were destroyed, with a large quantity of wheat.

In a tiny cottage at the bottom of Well Hill, part of what is now 'Stratford Cottage,' lived a Mr. Brook, who got his living painting miniatures and playing the violin. I have portraits of my grandfather and father which he painted on ivory. The latter was painted in 1826.

FIELD NAMES

Bun-ges; Brook's Field; Sideland; Bratch; Dry Close; Old Close; Cow Pasture; Maynards; Pear Tree Close; Copse; Ward's Ground; David's Hill; Down Field; Squire's Piece; Dog Kennel; Springs; Hillcotes; Little Park; Castle's Meadow; Lerton Ground; Shepherd's Piece; White's Field; Topples; White's Close; Gadden Hill; Assarts; Walkases; Mill Ground; Finstock Field, No. 1, 2, 3, 4, 5; Finstock Meadow; Tandrus Meadow; Ten Acres; Top Ground; Hobsthorn; Stock Field; Green Acres; Tay-a-Nay; Wilkins; Stockey Hill; Lammas Leys; Big West Field, Little West Field; Little Warborough; Big Warborough; Little Park Field; The Constable's Plot; Paintin's Ground.

CERTIFICATE, FINSTOCK AND SPELSBURY

Formerly when a person changed his place of residence to another parish if his rental was less than £10 per year he had to get a certificate from the overseers of the parish he was leaving and take it to the overseers of the parish to which he was removing; one of these certificates relating to the removal of John Souch from Spelsbury to Finstock is given. Several of these old documents are in my care. They were signed by two Justices of the Peace.

One relates to John Silver, who had come without a certificate from Deddington, and 'These are, therefore, in his Majesty's name to order and require you … do forthwith remove and convey John Silver and Katherine his wife from the town of ffinstock to the parish of Deddington,' 1738. Signed by W. Osbaldiston and Jona. Cope.

Finstock, 1707.

John Souch. Certificate

Oxon.

We John Trender and Henry Issard John Ryman and Thomas Couling, Churchwardens and overseers of the poor in the parish of Spelsbury in the County of Oxon aforesaid do hereby own and acknowledge John Souch to be an inhabitant legally settled in the parish of Spelsbury aforesaid in witness hereof we have hereunto set our hands and seals the 9th day of April in the 6th year of the Reign of our Sovereign Lady Ann by the grace of God of England, Scotland, ffrance and Ireland queen defender of the faith.

Anno Domini, 1707.   John Trinder
Attested by   Henry Issard
Thos. Couling.   John Ryman
               Thomas Couling

Richard Sesiens.
The Ch. wardens and overseers
of the poor of ffinstock in the
parish of Charlbury in the
county of Oxon or to any or either of them.

Primitive physic

One night our village tailor and parish clerk called with some work he had done for my father and I heard him say to my parents: 'The other night I was coming from Fawler along the footway and on climbing the railway embankment to cross the river by the bridge I stumbled and went rolling down to the bottom. The fright and fall made me feel quite ill, so when I reached home I took a teaspoonful of gunpowder.' Not bad, was it? when one remembers what the old black gunpowder was composed of.

The virtues of herbs were known, and tea made from stinging nettles, wormwood, agrimony, dandelions, rue, etc., was tried by those who suffered from some of the many ills our flesh is heir to.

Once when I felt ill, as I often did as a lad, Mrs. Bolton got me something I was to drink. I do not know what it was; I dared not refuse it, and I stood before her in her kitchen and somehow drank the cup of horrors. The taste was vile, but perhaps it did me good; she was a wise and gracious woman.

Roasted onions played quite a useful part in home doctoring in many ways. Just the middle, not too hot, put into the ear often gave relief from both ear and toothache. A toasted raisin, split, was used in the same way, but a hot wire or knitting needle thrust into the hollow of a raging tooth was drastic in the extreme. A visit to the blacksmith, who drew teeth with a big strong steel key with a hook which gripped the tooth, his warm anvil the dentist's chair, was perhaps a better remedy. I have a fine old tooth key obtained at Finstock. Leafield blacksmith was a famous tooth puller.

A child's first teeth as they came out must be burnt, else if a dog should swallow it you would have a dog's tooth, so the children said.

'Four doctors tackled Johnnie Smith.
    They blistered and they bled him,
With squills and antibilious pills
    And ipecacuan they fed him;
They stirred him up with calomel,
    And tried to move his liver,
But all in vain, his little soul
    Was wafted o'er the river.'

This verse was recently given on the wireless. I learnt it when I was a lad.

CHARMS ETC.

Charms of one kind and another were looked to for healing, as they seem to be to-day. Mysterious little packages sewed up in leather, which as a boy I should have loved to have cut open; so many strokes with a wedding ring for a wisp on the eyelid; a double nut or some curious object carried constantly and looked to for relief. I remember hearing a man whose wife had an enlarged neck tell my father how she had gone to a man going up the street with a stallion horse and asked him for a few hairs out of the horse's tail. She was not to tell him what she wanted it for — that would have broken the spell — but the man she asked gave them to her; he had had previous requests of the same kind and he knew. These hairs were to be worn tied round the neck.

An old bill shows how the overseers paid Dr. Horniblow for his care of the poor in 1828:—

The Parish of Finstock.

To George Horniblow. Attending to the Poor from the 25th March, 1827, to the 25th March, 1828, £6 0s. 0d.

Settled, April 14th, 1828, George Horniblow.

Pudlicote

The Chapel of Pudlicote is not in existence to-day, but it was given by Philip of Pudlicote to Eynsham Abbey before 1166, and it is mentioned in the Eynsham Cartularies in 1181, and is spelt Pudelicota, 'the cottage by the puddle,' or stream. The present mansion was built in 1810 by a Mr. Gorges. It is pleasantly situated in the Evenlode valley and has been improved by its present owner, B. Whitaker, Esq.

JOHN DE PUDLICOTE, 1303

The Chapel of the Pyx at Westminster Abbey was for many years the Royal Treasury of England. For centuries it was the depository of the box in which the standard gold and silver coins of the realm were kept for comparison with the current mintage. There the Normans and Plantagenets kept their reserves of cash, their barbaric store of gems, the gold and silver vessels for the regal banquets, and other famous treasures that to-day, if they existed, would be unique. The regalia of the Saxon kings, the royal diadem of the Plantagenets, the Ampulla of Henry IV, and other rare and priceless things.

It is one of the Norman sub-structures of the Abbey, and save to a few officials this remarkable chamber with vaulted roof and massive walls is almost unknown, seven locks with seven enormous keys being used to keep all secure.

Had such vigilance been observed while Edward I was gone to thrash the Scotch, John de Pudlicote and his confederates would have been unable on St. Mark's Day, 1303, to carry away such a booty. No modern burglar has ever dreamed of such loot. A vast, almost unbelievable, amount of money and valuables was taken. Three of the robbers were hanged, but John de Pudlicote's skin was taken off, and is to this day on the Treasury door. I think the way the doors were fixed up when this was done was that the skin was put on to the boards and ledges, and perhaps hinges fixed across, so the skin can be felt or seen at the edge of the door between the boards or underneath the hinges

The whole of the monks at the Abbey were confined in the Tower of London for two years, as they were thought to have been confederates of John and his mates.

They all found 'the way of transgressors hard,' and the Pudlicote star seems to have set, save that the name is here to the house and estate and as the name to one of the aisles in Charlbury Church.

ShoRThampTon, WalcoT and Chilson

1216–1307. Spelt 'Shorthimpton.'
1274–9. 'Scorthampton.'
1293, Eynsham Cartularies: 'Schorthamptone' and 'Schorthamtone.'

Shorthampton Church

It was purchased by John de Langelee in 1302 and in 1316 he is returned as lord of the township of Shorthampton. In 1322 he had to leave these parts and go to help fight the Scots, and it is thought that he became a prisoner and a heavy ransom had to be paid for his liberty. Three hundred pounds was borrowed on his estates and at his death in 1324 his son Thomas inherited his father's acres and the debt, but the de Langelees were great wool producers, and the trade being good, wealth and knighthood came to him. For years he represented the county in Parliament. He built Langlee Mill, and built a grange and sheep fold at Shorthampton, and then in 1361–62 the plague swept the land and Thomas and his three sons passed away. His widow married John Gifford, and changes came. Other names appear.

Bruern Abbey had possession of some part of Shorthampton at one period.

The Church of 'All Saints' was originally about thirty feet by fifteen, built in the Norman period, with a northern entrance, the recess inside the church showing where the doorway was situated before alteration. The stone work of the Norman doorway was removed and inserted in the west wall to make an entrance to a gallery that used to be across the west end of the church and was reached by a flight of stone steps outside that has not long been taken down. The buttress on the north side was built into the place that had been the entrance doorway.

The chancel arch is four feet six inches in width, and when the nave was made about six feet wider on the south side the arch was out of the centre, so a hagioscope was pierced through the wall close to the chancel archway, and worshippers could see into the chancel from the widened part of the church.

The bell cot is on the gable overhead, with openings for three bells. One is missing. The ropes of those in use come down inside the chancel and have cut grooves into the stone of the arch. The south wall is two feet eight inches in thickness and contains two perpendicular windows of very good design. The entrance doorway is possibly late Early English with the original (?) door and hinges. There is a small perpendicular window in the west end.

The chancel was rebuilt about 1820. The east window is of poor design and the flat gable is surmounted by a ball. The small window in the south-west corner is sure to be noticed. It is made up out of the remains of an old window fitted into a kind of frame and sill of plain stone.

There is a plain looking piscina with shelf and sink that was cut very deep and moulded inside. The front is, as usual, broken away.

A very pretty Norman window is in its original position in the north wall with wide splays inside and a neat label on the outside.

The big tub-shaped font is very ancient. The lead-lined basin-shaped cavity is not only, as all fonts must be, large enough to immerse an infant if the parents so desire, but a good-sized boy or girl could be put into it. The marks of the hinge and locking staple, used in days of yore, when fonts (1236) had to be locked, are still visible.

A high pulpit, so that the preacher could command the gallery, is in position, also the pews with doors.

The Belief shows dimly, painted on the wall over the entrance doorway, but the paintings discovered in 1903, when the church was restored by the generosity of the Lord of the Manor, are of great interest. They were executed some 300 years ago.

A figure with Benedictine dress with a crozier is on the north wall. Near by is St. Frideswide teaching a child. A figure of an archbishop, cross staff in hand, his right uplifted in blessing. On the south splay of the hagioscope is painted the Virgin and Child with other children, illustrating the legend where Jesus is said to have made clay birds, or the other children did, and He touched them and made them fly. On the eastern splay of one of the south windows is a picture of St. Sitha, the patron saint of housekeepers. She carries a bag and keys in her hand.

High up on the wall is a cauldron full of figures, most likely to represent the cleansing of souls in purgatory.

Across the east wall is the Doom. The resurrection is in progress, the whale's open mouth, to represent the abode of the lost, from the words of Jonah, 'Out of the belly of hell cried I.' Into this mouth the lost are being hurried, with a horrible chain about them. It is gruesome, of that there is no doubt.

On the south wall St. Eligias, the patron saint of blacksmiths, is shoeing the leg of a horse. This he had taken off because the animal would not stand to be shod. Then he put it back on to the horse again.

There are fragments of perhaps a representation of the Agony in the Garden, and other subjects.

Many years ago, at Hailey, I saw an old black-letter Bible that was said to have been the copy that had been chained in Shorthampton Church when it was ordered that a copy of the Scriptures was to be set up within the church, 'whereat your parishioners may most commodiously resort to the same and read it.'

The report of the Charity Commissioners for 1837 says: 'There are three small tenements near the church, one occupied rent free by the parish clerk for the time being, the others by two poor families. The houses are kept in repair out of the parish funds.'

The River Evenlode flows near by and is crossed by a bridge, 'Catsum' (the road from the forest down to the bridge being also 'Catsum Lane') leading to Chadlington. At Chilson there is a bridge connecting Chilson and Pudlicote.

Shorthampton chapelry includes the hamlets of Chilson, Pudlicote, and Walcot. There are but a couple of farm houses and a few cottages at Shorthampton, but Chilson, just across the fields, is a pretty little cluster of houses and farms, with a day school and a Primitive Methodist Chapel erected in 1867.

Ann Robinson opened her house to the first Primitive Methodist missioners in 1835, as recorded on a tablet recently erected in the chapel, and her niece, Lucy Milton, became the wife of Richard Norton, a preacher who settled at Chilson and carried on the business of a builder. He built the chapel, and very many have gone out into the world to play a noble part fired with ideals and hopes gained in association with the above place of worship.

The stocks to confine and punish the unruly at Chilson were placed near the corner where the lane joins the village street leading from Shorthampton. Hands as well as feet could be fastened and locked in them, so woe betide any rowdy man the constable put into their strong keeping.

Those who were bent on fighting and other things likely to bring the law upon them used to adjourn over the parish boundary up on the hill into Wychwood parish, and there Mr. Baskett, the constable, with his staff, handcuffs, and his terrible stocks, was unable to touch them.

Just over the forest wall near the Burford road where the 'Wychwood' farm house is now situated was a nice bit of grass, and if there was a buck in that part of the forest he was sure to come there to graze.

Two Chilson men thought they would have a try to get a buck one day if there was one handy, and though the wall was too high for a man to see over it they found means to overcome that difficulty. One of them bent his back and held the gun, whilst the other man mounted on to his shoulders, and there was the buck, quietly feeding, right enough. 'Give me the gun,' he whispered. It was handed up, there was a report, the bullet went home, and the buck went to Chilson.

SHORTHAMPTON, WALCOT AND CHILSON FIELD NAMES
(Some not now in use).

Barrow Piece, Woodstock Green, Cubridge, Barrow Ash, Castle Furlong, Old Horse Hitchin, Small Gains, Cannons Grove, Wake Stone, Pibly Furlong, Barrows, Bradham Napp, Ox Hay, Swift Water, Helm and Hatchet, Hop Yard, Dove Cote Close (now included in field opposite Shorthampton Church), Upper Biggersden, Langley Piece, Golly Copse, Easy Furlong, Wading Furlong, King's Mead (a small part in the bend of the river was called 'Catherine's Hook'), Chadwells, Broad Close

CHILSON

An echo of Waterloo days is in this Chilson story: A lad went to Chipping Norton Fair from Chilson with fourpence to spend, and it is pleasant to know that the first hole he made in his spending money was to get a fairing for his mother, at a cost of twopence. Then as he went through the fair he came across an invitation to step inside and see 'Boneypart' and he joined the crowd, paid his twopence, and exhausted his store. When the audience was big enough up went the curtain and there on a wire was suspended a sheep's head. He saw bony part right enough, and learned a lesson for life — not to let his curiosity ever again ruin his pocket.

WALCOT

1216–1307. Walecot, 'the homestead of the strangers or serfs.'

It appears to have been the property of John de Langelee with Joan, his wife, in 1302, and his son, Thomas de Langelee, built a sheepfold at Shorthampton in 1352. He held his manor on the service of carrying the King's horn when he hunted in Wychwood. He died during a visitation of the plague, as did his three sons, in 1361–2.

Walcote was probably the residence of someone of lesser rank than the de Langelees, and did not take its place as a mansion till later years, when it became the beautiful home of the Jenkinson family, one of whom, Anthony Jenkinson, was famous as a sea captain and traveller-ambassador, and one of the founders of the Muscovy Company. The mural tablets of this family are on the walls of the chancel of Charlbury Church. The one on the north wall has an angel choir of beautiful singing cherubs, carved in marble, beneath it, whilst many names are graven in ponderous black marble slabs in the floor.

The wall around Walcot, with its loop holes for observation purposes and to shoot the deer that came within range, would give one the idea that the name arose from the fact that it was a walled-in dwelling place, instead of, as those learned in the ancient lore of languages tell us, 'the home of the servant,' as it originally was.

When work was being carried out at the present residence a few years back a chamber up amongst the chimney flues was found — quite a fine secret hiding place. There are fish ponds, lawns, and a fine levelled piece of ground, evidently for a bowling green, on which the Jenkinsons and their friends played, or strolled down pretty ways to the winding Evenlode just below, with no railroad and rushing trains to disturb the peaceful retreat, as now.

The Jenkinson motto, 'I obey, I do not serve,' is quite a suggestive one.

The first five baronets were successively Members of Parliament for Oxfordshire. The seventh, the celebrated statesman, was created Earl of Liverpool, and his son, the eighth baronet, was for many years Prime Minister of England. He is the man who not only talked about sending Napoleon to a lonely island of the sea, but he did it, sending him to St. Helena, and a Finstock man was put to help look after him. The world knows how securely they kept him, and when guard Langford came home to live at Finstock he used to go up to Cornbury to give lessons in swordsmanship to the then young Lord Churchill. My father told me he used to cut the sword exercise as he rode home on his horse along Finstock street.

I have an autograph letter of Earl Liverpool's to Earl Bathurst:

Coombe Wood,

Dear Bathurst   August 1, 1815.

I send you the Dispatches which are very important and upon the whole I think satisfactory.

I wish you would take them to the Prince but they had better not be left there. It will be time enough to answer them on Friday, particularly as my last Letters can not have reached Castle Maze when these Dispatches were sent off and they will help up his L—as to the application of the principles on which they have agreed. I intend forthwith to explain to the Prince that I could not conveniently come to town to-day, being engaged to arrive at Hampton at four o'clock in consequence of having been elected High Steward. Shall we have a Cabinet to-morrow or Thursday. If you think it better to have one to-morrow, send out invitations for two o'clock.

Ever yours sincerely,

LIVERPOOL

In 1302 the Abbot of Eynsham sued the Lord of Walcot for the crop of two acres of corn. The jury decided that the payment was due *from beyond the memory of man.*

Trades and Crafts

In days not so long ago each district was self-supporting, things necessary were, so to speak, made on the spot. Except in the case of very unusual articles, men could be found, if not in one's own village, in the next, or not far away, who could supply the skill or ability to make, do, or produce what was wanted, was it a tobacco pipe, a bell, a lock, or a clock, or a new wheel for the mill. They might not be able to read, or even know how to play tennis, but they could do the work sound, effective and durable. I want to put on record a few names, memories, and stories of these worthy people who did their part in the past in this place and neighbourhood.

BAKERS AND OVENS

Names connected with the important trade of providing bread in former days were 'Spendlove' (he built the Corner House with the observatory on the roof, and left or gave one hundred pounds towards founding the British School. His name is kept green as the name of the field opposite the Playing Close as 'Spindlus's Close' as it is pronounced in our dialect), 'Bolton,' 'Barnes,' 'Cross,' 'Dell,' 'Draper,' 'Jones' — all were bread makers at Charlbury or Finstock.

Many people baked their own bread in days of yore, and many cottages had a small oven, generally indicated on the outside of the house by a small circular projection roofed over with a few stone slates or a bit of thatch, adding a pleasing little feature to the appearance of many a house.

Baking day was a busy one, and also a day of rejoicing. New bread, and possibly a cake or two, a flat cake, a 'lardie,' the flat top divided into squares with a knife before baking, and maybe a currant cake.

A lad I heard of said, 'Mother, where did you stand when you put these currants into the cake?' She replied, 'Just behind your father's nine shillings a week, my lad.' Not many currants were possible on a wage like that.

Then faggots were used as fuel to get the oven heated. The right temperature in some cases in these ovens was known by looking inside at what was called the 'Dick Stone.' That was a pebble about as big as the fist built into the brickwork, which changed colour in the heat and was an effective thermometer.

Some ovens were built from ironstone such as could be easily dug at Fawler, and pieces of old gravestones have been known to get put in to repair the floor of even a baker's oven, hence the story of the old lady who was much alarmed to get the word 'Died' on the bottom of her loaf, or some word of that kind. It came from the piece of stone used to repair the oven on which the loaf had been placed to bake.

Some ovens had no proper 'shet,' as the iron door was called, but a thick block of hard wood was stood up against to close the opening after the batch was put in and 'stopped,' as it was called, by being plastered round the joint with nice soft clay.

Some ovens were underneath the hearth. The house with the quaint thatched gables near the top of Ward's Lane, Finstock, had one of this kind. They were made underneath a broad iron plate on which the domestic hearth fire was made. A long shallow door shutting along the front down on the floor level of the house. I know these ovens would do good work, for I once had a splendid dinner off a leg of mutton that had been baked in one of these ovens in the house next below the Primitive Chapel at Chilson.

Quite a tragic story was told about an oven in a deserted cottage when I was a lad. When not in use ovens were handy places to store things, or put them out of the way. The man had got a deer, and his wife is reported to have said, 'We could do very well if they would leave us alone,' referring, no doubt, to the dread keepers coming to search, as they did occasionally. When later on she went to put the gun out of the way by throwing it stock first into the oven, holding it by the barrel, it was loaded and went off and killed her.

Poor people who had no oven sometimes used the three-legged iron pot not only for boiling but baking too. One of my playmates astonished me one day by telling me his mother had made a cake by baking it over the fire in the pot. No doubt it was a treat and was much enjoyed. Life is very different now, though many seem to be able to find much to complain about in these days of plenty.

BLACKSMITHS

No village community could be self-supporting without its smith. Clayden, Draper and Widdows are names. Railings and entrance gates at hand show the work that was turned out beyond the ordinary work of the smithy.

A locksmith long ago at Chadlington made his locks with a keyhole like the letter 'S.' Blacksmith Hunt, of Finstock, grandfather to the Mrs. Oliver with the generous heart, lived and worked in Patch riding. The following bill gives us an idea as to the prices he charged and the way he spelt:—

1821.—The Parish to Thomas Hunt.

April 4.—New hooks to Patch get	1	6
May 2.—Mend and Sht Peck axe	1	0

For the use of the sledge hamer   0 6
   21.—Shpt Peck axe both end   0 3
Sept. 26.—For fixing the well handle and sht him   1 0
Nov. 1.—New Stapel for the Well, put in   0 4
Dec.—Sharpt a Peck axe both ends   0 3
   29.—New Peck axe, 5 lbs.   3 4
1822.—For fixing and sharping a stone hamer   0 6
Jan. 3.—A stone hamer and steal   0 8

——

£0 9 4

Jan 19.—Settled this bill and received by me.—Thomas Hunt.

T. Cox, Finstock, Lock and Gun smith and Bell hanger, Tinplate worker, etc. He said he had put the clapper in the fourth bell at Worcester Cathedral, and no doubt he had — he could do most things in metal, and must have been a most valuable asset to the whole district. From what I have heard he was quite a character.

CLOCKMAKERS

Larcum Kendal is, perhaps, the most famous amongst these local craftsmen. He was born here in 1721. He became one of the most skilful craftsmen of the day. John Harrison had made his famous chronometer so that time could be told at sea, and this proved a great boon to those that went down to the sea in ships, saving many lives.

Parliament had offered £20,000 as a prize for a machine that would keep time at sea, so that longitude could be known. It must be such that another workman could reproduce it, and the Government set Kendal to copy Harrison's watch, which he did, and though it is a sorry tale how our Government treated Harrison yet the timekeepers did very well. Kendall afterwards made a much simpler instrument than Harrison's, the date on this is 1771. It was presented in 1854 to the United Service Institution by Sir Thomas Herbert.

Captain Cook took this watch on his ship, and readers will remember how in his 'Voyages' he speaks of the 'excellent timekeeper made by Mr. Kendall.' It was taken again to the Pacific by Captain Bligh in the ill-fated *Bounty* in 1787, and was taken by the mutineers to Pitcairn Island and was sold by Adams to an American, who sold it in Chili, where it was purchased by Sir Thomas Herbert. There is a fine watch by Kendall in the Guildhall Museum, London. He died in 1795.

Thomas Wise and his son Sam lived and worked at the house with the big old-fashioned windows, where Mr. Hopkins now resides.

Gilks was a good maker. His clocks are going yet, like Longfellow's
   'For ever never, never for ever.'
He, like Dan Quare and George Graham, was a Quaker.
Richard Street, Wm. Harrison, Fairbrother, were clock makers here.

GLOVE MAKING

Since the days when William Albright introduced the manufacture of leather
gloves to Charlbury it has been carried on with benefit to the town and neighbourhood.

No doubt there have been glove makers here for many years, but not
preparing the leather and cutting.

Shakespeare compares someone's beard with 'a big round paring knife,' and
in preparing the leather these cornerless knives were used. Twisting the skin
about a post and stretching tightly with the left hand the worker gripped the
knife with the right hand through a hole in its centre and deftly pared the skin.

Cut to shape and size by skilful men, adepts in stretching, pulling, and
detecting faults or flaws, they were handed out by the 'glove master' to the
women who made them at home, beautifully sewing by hand all the various
seams, adjusting the 'forgetts' and 'quirks,' and it was quite an interesting thing
to see a 'gloveris,' as they were called, sew a glove, every stitch in its place, like
print, fit for a king.

Machines have altered this, but some hand workers are left and are still
working. The pay used to be 4½d. and 5d. a pair.

As many as 25,000 dozen gloves have been made in 12 months in our little
town and neighbourhood.

MASONS

Roger the Mason was in this neighbourhood, it is recorded, in 1346.

Harwoods, of Charlbury, quarried stone and did masonry from very early
times; men of sterling worth and skill in the mason's art; now all the local representatives of the family have forsaken the ancient family craft.

Hutts, of Finstock, did Cornbury estate work for generations, and Danbury
used to be there, and on the chimney of a quaint old cottage at Finstock is a
sundial that most likely Stephen Danbury made and set when he lived in the
house, which was his home. The sun was lighting up the figures and casting the
shadow across them as I passed by on a recent day.

SLATERS

In the part of Fawler parish near to Stonesfield were quarried and dug from
mines what are known as Stonesfield slates, used on very many roofs in all this
district and on many of the ancient buildings at Oxford.

They used to be made in great quantities, the vast heaps of rubbish about Stonesfield left from making them is evidence of this.

There is no roofing material more pleasing to the eye than these 'slats' as they are called in local dialect. Their rough surface and irregular shape, and starting at the eaves with big ones and ending at the ridge with quite small, all through the different lengths known to the workmen as 'Cussems,' 'Long Elevens,' 'Muffities,' 'Long Becks,' etc., all tend to give a pleasing, harmonious effect amongst nature's setting of field and tree and sky.

William the Slatter is mentioned in 1345, and all down the years till just recently men have worked, in the last part of the year mostly, underground in mines, about three to four feet from floor to ceiling, almost creeping on hands and knees, kneeling, and sitting on a plaited straw mat, pecking out the waste and breaking up the 'pendle,' loading the rock for sending to the surface on to a jack barrow, with wheels where the legs usually are, and these were pushed along to the shaft and hauled up by a windlass (sometimes a horse was used) to the surface, where they were laid out all over the ground. If one week's frost came in January, good and well-split slates were the result, and the men who made them were busy.

Some men were very skilled at this work. Using a few simple tools, sitting under the shelter of a hurdle or two covered with straw, or in a little cave-like workshop made by building up some waste stone, gradually reducing till the top was completely domed in, and sitting round, each man with a stone for a work bench to rest the edge of the slate upon, whilst he tapped away, turning out the slate shaped something like a luggage label with its hole, but in this case to have a wooden peg driven tightly into it, by which it was hung on to a lath when it was in position on the roof.

Some old roofs are made with a hollow curve from eaves to ridge, the rafters pulled down to the side pieces or purlins so the slates pitch as they are hung, giving greater security against the wind lifting them, besides giving a better bed for each slate. Gutters and hips are both sometimes formed with slates without lead or cresting, the slates neatly fitted and carried round and over, the result being a splendid roof, cool in summer and warm in winter.

If sufficient frost did not come to make the slate split the stones were buried in soil and vetches or green stuff to shade them was sown over, as if the quarry sap dried out they were not of much use.

A curious system of counting prevails, some slates counting as three if over a certain size, and some counting as five.

The strata is remarkable for its fossils, and many celebrated and beautiful specimens found there can be seen in the University Museum at Oxford.

SHOE MAKERS

Ward's Lane, Finstock, I expect, got its name from a family of that name who lived in it. James Ward was a boot maker, and his bills are, some of them, before me for work done for the overseers for the parish:

'New pair shoes, six and sixpence.'

'Shoes four and sixpence.'

Such charges are, or seem to be, surprisingly small charges; yet these are items from James Ward's bills.

There were several shoe makers at Charlbury, and the name 'Parrott' was in the first rank amongst them.

Old Mr. Parrott in Watts Lake had been a soldier when Sir John Moore retreated with his army of 25,000 men before Napoleon, who had 70,000, marching in December, 1808, from Astorga to Corunna, a march of 250 miles through mountainous country in snow and rain, Sir John on foot with his men, now and then carrying a tired soldier's musket for him, and then on January 16th, 1809, defeating the French but being killed by a grape shot at the moment of victory. Everyone is acquainted with the poem—

'Not a drum was heard, not a funeral note.'

Our Mr. Parrott was one of his men and went through that trying time.

'When shall come the day when
    The stormy clangour
Of wild war music o'er the earth shall cease,
Love shall tread out the baleful fire of anger,
    And in its ashes plant the tree of peace.'

Mr. Townsend at Chadlington was a member of the cordwainer's craft, and Mr. Kerry, of former days here at Charlbury, came from that village, I believe. He was a most excellent man; he filled the important office of Parish Constable, was a Wesleyan local preacher, and from what I have heard was quite a man above reproach. He used to quote Matthew Henry in his sermons, and his doctrine was sound, no doubt. He little thought, I dare say, that he would have a bishop for his grandson.

TOBACCO PIPE MAKERS

A document (1711) with signatures of Ro. Jenkinson, Rog. ffranklin, Edward Copeland and others, to the parish officials at ffinstock:—

'We do hereby desire you to permitt and suffer John Willis, pipemaker of Charlbury to inhabit and abide in ffinstock and to follow his lawful calling there without any molestation.'

I wonder why and who objected. Was it the dames and damsels? They would not shame their fair lips by using themselves the noxious weed, and did they resent its use by the sterner sex? I wonder!

Another document (June 7th, 1714) relates to the settlement at Finstock of Joseph Cox, Tobacco Pipe maker. His kiln and dwelling was, I think, where the late Mr. John Kite used to live.

The craft is gone, but the tiny bowls with short stems turn up all about us.

Though we are told 'No man is at his best who smokes,' the use of the weed continues, and even— A skeleton nearly popped out, but I had the key.

WOODWORKERS

In 1216 'Hugh de Barintin, the King's carpenter, is to have possession of the land at Cotes which the King has given him.' So runs the record, and as in his day woodworkers were an indispensable part of the community; there have always been in our manor men of skill in woodwork, be it to frame the timbers of a roof, to build a stair, or make a bow or an arrow shaft when such were used, or hurdles from the willows that grow on the banks of the Evenlode.

Many workers' names are lost, not being recorded as Hugh, the King's carpenter, who was to have Coate, and a later record states that he is to have twopence a day pension, but a few names of more recent years I want to mention. The names of the men who did our Church roof timbers, put our ample chest together, or built the quaint stairs to the belfry, turned the balusters in Merton House, an early craftsman who made a door I have that did its last important service as the outer door of the 'Blind House,' or lock-up on the Playing Close, with its inside dowells, so that neither rails nor ledges were used in its construction, but it was like one plank exactly alike on either side, as though made from one board.

Also the beautiful stairs at the Manor House, Finstock, and the curious roof timbers in a tiny cottage nearly opposite the Crown Inn. Panelling on the wall of one of the houses at Shorthampton, a few caned lintels at Charlbury and Finstock possibly cut by the same hand, also a couple of carved corbels carrying the porch at the house this side Finstock School playground. These things have come down to us each with a message for those that can take it, and where a line of beauty appears the gift of the man who made it long ago, to this world of hustle, we are grateful for the legacy.

The window sashes at the Wesleyan Chapel here are remarkable examples of fine work of about 1823. I wish I could give the name of the man who made them.

Some names — Baughan, Compton, Coombes, Collett, Dore, Hill — were connected with woodworking, also Paintin, at Finstock. Can give one of his bills (1828):

> Mr. Stait, the overseer of Finstock Parish to Richd. Paintin for a coffin, 17s. 0d.
>
> April 7th. Settled this bill.— Richd. Paintin.

Malins, the cooper, was the clever man whose workshop used to be in Watts Lane opposite the brewery, now Wool Warehouse. He would make one of the small wooden barrels like bottles that men used to take into the hay and harvest field, for one shilling and sixpence. Fancy jointing all the little staves, making and fitting the heads, also several hoops of iron with a carrying handle, for that sum. I know this is correct, for Mr. Henry Hall told me he paid that to have his made. Buckets and other utensils of galvanised iron had not come in and the cooper's trade was in great demand.

An old lady at Spelsbury not so long ago persisted in the use of the big lumbering wooden buckets for her drinking water. She did not think water was fit to drink from a galvanised pail.

Public houses

Previous to the fifteenth century beer was made without hops, indiscriminately from barley, wheat, or oats — some with a mixture of all. It was drunk as soon as made before it got heady. Malt houses there were in plenty. Many have been altered and put to other uses.

Charlbury Brewery is now converted, and is the central depot and offices of an extensive wool trade.

At Finstock the 'Plough' and the 'Crown' are old inns, but Charlbury for its size was some years ago hard to beat for the number of its inns and public houses. There were 'The Ball'; 'The Bell,' with a stone sign carved in panel with date 1700 over the door; 'The Bear'; 'The Black Horse'; 'The Bull' (this property came into the hands of the Lord of the Manor some years ago because of no claimant or title, or something); 'The Crown'; 'The Dog'; 'The Lion'; 'The Mason's Arms'; 'The Oak,' now a temperance hotel; 'The Orange Tree'; 'The Star'; 'The Swan'; 'The White Hart.'

'The Waterloo Arms' at Finstock Heath was so named because the house was built by a Mr. Poole, who also had built the two cottages down the street at Finstock with a stone tablet with 'Waterloo Cottages' on it. He was at the battle of Waterloo, and his wife's gravestone in the Churchyard records the fact that she was a native of Portugal. I believe he was keeper at Cornbury after his army career was ended.

'The Malt Shovel,' at Chadlington, used to be connected with a malt house on the cowl of which was an interesting figure. I wonder who made it, and what became of it.

'The Sandy's Arms' sign takes us at once to the Bayton Sandy's family, formerly connected with the parish. See the names on the wall in the north transept in the Church.

The word 'Tite' is an old name for a bursting out spring, in this case taken by John Barleycorn as a sign where his manufactures are sold.

Customs

Finstock youth ale

In the year A.D. 601 it was ordered that the natives who had embraced Christianity were to have their annual heathen feasts turned into Christian festivities. Huts were to be built from branches and gaiety and feasting to be the rule. These things degenerated into drunken orgies, to be banned and shunned by those of enlightenment and refinement. Corn was planted to make cake, barley to brew ale for these. 'Whitsun,' 'Lamb' and at Finstock a 'Youth Ale.' Webb's barn, now pulled down, near the Plough Inn, my grandmother remembered was the scene of the last. My Lord and Lady sat in state, an owl in a cage was referred to as 'My Lord's parrot,' and a flail on the wall 'My Lord's bagpipes.' It appears a tree used to be cut in the Forest and brought and laid for a year on the green, when it was cut up and the timber sold to find funds for the youth ale at Finstock.

Spanish water

At Finstock on Palm Sunday, the youngsters indulge in 'Spanish water,' as it is called, that is a liquor made by dissolving a few bits of liquorice and a couple of black sweets in water. Made on Saturday night, given a shake in the morning, and it is prime. Before the forest enclosure the young folk, carrying their bottles, used to walk to a spring in the forest or to the Lady's Well at Wilcote. It is a remnant of the old heathen custom when wells were worshipped. It was forbidden in 963, so it has persisted for long, and the 'Spanish water' part, it seems, will never die.

Spitting

The boys in Finstock had the old custom of 'spitting their faith' or their 'soul' when anything was to be very binding, or assured. One would say, 'Will you spit on it?' and a stone was picked up and spat upon. This is a very ancient custom, according to Pliny, as is spitting on the hands before fighting — it would avert witchcraft, and a shrewder blow could be given, so it was thought.

Carol singing

Some time before Christmas the children at Finstock used to sing at the doors and windows of the cottages, after dusk had set in, as a carol:—

'As I sat on the sunny bank, the sunny bank, the sunny bank,
As I sat on the sunny bank, on Christmas Day in the morning,
I saw two ships go sailing by, go sailing by, go sailing by,
I saw two ships go sailing by, and in them were Joseph and Mary.
He did whistle and she did sing, and all the bells in Heaven did ring,
For Jesus Christ is our King, on Christmas Day in the morning.'

This was done night by night till Christmas Day came.

29TH MAY
On the above day sprigs of oak used to be worn with the oak apple gilded.
I had once in my possession the remains of a book of gold leaf. Part had been
used, I understood, to gild oak apples for May 29th.

THE FLITCH OF BACON
The late Mr. George Huckin was the last man, I believe, many years ago, to
have presented to him the bacon, given once in forty years in Charlbury, to the
man 'who did mind his own business and did leave other people's alone.'

Charlbury Whitsun Ale was celebrated once in seven years. A maypole from
Wychwood stood in Church Street and for a week things not pleasant to think
of were to the fore.

Dialect

'Thy speech bewrayeth thee.'

The speech of a county, place or district has kept fairly constant amongst working people that remain in the same place from generation to generation. The pronunciation of a single word may proclaim the village a person hails from, and though the schoolmaster and contact with the outer world may have done something, yet — unconsciously often, words and old pronunciations and intonations abide.

It is far more easy to talk our various dialects than to write them, but I have tried to give some idea of our local English, as it is 'spoke.'

A. — The letter is pronounced 'ah,' the same as in Welsh. An old man said to me one day: 'It's Oxford 'Ah' and Cambridge 'A', referring to the way clergymen pronounced the word 'Amen.' It is used instead of 'he' and 'it' and 'in.' 'Where is a gone?' 'Abed.'—In bed.

Account.—Of worth. 'Not much account.'

Addle.—Rotten egg. 'Be um addled.'

Ashore.—Ajar. 'I left the door ashore.'

Arter.—After. 'Arternun,' for 'afternoon.'

Baffle.—To hinder; or better, to confuse.

Be.—Used for are and am. 'Yer us be' for 'Here we are.'

Beant, or Beyent.—Are not. 'No us beyent.'

Bisnt.—Art thou not.

Bwyle.—Boil.

Buttie.—A mate.

Bwoy.—Boy.

Bash.—To beat a tree, as for walnuts.

Call.—Reason, or need. 'No call to go.'

Cas-ul-ty.—Uncertain, as the weather, etc.

Cha-ney.—China-ware.

Cheer.—A chair

Cherkey.—Stale bread said to 'eat cherkey,' dry.

Chimbley.—Chimney.

Clackett.—A noise. 'Stop that clackett.'

Clats.—Clods.

Close.—A small field.

Clout.—A blow. 'A clout o' the yer.'

Crack up.—To praise.

Crap.—Crop.

Cup, cup.—A call for cows.

Cwot, Quott.—A coat.

Deep.—Knowing, wise, crafty.

Did'st.—Did you.

Dillin.—When there is a small pig in a litter, that is the 'dillin'.

Dinks.—To toss a baby, or jump it up and down quickly.

Dout.—To extinguish. 'Dout that light.'

Dum-el.—Slow, dull, stupid.

Egg on.—To encourage to quarrel, or fight.

Ese.—Yes. An old man said: 'When I was a bwoy and anybody asked me to have anything (food, etc.) I used to say, "No, thenk 'e," but now I says, "Ese if a plaze."'

Ethering band, or bend.—The twisted top twisted along the top of a cut and laid hedge.

Fet.—To fetch.

Fettle.—To repair or put in order.

Form. Condition, appearance. 'What a form you did it in' or 'did that work.'

Forrust.—First.

Fut.—Foot. 'You trod on my fut.'

Gallied.—Confused with noise. 'You children gallies my brains.'

Ghet.—A gate.

Go at.—To set about. 'Go at him,' or 'it.'

Grace.—Grease.

Hale.—Well and lusty.

Haw wut.—To a horse.

Haps.—A fastening, not a latch.

He-ah.—A dog's call. He-ah, 'come here.'

Heft.—To lift. Anglo-Saxon hefan, to lift.

Hi-nuns.—Onions.

Holler.—To shout.

Hood.—Wood.

How-zen.—Houses.

Hoxey.—Sticky dirt, as after a shower.

Hud.—A pea or bean shell.

Hut.—To hit, as 'I hut him.'

Kangle.—Tangle.

Keck-handed.—Left-handed, awkward.

Kerlick.—Charlock.

Lap.—To cut branches off trees as they stand.

Lappen.—Foolish. 'You gret lappen.'

Lollipops.—Sweets.

Loppeting.—Lolling idly about.

Maggled.—Hot and tired.

Mated.—Very much bothered.

Med.—May. 'You med if you like.'

Mom-erd.—Anything said or done over and over again till confused.

Moot.—The stump or root of a tree.

Motherish.—Wine, etc., got rather thick.

Muck.—Dung, manure.

Muggy.—Hot, close. 'What a muggy day.'

Nacker.—An old-horse.

Ok-kurd.—Awkward.

Ood'st.—Would you.

Oodn't.—Won't you.

Parkie.—Cold.

Paingers.—Broken bits of pottery.

Peek.—To peep.

Pelt.—To throw at.

Pen.—A sheep fold, or for cattle.

Pick-ed.—Pointed.

Piller.—A pillow.

Pinner.—A pinafore.

Plim.—To swell in cooking. 'This bacon plims.'

Rackett.—A noise.

Rubbage.—Rubbish.

Ruckett.—Lumber.

Saa-ser.—A saucer.

Scart.—Walking vigorously. 'How you scart along.'

Scaut.—To hang on with feet forced against the ground.

Scrimpy.—Little, poor.

Scrobble.—To scrape, to claw.

Scrunch.—To bite with noise, as crust.

Scrunge.—To push through amongst people or to push them along a seat or bench.

Sheth.—A sheath.

Shet in, or Shet off.—To put in or take out of harness a horse or other animal.

Shick shak.—Oak leaves carried on May 29th.

Shick-el.—A reaping hook.

Ship.—A sheep.

Shirty.—Cross, touchy.

Showl.—A shovel.

Skimmer lad or laddie.—Pudding put without a cloth on to a skimmer and so placed in the pot and cooked on it.

Slans.—Sloes.

Slummox. —Sloven, slatternly.

Smartish.—A number, amount. 'A smartish frost last night.'

Sock.—A blow.

Squatch.—To keep quiet, not tell about.

Squez.—Squeeze.

Stale.—A handle, as of a hay fork.

Stwun.—Stone.

Sum-mat .—Something.

Swiffet.— To be cross.

Swig.—A hearty drink, as from a bottle.

Take off.—To make fun of.

Tay.—Tea.

Tollet.—A loft over a stable.

Tur-nup.—Turnip.

Tewer.—A passage between fences.

Unked.—Miserable.

Var-nigh.—Very near.

Wapps.—A wasp.

Watchered.—Wet feet, wet shod.

Werks.—A fuss, a row.

While.—A long, or short time.

While away.—To kill time.

Workey day.—'Sunday or workey day.'

Worrit.—Worry.

Yaller.—Yellow. Yella bwoy, a sovereign.

Yawn-ups.—A silly. 'What a gret yawn-ups.'

Yelm.—To get straw out straight for thatching.

Yed.—Head.

Yer.—Here, or hear.

Yet.—Heat, or to eat.

Not long ago a man in a trap met a woman evidently he was well acquainted with, and pulling up his horse I heard him say, 'Yer us be,' and she replied, 'And yer be I.' This was quite an old style Oxfordshire greeting.

An old friend of mine went to London on a visit, and one day asking a policeman the way was greeted at once with, 'I be Oxfordshire, I be.'

A rustic poet one day at a very bad gate on his master's farm came out with:

'Is this the best ghet (gate) the man can affoord?
Hung with a chain, and tied with a coord.
Is this the best ghet that goes into the clover,
Neither opens nor shets, and you can't get over.'

On another occasion at the farm house to the servant girl—

'Baking and brewing, and all things a–doing,
But it all lies on John Jones's daughter;
But she is to make haste, and put all things in place,
And go up in the field, and rake arter.'

Things found

A lovely piece of coral which my father found in his garden, in the 'Bottom,' near to the Plough Inn, Finstock, always stood in a place of honour on the best table in our cottage, and later on I found a stone the size of a penny with markings like a star fish upon it, in the rough edge of the bank by the roadside on the 'Wellhill,' and ever since I have been on the lookout for these remains of life in past ages.

In the rocks, clays, and gravels of our neighbourhood there is abundant food for thought, and much to excite delight and wonder.

This tiny spot of the globe's surface has been rent and broken, washed and swilled, lifted up and cast down, till it got to be the lovely bit of hill and dale as we know it.

Ironstone peeping out here and there, clay many feet in thickness, known and used in the preparation of gloving leather, and at the bottom of this clay lovely fossils are to be found: Ammonites, Belemnites, delicate Pentacrinites, etc., and bits of black wood.

The gravels are full of wonder to those that can see; many kinds of fossil remains are easily found.

There is a fine stretch of gravel deposit along the north bank of the Evenlode, extending from our parish away into Chadlington, at about 50ft. above the river level according to Dr. K. S. Sandford. This he considers belongs to the Wolvercote terrace, and is not so early as the Handbrough gravel deposit.

I found a beautiful small pennanular brooch in the edge of the bank at one of the gravel pits, about 6in. from the surface.

Roman coins turn up everywhere in our neighbourhood, also fragments of pottery, and oyster shells. In Roman times how did they get oysters into our neighbourhood quickly enough from the sea so they were fresh, or had they means of keeping them sweet and good for the long journey here?

Fragments of pottery, from British or very early days, made without a potter's wheel, down through all the periods to 'Field town chaney,' as the red ware made at Leafield was sometimes called, is to be picked up in our fields and gardens. Franklin's at Leafield were good potters. In my time I have seen the clay dug, then put through the Pug mill, then cut with a wire, back and forth, to remove stones, etc., then most cleverly turned and fashioned on a swiftly revolving table, put to harden, then lead glazed if to hold liquids, then put into the furnace and burnt, brought out when cool enough, all rough bits filed off with a rasp, and it was ready for the hawker to take round to sell, or for any other market. Franklin's wharf, for so many years at Oxford, was I believe founded by one of the Leafield family going there to sell goods made at the home village in the Forest.

In the district interesting things have come to light. I bought a Posey ring that the plough turned up, that had engraved inside it, 'As God hath appointed so am I contented.'

I heard of another of these quaint rings that a man found in his cottage garden. He had planted his runner beans in the same place for some thirty or forty years, and then found this ring, which had inside it, 'Happy in thee hath God made me.'

A groat of Henry VIII was found in one of the Walcot fields some time ago; it is in my possession. A Testoon of Edward VI was found during some alterations to property in Sheep Street, but more interesting I think, is a Silver Penny of Edward I, Bristol Mint, found along Hundley recently.

A more recent find is a hammer struck Shilling of Elizabeth, found in the garden at the back of the White Hart.

If anything is found in the earth, handle it carefully. If pottery, do not smash it, if metal, coin, etc., do not scrape, or file or rub with a piece of brick, at most only scrub it with a brush and water and set up to dry, and, in your ear — 'Let me have a look at it.'

Spelsbury

Though not in our manor, yet is our near neighbour, and we will jot down a few items.

The Manor of Spellesbury was given by Berthalf, King of Mercia, to the Bishop of Worcester about A.D. 798, and in a charter A.D. 1005 Spellesbury is mentioned. In Edward I's time the Beauchamps, Earls of Warwick, held it, and it was worth £30 19s. 10d. The names of 55 heads of families are given. After the Battle of Barnett, 1471, it was, with over 120 manors that Earl Warwick owned, forfeit to the Crown, and it remained Crown property till near the end of Queen Elizabeth's reign, when she gave or sold it to Sir John Fortescue, and he sold it to Sir Henry Lee. In Edward VI's time it was called 'The King's Hare Warren.'

In 1391 the rectorial tithes were given to the Church of Our Lady at Warwick, 'that they might pray for the soul' of the donor, Sir William Beauchamp. Henry VIII gave the Rectory to Christ Church College, Oxford, who possess it still.

Spelsbury Church was built by a Beauchamp, and in ages past had monuments to that family, but they have entirely gone. I wonder if the fine old stone coffin in the churchyard is one of theirs.

The spire was taken down, as was much of the church, leaving the Norman tower, in 1775. Robert, Earl of Lichfield, rebuilt it at a cost of £1,000, but did not replace the spire.

The bells stood in the churchyard for 13 years, and were recast in 1788 to weigh 40 cwts, instead of 68 cwts. original weight, and were a maiden peal. Beautiful and tuneful music from them has been borne on the northern breezes across this way many times.

In 1631 Sir Henry Lee, cousin to the great Sir Henry, was laid to rest in Spelsbury Church. His tomb is in the place of honour in the chancel and is worth study. There are fine monuments to the first, third, and fourth Earls of Litchfield, and a recumbent effigy to Lord Charles Dillon, died November 18th, 1865. Other Dillon monuments are in the churchyard.

The three Wilmots, Earls of Rochester, were buried in the vault in the north aisle in 1659, 1680, and 1681. John the wit and profligate died repentant under the ministrations of Bishop Burnet at High Lodge in Blenheim Park in 1680.

I have a copy of the funeral sermon preached by Robert Parsons at Spelsbury.

A plain brass in the floor in front of the chancel steps bears this inscription.

'George Pickering, gentleman, having been XXX. yeares a servant to the hon. familie of the Lees of Ditchly about the XIII. day of March Ao. Dni. 1645 departed this life and lyeth here buried.

> Not to prophane (by a rude touch) the dust of his great Master's doe we bouldly thrust this aged servant's bones whose humble love and innocent ambition did move by creeping neere their tombes adored side to show his body not his duty dyde.'

The four Almshouses of quaint design were built and endowed with £10 10s. yearly by John Cary, of Wilcote.

The schools were built and maintained by Viscount Dillon.

A memorial fountain to Constantine Augustus Dillon, drowned 16th April, 1853, is in the centre of the village. Nearby is a good village hall.

In the plaster on the Church tower are the names 'John Trinder, Henry Issard, Ch. Wardens, 1706.'

1346 Robert Frankeleyn and John Taillour and others carried away goods of the Abbess of Godstow, Bloxham and Whichewod, and assaulted her servants there.

In 1569 someone stole from the Church box.

1537 every communicant is to give a halfpenny for bread.

At Dean, a hamlet of Spelsbury, is a monolith called 'The Hawk Stone' and 'Dean House' nearby was formerly the residence of Governor Eyre, the first white man to cross Australia. The record of that journey in a book, *In Danger's Hour*, is worth reading.

At the roadside is the base stone of an ancient cross.

Taston, another hamlet, has an old cross with lofty steps, and not far from it 'Thor's Stone,' standing about 7ft high by 3ft by 1ft 3in.

The 'Mace' family, blacksmiths and clock makers, lived and worked here.

Methodist services were formerly held in a house near the fountain and at the Cross steps.

On a bedroom wall of a cottage towards Coate were wall paintings similar to those in churches. My father saw them many years ago.

Charming Charlbury

Gleanings of an Oxfordshire countryside,
with notes on
Chipping Norton, Churchill and Kingham

Contents

Introduction

Charlbury from near railway station

'Where do you get your information?' I am asked by kind readers of my books. 'He that asketh receiveth, and he that seeketh findeth,' said our Lord, and this applies in more realms than one.

Memories recalled; the village Fathers; old letters and records; newspapers; observation and reading; and so I have set down some things never before in print, and others not generally known, of our charming Charlbury and Wychwood district.

Some things past, gone, discarded cause a pang of regret, whilst others are best done with for ever.

> 'Tossed out to wither like unsightly weeds
> From the world's garden banished.'

There is much pleasure (mixed with a sweet pain) to go back in thought to one's early memories of cottage life and doings, within and about it. Father, alert and strong, filling my mind with what he knew, and kindling my desires to see and know all I could of our beautiful district, dear good mother seeming to live again amid it all:

> 'A kiss when I woke in the morning,
> A kiss when I went to bed,
> A kiss when I burnt my finger,
> A kiss when I bumped my head.'

All life centres for me about a little cottage at the foot of the Well Hill, Finstock, and the 'Bottom' there; our neighbours; their doings, dress, sayings, and ways. Hey! but it is a pleasant picture. What splendid companions I had, what rare times the different play places witnessed in those happy days!

Life was full of interest in our village:

The Postman blew his tin horn in the evening as he entered the 'Bottom,' coming down the Plough Lane from Ramsden. Letters had to be taken to him.

The carpenter's workshops to see, and sometimes a pair of pit sawers to watch, one on top of the tree trunk, the other man below in the pit.

A big old cider mill with a ponderous revolving stone travelling round and round in a circular trough as a horse walked round.

Mr. Greenshilds coming to bring the Parish relief for the worthy decent old people that gathered in Ward's Lane every Friday, half-a-crown and a big square upright loaf to each one, to some cases he gave a paper with which a half pint of gin or a pound of neck of mutton could be procured.

We were in touch with the highest in the land, was not Lady Churchill away with the Queen? And when she came home she would come to the school, and call at our house perhaps.

One day in the year our school was turned into a shop, a vast tilted waggon came from Oxford full of drapery goods and smart shopmen. It was the Clothing Club Sale.

Wonder of wonders was an annual event, our Vicar gave us a Magic Lantern Show, and the second night to the adults.

Then Mr. Groves the builder would go through to Wilcote and he would give a boy a ride in his trap and very likely a penny or more. One of my talented playmates was learning the harmonium so that he could play in church. Mr. Groves promised him a shilling when he could do it; that money was claimed, you may be sure.

One of our honest old men who was deaf and lived alone, not so long ago, drove away his tedium and found comfort in beating a drum he possessed. I fear his 'Drum Solos', long continued, were not altogether acceptable to the neighbours about him, but he was happy as he thumped away.

We had men and women of character, and they spoke with a glow and zest of life and its doings, words sometimes full of simple wisdom gained by patient continuance in well doing, was it in the woods, or in the fields, or at home, facing up to pain, and sorrow, and death.

Work, our master word, was first to be considered in village life. Work or the Union. A few escaped it, dodged it by wit or skill, but to most it was work first, and work last.

Some heard the eternal music and with face aglow led us towards the heights and everlasting things. 'Many are called, but few are chosen.'

Was not all nature about us? Summer and winter with its store of interest never ceasing. Fields, lanes, woods, and streams, flowers, birds, beasts and butterflies. God's great sky of changing beauty arching all by day, and at night the wondrous stars. My! they were glorious at Finstock, who could fail to see the stars, *our* stars? We knew:

'There's not a bird or plant or tree,

No song-bird's carol wild and free,
But is a messenger to thee
God's wealth of love revealing.'

I am glad I was born in the country. Life is so varied, so arresting, so much to demand attention, so sweet and wonderful.

The breeze so gentle fanning the face, and then the boisterous wind rising to a tempest, you fought through it holding your breath and rejoiced.

Books were a joy. Bunyan's *Pilgrim's Progress*, *Robinson Crusoe*, Huntington's *Kingdom of Heaven taken by Prayer*, Jordan's *History of Enstone*, and do not forget *Uncle Tom's Cabin*, and that wonder book, *The Bible*, was always at hand, whilst many others came our way. What a debt I owe to those who put reading in my path and lent me many, many books. I remember vividly how difficult I found it to learn to read.

We were in constant touch with our manor town, Charlbury. There we had:— The Bank, the Railway, the Doctor, the Grammar School, Gloving, Shopping, and Newspapers. Any Post Office business we did at Charlbury — up a passage, through an opening in the partition, one at a time.

The letters formerly, we hear, came from Enstone in a little cart drawn by two dogs, coming down Banbury Hill at a gallop and full rip round the Bull corner, the driver in a heap on top of the mail.

The Market House we saw in Church Street, the 'Blind House,' a dungeon on the Playing Close, with nail-studded door, and iron plate with air holes, bolted thereon.

We could buy three-pennyworth of wonderful cough mixture at the chemist's shop, and, tell it not in Gath, laudanum could be had as easily by those who ventured with the deadly drug.

We were always hearing of Chipping Norton, our hawkers went to its markets and fairs, tasty bloaters and sprats in season came to us from the sea, via Chipping Norton.

If any one got 'pull'd' (summoned), the magistrates sat at Chipping Norton. The whales' ribs in Back Lane, as it used to be, the tall factory chimney shafts, a clock with a curious escapement in Sims' window, and Charlott's coffee house in New Street, stand out in my first recollections, as a lad, of the ancient market town.

Then for a time I stayed at Cornwell, later on for some time at Churchill, lodging at good Mrs. Widdows'.

At Kingham I spent a winter, staying at Mrs. Brick's, and I got to know the feel of the place pretty closely, as to who and what things were, at that most interesting village.

With thanks to all who have lent a hand in my search for village lore.

Here is the book, read it, and if you pick up a pleasant or helpful thought amongst my odds and ends, I shall not have written in vain.

'To be a Seeker is to be the best sect next to a Finder, and such an one shall every faithful humble Seeker be at the end. Happy Seeker, happy Finder'!
—*Oliver Cromwell to his daughter Bridget at Cornbury.*

Charming Charlbury

A treasure ground of antiquity

A veritable treasure ground of antiquity is this Wychwood countryside. Our hills are dotted with numbers of earth mounds, the burial places of prehistoric man.

The long or egg-shaped earliest type occur at Slate Pits Copse in the Forest, whilst tumps like a big mole-hill occur again and again in our fields. Grim's Dyke can be easily traced zig-zagging across our parish, and beyond.

The standing stones on some of our hill sides and open places are more arresting than the earth mounds. Rough and unwrought, they raise many questions as to who? when? how?

The Hawk Stone, Dean (left).
Slate Pits Long Barrow in Wychwood Forest: burial chamber stones (right).

The upright solitary Hawk stone at Dean, standing like some giant sentinel, a cenotaph to mark some great event in dim forgotten days.

At Taston (with a dry wall built against it) is Thor's stone; once it stood clear, an honoured monolith, perhaps with rank, and much meaning, in its prime.

It was no child's play to stand upright and fix the largest of the three of 'The Devil's Quoits' at Stanton Harcourt, whilst to raise and balance the table stone, some ten tons in weight, on top of its supports about eleven feet in height at Enstone Hoar Stone, meant resource and skill of no mean order, whatever the date or period.

Viscount Dillon of Ditchley, who owns the land, has had the holly bushes cleared away that for long years had hidden this remarkable relic of antiquity, so now all may enjoy the sight of it.

In the field at Lidstone is a big standing stone, and till recent years one stood near to the cottage at Cuckold's Holt, Gagingwell.

Thor's Stone, Taston

THE ROLLRIGHT STONES

My father had fired my imagination about these stones, Circle, Whispering Knights, and King Stone, so when one of the first places as a boy I went with him, was to help build a new water bridge, in Choicehill Bottom, at the foot of the hill on which the stones stand, here was a fine chance to see them. The world to me was fresh and young and full of glamour.

We lodged at Over Norton at the house of a Charlbury woman, who had married a man of the romantic and suggestive name of Gulliver. On the wall hung a sampler, some words on it I remember:

'Weigh well your part and do your best,

And leave the rest to God.'

One night a canary hanging in a cage on the wall was in some mysterious way got through the bars and eaten by rats. Cement and broken glass my father used to stop the holes that were in the house after that.

The foreman at the bridge, Arthur Timms, father and I went one day to visit the famous stones. I did not quite walk on air, but it was a wonderful time. I can almost see my father stepping the circle to get the diameter.

There were no railings about them then. Of the baker putting his loaves upon them in a vain endeavour to count the circle stones, I heard, and amongst gentle and simple, many things are told about them.

The King Stone, Rollright

An early manuscript speaks of them as the second wonder in the kingdom, I believe. Camden in 1634 gives a drawing. Other authors have things to say about them.

A king with knights, and soldiers, called on Mother Shipton, asking his prospects; he wanted to be England's king. She worked her incantations, boiled up her witches' pot 'with babies' blood and graveyard mud' and then she said:

'Seven long strides shalt thou take — and if Long Compton thou canst see, King of England thou shalt be.'

Thinking the prize was sure he cried: 'Stick, stock, stone, as King of England I shall be known,' and took seven strides forward, but lo, not quite far enough did he go, and he heard the fateful words:

'As Long Compton thou canst not see,
King of England thou shalt not be.
Rise up, stick, stand still, stone,
For King of England thou shalt be none.
Thou and thy men hoar stones shall be,
And I myself an elder tree.'

There stands the king stone, his army seventy yards away, his five plotting knights about 300 yards down the field.

The eldern tree is said to bleed if cut on Midsummer eve.

How many things are missed by not going quite far enough, just short of success we go, and all is lost. In sacred story the dying prophet reproved the king when he smote the arrows on the floor, he had come short of complete victory. I was told that if you climb the king stone and put your chin on top of it you *can* see Long Compton.

An attempt to use any of the stones leads to trouble. One horse could bring back a stone it took several to take away, and the same is told of other stones in other parts, even overseas.

Sober thought and research has not with certainty grasped their secret. The whispering knights a fallen cromlech. The circle possibly a temple. Men have always found it good and strengthening to the inner life to assemble together (though this does not take the place of individual meditation and worship) and in the Gospel days we have our Lord's words as to His presence 'where two or three are gathered together in My name, there am I in the midst of them.'

FLINT

Not so noticeable, perhaps, but none the less remarkable, is the abundance of flint, weapons and tools, that lies in the soil all over our district, shewing that in the Stone Age, much life and activity was here. Early man favoured these parts in, to us, those dim and distant days about which we know so little. Whatever his appearance or his language, he possessed no small degree of ability and skill, the make and finish of his flint work plainly tell us that, and was he here today, he would have taken his place alongside our most skilled artificers without a tremble or a blush.

Rough hand-made vessels of pottery from our early graves, objects of bronze, also British coins, plainly tell us of life and movement in days of yore. The mill ponds, as ours, in use in the eighth century, all have their story to tell us.

Deeds, charters, wills and documents exist for those who can read them. The learned ones in ancient lore are putting these things into modern English, so that all may read these old records, and they tell us that the first mention of Oxford recorded was in 912, whilst Charlbury has earlier mention as the burying-place of St. Diuma of Lindisfarne, the evangeliser of Mercia 656 A.D.

Henry III., Feb. 7, 1256. 'Charlbury to have a Market every Monday and a yearly fair to last 4 days.'

Many I hear are visiting Shorthampton, one of our hamlets a mile and a half away in the fields, to view the interesting wall paintings within the quaint little church.

Ancient memorial brasses

Our district shares in the heritage of brasses that are to be found in many churches, laid down to commemorate the departed.

Since the conquest an engraved plate of latten, a mixture, or blend of copper, tin and zinc, let into the surface of a slab of stone, generally over the grave of the departed, has been a favourite and most enduring form of memorial. Many thousands were put down before the Reformation and many have been destroyed. Some because of reforming zeal against what was considered superstitious or wrong, emblems also invocations for prayers for the dead, and the words '𝔒𝔫 𝔴𝔥𝔬𝔰𝔢 𝔰𝔬𝔲𝔩𝔢𝔰 𝔍𝔥𝔲 𝔥𝔞𝔟𝔢 𝔪𝔢𝔯𝔠𝔶 𝔄𝔪𝔢...' were torn up. Some brasses executed during the life of the person commemorated never had the dates, etc., filled in.

Most of our churches have at least one, or a matrix from which it has been taken; sometimes, as an early tomb at Churchill, there is a sinking shewing where was formerly a plate of brass.

There are many things to be learned from them besides that they are to the memory of those 'loved long since and lost awhile'. Armour is depicted, form, shape, style, as Goliath, 'a helmet of brass upon his head, and he was armed with a coat of mail, greaves of brass upon his legs, and a target of brass between his shoulders.'

Female dress is shown in detail and splendour and the different phases that have obtained in days past can be seen from the early 14h century, onwards. 'Reticulated', 'Horned', 'Butterfly', 'Pedimented', to give but some of the head dresses depicted in many of our churches.

The girdles, represented with buckles, ornaments and pockets, or pouches, are worth notice.

In the great days of architecture, the canopys, and other features introduced about the figures, shared the glory of these wondrous days, when men wrought amazing well, and with a stroke of the tool could give you insight and feeling that later men with endless labour have utterly failed to do.

From the 10th century the metal plates were imported from the Continent. Sometimes they are found to have been reversed and used again, another figure and lettering appear; 'Palimpsest' they are then called. There is one hinged in the corner at Shipton-under-Wychwood church near to the organ.

Very few of our churches but have one or more, from elaborate ones as at Great Tew to tiny ones but a few inches square with a few letters upon them.

'The Badge of Poverty'

'It is agreed that from the Growing Charge and the Insolence of the Poor, that all the Poor that Reseave pay shall ware the Letters according to Law.'

The letter 'P' for pauper had to be worn on the sleeve or other conspicuous place, generally on a piece of red or blue cloth, by those in receipt of parish relief. Sometimes the initial letter of the parish was given and the two letters stamped on a metal badge, hence the term, 'The badge of poverty.' Poor people (females especially) resented wearing it and so lost their pay, perhaps, till they put it on. Women used to pin or sew it under their skirts, so, though not seen, they could not be charged with not wearing it.

In days past all Jews had to wear a badge. In 1218 at Worcester the mark of a Jew was two white pieces of cloth sewn upon the breast. Theirs was not a 'badge of poverty.'

The rate of wages was fixed by assessment and was proclaimed aloud on market days and a copy was fixed upon a post or wall, so no one could plead ignorance. Any person paying more saw the inside of a prison for ten days and had to pay £5, whilst the worker was imprisoned for twenty-one days.

Anyone joining or combining with others to raise wages or interfere with work to be fined £5 or prison with bread and water for twenty-one days, the second time £20 or stand in the pillory, the third time cutting off one ear and loss of all citizen rights. Artisan's pay was 6s. a week, mason's 8s., labourer's 4s. Time, five in the morning till half past seven from March to September, the other part of the year from daylight till dark.

In the 13th century the law fixed prices so that three pigeons were to be sold for a penny, Lamb 4d. a pound except between Christmas and Lent when the price was to be 6d.

The aged poor suffered greatly in days past especially in cold weather. Parish workhouses were established, the poor were farmed out, contractors were found who fed and cared for them by contract. A most heartless way of dealing with the business it seems today.

Parish accounts show how small was the cost at some places of keeping the poor. '1738, July 1. 35 people in the Workhouse maintained at 1s. 0 1/2d. per head per week.'

The workhouse at Finstock was where are now the day schools, and the old building at the rear was always called 'The Workhouse barn'!

Items from Finstock Parish accounts:—

'Broom for the poor house 4d. Beesam 4d. Faggots and soap 9d. For Breeches and Jacket 7s. 6d. Gin 10d. Beer 3s. Bread 1s. 2d. Cheese 1s. 3d. Soap 4 1/2d. Beer to the teems 1s. 6d. To funeral 2s. Repairing the draw well 1s. Box of pills 2s. Packet powder 4s. Ointment 1s. Blister to the neck 2s. Pills repeated 2s. Aperient powder 1s. 6d. Beer and Liquor 3s. 3d. Gin 5d. Lining Hanchif 1s. 3d. Stockings and Bonet 2s. Thread 7d. Rapering 9d. Rushlights 2d. Tea 3d. Sugar 2d. Paper 1/2d. A strengthing Plaster 1s. Half pint embrocation 2s. A letter from Oxford 8d. Beer for men putting up the Stocks 1s. 9 1/2d. Reducing a fractured rib 10s. 6d. Horney Blow and Walden 7s. 6d. Expenses at the Churchwardens meeting 2s. 6d.'

'Caring Saml. Dring and famaly to Ascot and Expenses 9s. 6d.'

'Order for removal 6s. 6d.'

'Pare of Stocks painting and putting up and all complete £2. 10s.'

The following bill was charged to Finstock parish accounts, but there is no clue as to who consumed all this liquor, etc.:

3 glasses of rum and water	5	3
21 quarts of strong beer	12	3
Tobacco	1	1
Paper		1
£1	9	10

Another bill:

'Overseers of Finstock to Henry Early assignee to the Estate of William Barnes

4 months pay for maintaining the poor of Finstock from April 16th, 1815 till August 16th, 1815 … … £83 6s 8d

A true Statement.'

Charlbury workhouse was in the old building at the rear of Bull Lane. Mr. Jesse Clifford says:— 'such food as I have seen given to old people there to eat, no decent dog would touch now — bread made of barley and bean flour mixed.'

There was a hand mill with stones about two feet in diameter. The men in winter were despatched with wheelbarrows to Gibraltar wharf to fetch coal, wheeling it to Charlbury.

Advert. in *Oxford Journal*, Feb. 18, 1819:— 'The Parish Officers of Charlbury hereby give Notice that a Vestry will be held on Tues. 16th Feb. at the Crown Inn Charlbury at 2 o'clock for the purpose of contracting with some person for the Maintenance and Employment of their Poor. Particulars of the Overseers,

John Haines, Vestry Clerk.'

To live with friends who felt them a burden must have made life very unpleasant, one old man who was deaf used to say the Lord's Prayer aloud before he got into bed at night, and later on he used to finish his devotions with the following in the same voice:—

'If I can't hear, I can see,
The sooner I be dead, the better it'll be,
When I be shoulder high, there'll be
All to laugh, and none to cry.'

Poor old chappie!

Gifts to the poor were not always wise or discreet, as the following, recorded by S. Baring-Gould, M.A., of the story of a night errand for a Vicar:— 'Take them these feur bottles of brandy,' he says: and he brought up feur bottles with never so much as their cerks drawed. 'Now,' says he, 'what will yeu have yeur-self? 'And I says, 'Gin if yeu plase sir,' I says. And he poured me out gin and water: and then he gi'ed me a lemonade bottle of gin fer me to put in my side-pocket. 'That'l keep you alive before yeu come back.' So he fulled me up and sent me off ... to feur old people's houses with a bottle of brandy fer each. An' then he says 'There's two shillings fer yeurself: and yeu keep pulling at that bottle and yeu'll keep yeurself alive afore yeu come back.'

It is told of George Eglestone, a character of this district who did very little work and lived by his wits, that one day when on the road he fell in with another of the same stamp but not quite perhaps as smart as George. They heard that a retired seafaring gentleman, whose residence was just off the road, was always good to sailors, so they agreed to go down and pretend they were sailors and laid their plans that they would go down singly, and then halve out the proceeds, whatever they were. They tossed up a halfpenny and it came to George to go first. He went, and on the gentleman asking, 'What are you my man?' George replied, 'A sailor Sir.' 'Come this way!' Taking him into his grounds where he had a mast with ropes erected, he soon discovered that George was no sailor, he reached a big whip and thrashed him well and George made tracks back to the highway where his mate was waiting with 'How did you ge on?' And in response to George telling him to 'Go on down' without betraying anything as to the thrashing, away he hurried to be put through the same examination till, reaching the dreadful whip, the angry seaman said, 'I had another rascal down here just now, be off with you,' and he slashed the whip in style.

George was waiting. On his arrival he wanted to fight George, to be met with 'Did we not agree to share whatever we got, and you couldn't have your share without going to fetch it, could you?'

It is said George one day met Mr. Whippy of Lee Place, who enquired how he was. 'Very middling Sir, thank you, how are you ?' 'Well, George, I am not very well, in fact I am out walking now to try to pick up an appetite for my dinner.' 'How very strange,' said George, 'why, I am out trying to pick up a dinner for my appetite.'

FROM AN OLD GLYMPTON ACCOUNT BOOK

Hannah Neal spinning 6 lbs. Flax 2s. Rich. West cutting 38 bolts of Osiers at 3d. 3 Beehives at 1s. 6d. each.

Poor man a traveller 1s. Poor man 6d. Thomas Hall rending Laths 400 — 2s. Caroline Castle one day picking up potatoes 9d. Chafe money for wheat 1s. 9d.

Turn pikes to Chipping Norton 3s. Wm. Hosier one week's work by the day 8s. Beer for Masons at work at the Asserts Farm oven 5s.

Wm. Hanks making 2 dozen Hurdles 9s.

Lord Dynever's Bill for Stone troughs, the stone 1s. 6d. per foot.

Bell rope and twine 4s.

A CHRISTMAS DINNER

Many years ago a Charlbury man with no regular work, and blessed with ten children, put his gun into his pocket and went in the night up into Ditchley Riding and there under a tree, gun in hand, he waited, hoping to see a hare come along over the snow with which the ground was covered. After some time, something partly white was coming along which as it got nearer he could see was a fox with a goose over his back, its head in his mouth. There was a report, and Reynard's supper, instead of reaching his 'den O, where the little ones scrambled for the bones O,' was on its way to Charlbury, where the proceeds of the sale of the goose found that family with their Christmas dinner.

The next year the same man was proceeding along Hundly on the same old errand, over the snow, when to the right hand of the lane he caught sight of a covey of partridges. He paused, and thought, 'If I go further they will see me on the snow, and fly,' so at once he turned for home where he got his wife to fix him up in white like a ghost, in a sheet, with a white night cap on his head, and white rag twisted round his gun. Away along Hundly he went till he got near enough to the partridges without alarming them, and he let fly both barrels and secured some sixteen birds. So Christmas found him and his numerous family with a Christmas dinner again.

Banks and bankers

'Thou oughtest to have put my money to the exchangers.' Matt. xxv., 27.

Banking was known to the Greeks and Romans, but they do not appear to have issued notes. Edward III of England owed 1,500,000 gold florins to bankers in Florence which he could not repay, the banks failed for large sums.

William Patterson devised and founded the Bank of England in 1694 .

The London Goldsmiths before that period used to have coin and valuables deposited with them, for which they gave receipts, known as 'goldsmiths' notes'; these were the first English Bank notes. The loans Charles I and Charles II drew from them were never repaid, and even their bullion deposits at the Tower were used in Civil War days.

In 1783 Bills payable in coin were permitted to be issued, whilst in America we had abolished in 1764 their issue (where they had been such a boon to trade and commerce), thereby ruining trade, and creating such feeling that resulted in the War of Independence, which was fought on paper money.

In the early years of the nineteenth century the forger was very busy. Between 1805 and 1818, 501 convictions for forgery were obtained, which resulted in 207 executions. In 1817, 28,412 forged £1 notes were detected, though the penalty was death, and numbers went to the scaffold. In 1821, £1 and £2 notes were withdrawn from circulation.

The names of some early banks give the impression that many people started in the banking business, some to succeed, and the names have been handed on as household words.

At Oxford, Lock's Bank was an early one. Parsons' Bank was known as 'Old Bank', now absorbed in Barclays.

At Banbury in 1784 Bignell, Heydon and Wyatt started a bank and in 1822 John Ashby Gillett and Joseph Gibbens became chief proprietors. The pedigree of the Gilletts is traced to one Nicholas Gyllat of Kingham, 1567. These bankers were Quakers, and Gillett a Conservative, and in those days his goods were distrained for Church rates. Here at Charlbury the vicar used to have the milk every tenth day from Mr. Albright's cow. Albright's kitchen table was sold in the market place for Church rates. At Banbury a Conservative, refusing to pay his rates, 'tell it not in Gath,' caused one to write:—

'Joseph Gillett, attend!
How canst thou, a Friend,
Attired in broad-brim and straight coat,
Like an orthodox saint,
Suffer Church rate distraint,
Yet give to the Churchman thy vote?
Joseph Gillett,
Yet give to the Churchman thy vote!'

A branch was opened in Oxford in 1877 and then Gillett's bank became associated with Clinch's bank in Witney.

At Chipping Norton in 1807 there were Messrs. Corgan and Winter, Bankers, also Atkins & Sons.

In 1835 Messrs. T. and T. R. Cobb had a bank there. Also in that year The Stourbridge and Kidderminster Banking Co's., founded the previous year, opened. Later on at Charlbury Mr. Albright conducted a branch, the late Mr. Henry Baskett (he told me he did it) put along the beam across the shop ceiling in gilt letters the name of the bank. This was carried on by Mr. Thackwell Smith, followed by his son, Mr. Gillett Smith, and is now absorbed in the Midland Banking Co.

At Witney in 1807 Batt & Co. were the bankers, later J. W. Clinch & Co. had a bank, now Barclays.

At Woodstock in 1806 Joseph Brooks conducted a bank. Mr. Wadley, the

Charlbury manager for the Midland Banking Company, has a five pound note issued by him, of which a copy is given here. I heard a joke when a lad that there was but one five pound note between Charlbury and Woodstock; when one place got it, the other was without it. Mr. Wadley's note curiously has written on the back the name Bennett, Woodstock, and also, Mr. Izzard, of Spelsbury, so is this the very note the tale started from?

Woodstock Bank. £5
No. 291 . Bk.

I Promise to pay the Bearer on demand the sum of FIVE POUNDS here or at Messrs Brown, Cobb, Stokes, Bankers, London.
Value received.

Woodstock the 3rd day of ffebry. 1806.

No. 291.

FIVE POUNDS. Jos. Brooks.

The Woodstock Arms, surmounted by a Coronet and the words 'Original Bank', are in the top left hand corner.

In 1835 I. and R. Morrell's Bank was at Woodstock.

TEN £50 BANKNOTES IN WOODSTOCK

When a house was being renovated at Woodstock, a workman discovered a cavity over a door frame, in one of the rooms, that had been pasted over with brown paper. In it was a case containing ten £50 notes. As the notes were very old they were thought to be valueless and lay about for some days till someone took one across to the bank to see if they would cash it. It was considered, on enquiry being made, that this was £500, mentioned in the will of someone who had died in the house about eighty years previously, and the money could not be found at the time.

The heir and the owner of the property agreed on a division I believe, and so the matter was settled.

The Battle of Otmoor

CHARLBURY TROOP CALLED OUT

About five miles north-east of Oxford a stretch of low-lying land, often for many weeks under water, bears the name of Otmoor, originally, according to an old story, Oat Moor.

This used to be an open space of free land where all could pasture their sheep or pigs, or geese, and the story is that, in ages past, the daughter of the lord asked her father to grant a portion of this land for the poor. He said she could have as much as she could ride round, while a sheaf of oats was burning, the sheaf seems to have been tied up rather tight, and she rode very fast.

The extract below from the pen of a former Charlbury resident may be of interest.

'Otmoor, or Oatmoor, was a large common on which the villagers could turn their geese or other live stock free. But the Lord of the Manor, on the principle that 'he should get who has the power, and he should keep who can,' enclosed the common, and by quickset hedges divided it into cultivable fields. The commoners resented the action of the lord, destroyed the hedges, and laid the common open again. To put a stop to this rioting, the D. troop of Oxfordshire Yeomanry Cavalry, under the command of B. J. Whippy, Esq., their captain, were called out one Sunday in 1832 to go to Otmoor to quell the riot, and arrest the rioters. I remember the hullabaloo that morning, the grinding of swords, the furbishing of arms, the saddling of war horses, the bugle call to horse, the address of the Captain to use forbearance, and not to use the sword but in extremity. They started on their twenty miles ride to put down revolution and uphold the majesty of the law, in this case of stealing the land of the poor from them. They arrived on the scene of strife and 'twas said (I never heard it contradicted) took two boys and a woman prisoners, who for a time defended themselves valiantly against the troopers with pikes. Next day they escorted a load of prisoners to Oxford amid the jeers, and some missiles, of the sympathisers of these asserters of their rights. A wine merchant of Oxford befriended the prisoners, became bail for them, and employed counsel for them at the Assizes. The jury acquitted them of all blame and their common was restored for the time. The Troopers came home with all their 'blushing honours thick upon them,' and some who were not used to riding, terribly galled in their seats. So ended the battle of Otmoor.'

It appears from the following there had been trouble over the Moor years before, but Charlbury was not amongst it then, with sharpened swords, etc.

'One Hundred Guineas
Reward
Otmoor Drainage.

Whereas the Banks made to promote the Drainage of the Moor have been several times maliciously cut through by some evil disposed person or persons,— *Notice is hereby given*, that whosoever shall give such information as shall be the means of discovering the offender or offenders shall upon their conviction, receive a Reward of One Hundred Guineas.

John Maughan, Esq., the Commissioner, at the Red Lion Inn, Islip, Jan. 16, 1817.'

Beds

'O bed! O bed! delicious bed!
That heaven upon earth to the weary head.'

What a place bed fills in life, rest and sleep, existence is not possible without it.

'In bed we laugh, in bed we cry,
And born in bed, in bed we die.'

In the seventh century the Saxons, settled in Britain, are said to have counted the bed chamber as most worthy of adornment in the house, whilst later, the Normans brought daintier ways, and embroidered sheets, velvet curtains, with quilts of silk, were in use.

The great lord or baron, had a gorgeous bed, whilst his retainers seem to have slept as they could, cattle men in early days sleeping with their cattle.

Thomas Ellwood the Quaker tells how when in confinement: 'I gathered up a good armful of rushes wherewith the floor was covered, and spreading them under the table, crept in upon them in my clothes and keeping my hat on, laid my head upon one end of the table's frame, instead of a bolster … for four nights together… I rested and slept well.'

William (Billy) Dawson, the famous Yorkshire local preacher preached at the opening of the old Wesleyan Chapel at Oxford, every one in the audience starting to their feet carried away by the wonderful sway he could wield over a congregation. Once where he stayed, the sacking of the bed broke away and his head and shoulders sank to the floor. Taking the pillow he opened the foot and got in that end, and slept on an inclined plane till morning.

There are proverbs and sayings about beds, 'He got out of bed the wrong side,' or 'He put out his left foot first this morning,' means 'He is cross,' or 'ill tempered,' or displeased, 'As he made his bed he must lie on it,' when one has gone into an unwise undertaking of some kind or a foolish marriage perhaps. Our grandmothers thought much of feather beds, so soft and warm and comfortable. John Wesley, with his strenuous active life, did not, even when he was an old man and had given up horse riding, want a soft bed. Someone went into his room where he was staying and was astonished to find his coachman rolling up and down Wesley's bed, which he explained was too soft for Mr. Wesley, so he was trying to make it firm for him.

In Earl Leicester's room at Cornbury is a very fine old oak bedstead.

Catholic children in our forest borders used to be taught before getting into bed to say as a prayer:

'Matthew, Mark, Luke, and John,
Bless the bed that I lay on;

> Four corners to my bed,
> Four angels round my bed,
> One at head and one at feet
> And two to keep my soul asleep.'

What mystery there is about sleep.

> 'Sleep is a death; oh, make me try
> By sleeping what it is to die,
> And as gently lay my head
> On my grave, as now my bed.'

Never shall I forget a bed at Bodicote, or rather two, in which I slept when a lad. Father and I after some difficulty got lodgings and went to bed with the brother of the woman of the house, three of us in one bed. Before going to sleep something fell, a knife out of a pocket I think it was, on to the floor. Our bed-fellow called to his sister and insisted she should come and see what had happened, which she did, he giving us the cheerful information that the house was said to be haunted, but after that all laid low, we heard nothing.

The next night a bed had been made for me on the floor. It looked inviting to a tired boy but, O horror, never shall I forget it. Being between the chimney stack and the corner, I found, as in sacred story, 'the bed was not long enough for a man (lad in my case) to stretch himself upon.' Some time in the night father awoke me, I was lying out of my corner bed on the floor of the room. Never again I hope shall I have a short bed.

'The son of man hath not where to lay His head.' How low He stooped for our sake, no bed of His own had He. A cradle hymn:—

> 'Hush my dear, lie still and slumber
> Holy angels guard thy bed !
> Heavenly blessings without number
> Gently falling on thy head.'

An early mural painting runs:—

> 'Whether you Rise yearlye
> Or Goe to bed late!
> Remember Crist Iesus
> that Died ffor yern sake.'

'The best of books' — Bunyan

'Which is the Best Book in the world?' said a man I knew to a company of children, and at once the reply was at hand, they all were ready with 'The Bible, Sir.' He was a quaint man, and a thought struck him, so he asked, 'which is the worst?' One solitary hand appeared and a little girl replied, 'The Shop book, Sir.'

In the day school at Finstock we read the Old Testament scriptures, book after book, in the years I was there, Mr. Butler, our schoolmaster, directing us as to the way to handle a book, and how to read it.

Under his guidance, with scarcely any comment, most mornings in the week, the first lesson was 'The Bible', and I look back with great pleasure to those golden happy hours, when, so fresh and wonderful to us, those words and records were on our lips, and in our minds. Where could children learn better as to the origin of life, and the world, than with such words as 'God said let there be light, and there was light?'

About this wide world, I expect there are many who look back as I do, to those hours with Mr. Butler and the best of books in Finstock day school with pleasure and much gratitude.

Some of us were privileged to be in Thomas Harris' Sunday School class, and his soul used to kindle, as he described Bible scenes and characters, 'Elijah on Carmel', and other subjects to us. His long tall body would sway, his face with its strong lines a study, his voice vibrant with thrill and feeling, we could see the prophets of Baal, wicked Jezebel, or any one else he pictured to us. I can feel, with all these years between, as though I was sitting close to his long arm now, and arrested by him and his story.

He could quote a great deal of scripture, knew it by heart, the music of the words and the truths contained in it had gripped his heart and soul, and in our Finstock dialect he gave us what is now a fragrant memory and a benediction.

Did not John Bunyan say in *Grace Abounding* he was 'never out of the Bible,' either by reading or meditation?

There is hardly a person amongst us over forty years of age who does not know something about the stories in the Bible, but from what I gather there is a generation growing up that does not know the stories of Abraham and Isaac, Moses in the bulrushes, the Israelites and the Red Sea, Daniel in the lion's den, the brave lads in the burning fiery furnace, Our Lord feeding the multitude, or walking on the sea.

The head mistress of an expensive and fashionable girls' school said recently that girls came to her thirteen and fourteen years of age entirely ignorant of the Christian religion and utterly ignorant of the Bible. The children in elementary schools have Bible lessons but the children of the well-to-do are not so fortunate it appears. Sunday is a day of motoring, golf, and tennis, and the children are not even sent to church, it is said.

For generations Bible lore has been at the root of our English life, in our thoughts, in our speech, in many ways past telling.

An old Dutch tile showing Jonah under the gourd tree waiting for the destruction of Nineveh.

On Saints' days we marched to Church for a service, and one thing to notice and perhaps remember was the Scripture lesson read by the Vicar. The grand old wording of the Authorized Version well read, not hurried over as though it was a part to be got done, so the really important part, the sermon, could come on, is, no doubt, arresting to young and old. Revisions and modern translations should be kept for use in the study, so it appears to me. Never is the jar, or worse, they give one's sensibilities compensated by perhaps one, or two at most, improvements they may give to the sense, and is it not a great pity to spoil the effect, for that which could be explained in a word, if at all necessary, in public worship?

As a small boy in Church one day I put two marbles on the margin of the panel of the seat in front and a movement made them drop on the board floor with a rattle and roll away. I lost them, but worse, when we got to school and we all stood in our classes, to my unspeakable horror, Mr. Butler said:— 'Someone dropped marbles in Church, who was it?' Where my heart went to I do not know, but after some tense seconds, there was never a word, no one spoke, and if any of my little comrades who were in the same seat and held their tongues should read this, I should like to tell them how grateful I am to this day for their silence. We dreaded our master's frown, the most daring amongst us, and I learnt my lesson that day, as to behaving myself in God's House, without having personal words on the subject directly spoken to me.

Our age is distinguished by its enormous number of books, periodicals and newspapers, much of it light, some muddy. Time spent on it wasted, and worse. The inspiring field of biography is of great value, the question 'How did you come to be you?' apart from Divine appointment, is in our mind as we read of notable characters. Also the books that have lived on, that seem to have a spark of an eternal quality about them, why not let it throb in me?

'How readest thou?' Our Lord's question to the tempting lawyer, we may well take to ourselves, and what else we read, let the sacred Scriptures, the Book of Life, be our daily study.

'Who its truth believeth
Light and joy receiveth.'

My grandfather Kibble was parish clerk at Wilcote, it being nearer than Charlbury. Finstock people walked across the fields to church there, from earliest days.

When I was a lad my father told me a story of a clerk who kept a public house and living near the church used to carry the Church Bible into his house to find the proper lessons ready to be read on Sunday.

One day the book was lying open on a table in the tap room at the 37th Psalm, and some waggish person cut the word 'horse' from similar type in a newspaper and stuck it over the word 'tree' in verse 35. On Sunday in Church it is said the clergyman read: 'I have seen the wicked in great power and spreading himself like a green bay horse.' 'Never, can't be,' said the minister.

So vain and perverse persons treated God's book, over-stepping the bounds of discretion.

Botellier – Botiller – Butler

Wilcote was a residence of this family and was called 'Botelers Court.'

Oaks were to be sent from the forest to Robert Botellier in 1279.

Thomas le Boteler Rector of Chipping Norton 1319.

In 1401 William Boteller wrote at Oxford a tract against the translation of the Bible into the common tongue, and it is interesting to see the objections he brings forward as follows:—

'It would lead to multiplication of faulty copies.

Human understanding is insufficient. Knowledge of God is better gained by prayer and meditation than by reading.

Higher angels teach the lower.

The apostles taught not by books but by the power of the Spirit. Christ himself asked the doctors and did not read.

Disputes would follow if men read the Scriptures for themselves.

In Christ's body each member has its proper office but if anyone may read then the foot became the eye: and who would offer a book to a joint of his foot.'

Wycliff's Bible was ordered to be burnt 1408.

In 1413 Stephen le Botiller paid rent to the king 5s. 7³/₄d. for waste land in Wychwood at Bradley near Akerman Street.

In 1448-9 Henry VI granted Sir Ralph Boteller rent and venison in Wychwood including a fee form of £7 18s. for land in the forest. He was Lord Chancellor of England and married as his second wife Alice, widow of William Lovell of Minster Lovell. He built Sudeley Castle on the site of an old Norman fortress of Stephen's day.

There are two ladies buried within the cloisters at Brasenose College, Oxford, and one of them was Lady Katherine Boteler in 1681.

Pickering's avenue at Wilcote, was planted by William Poole who was at Waterloo, he built Waterloo cottages at Finstock,

John Carey of Wilcote built Spelsbury Almshouses leaving a charge on his estate and timber also to be cut for their repair. He rests under a big erection with iron railings at the north side of Spelsbury Church.

Bull baiting

Butchers formerly when they wished to kill a bull at Nottingham were obliged to bait him. The animal first was led through the town, perhaps a man walking in front beating a drum. At Oxford the 'bull ring,' stocks and Whipping Post were at Carfax. At Reading it was ordered that there should be no bull baiting on Sunday 'on pain of twelve pence to be paid by every house holder where the baiting is.'

Mr. Jesse Clifford wrote: 'I saw the last bull-baiting in the Playing Close (Charlbury) in 1820. The bull was chained to a block let into the ground, and its poor face torn by the dogs, its eyes streaming with blood, when a bucket of brine was thrown into its face. Mad with pain, it broke the chain and dashed away to the turnpike. Caught there it was brought back; but neither men nor dogs could make it renew the attack, so it was taken to the slaughter house.'

Happily these things are gone and a better spirit prevails. It is a great day in the life of a boy who has thought it great fun to hit and destroy something when he takes the opposite idea, and finds out what a noble thing it is to love those creatures God has made and if needs be protect them.

It is curious to notice that many of the old nursery rhymes were concerned with animals and birds that are most unhappy, through some cruelty such as the farmer's wife did to the three blind mice, the tragic death by an arrow of Cock Robin, 'Pussy in the well,' Mother Hubbard's hungry dog, all perhaps helping little folk to fancy there is fun in cruelty. Is all the sport of grown-ups free from it even now? How about fox hunting? I shall never forget Mr. Butler telling us in Finstock school of the Ancient Mariner and the lines:—

'He prayeth best who loveth best,
All creatures great and small,
For the Great God who loveth us
He made and loveth all.'

1815—1929: Charlbury Council Schools

When good Robert Spendlove gave his hundred pounds to start the British School at Charlbury and a Committee was formed, engaging a room at the Bell for meetings, more than one hundred years ago, they never dreamt to what dimensions their work would grow.

Many fail to realise the remarkable developments that have taken place in and around the 'Playing Place' for which Charlbury used in far away days to pay to Eynsham Abbey four barbed arrows yearly rent. The school buildings are extensive, with headmaster's house near by.

Under the group system, Stonesfield, Finstock, Ramsden, Spelsbury and Chilson senior scholars are conveyed, most of them by bus, to and from school. The dinners (generally hot) for the sum of twopence, are possible through the cookery department, Miss Miln, teacher, and the school gardens. These are in Spendlove's Close and are

ONE OF THE SIGHTS OF THE TOWN,

and are well worth a visit, and hardly to be equalled in the County and beyond. Produce, flowers and vegetables, appeal to the beholder and reflect great credit on the work of the lads and their instructor and guide, Mr. W. Campbell. Bees and fowls are kept. Handicraft instruction, carpentry and other useful arts under Mr. Watt's direction is a strong feature of the school, whilst the girls are trained in useful and ornamental needle craft by Mrs. Brackenbury.

The headmaster is Mr. J. E. Barton, with his staff, Mrs. Thornett, B.A., Mrs. Maynard and others, whilst away on the hill in what was the Grammar School for so long, Mrs. Foster with the little ones is carrying on in grand style the work begun in such a small way by Robert Spendlove and his helpers when they founded a school in 1815.

William Spendlove, Maltster, bought in 1723 what is now 'Corner House' (the residence of Miss Crawley and Charles Crawley, Esq.), building the Market Street front, moving in, where was born his son Robert in 1727.

A stone in the Friends' burial ground records:— 'Robert Spendlove, Died 2nd, 12mo. 1822. Aged 96.'

Children

Child life was different in days past. Many children ran wild till they could go to work of some kind, scaring birds at six years of age or cattle minding. In days not long past every penny was ' handy ' as village folk say and some families were very large. Some years ago, I have been told, in three cottages just below where I write at Pound Hill, there were thirty children. I knew members of a family of nineteen; how they were all fed, clothed, and packed in to sleep is a wonder. Some of this family did very well, one member of it left a considerable fortune. An exceedingly well informed man I knew started work at six, and married on nine shillings per week.

Childhood was something to be got over as quickly as possible, and life's stern duties taken up. The pressure of want was never absent, the wolf always at the door.

Many got no schooling at all, though in most places there was some one who taught children their letters — Mrs. Paintin at Finstock, and Mr. Goodman and his daughter, [taught] the lads, before they were big enough to walk to the Grammar School at Charlbury.

Mr. Hall, the parish clerk at Spelsbury, had a night school for lads. Lord Dillon built the schools there and to all the girls he gave red cloaks.

The old teachers were great on writing. Quill pens were cut and used in grand style. Penmen challenged others to write for a wager.

The Testament, with books of Fables, were the lesson books.

Some village lads went to boarding school but the greater number could not afford this.

Surely childhood is as it should be when it can be thought of with pleasure — mother, home, lessons, and the first glimpse of the face of One who is the children's Friend, our Lord.

HOW TO SUCK AN EGG

An old man told me of a lad who had been away to school and coming home feeling very learned and important set about telling his mother the scientific way to suck an egg. Said he:—

'We perforate an aperture in the apex,
And a corresponding aperture in the base,
And applying the egg to the lips,
And forcibly inhaling the breath,
The shell is entirely discharged of its contents.'

'Why,' said his mother: 'You makes a hole in one end, and a hole in t'other, and sucks en.'

'JUST COMFORTABLE'

Another lad, a little chap, when his father returned home and asked him: 'Well, have you been a good boy?' heard: 'Not very good, or very bad; just comfortable.'

'TELL ME ANOTHER?'

A lad about ten, or eleven, was sent from Milton-under-Wychwood to Little Faringdon, to collect seven-and-sixpence, owing for a stone trough his father had supplied to someone there. On the way he found another lad driving some pigs and these he helped to fetch out of a field of growing corn, getting wet about the legs. After the long walk, he found the man was out, and the woman could not pay, so he set off for home. Arriving at Filkins, he looked and felt so ill, and done up, that a kind woman asked him into her cottage to sit down. She could offer him only some crust, broken from off the brick work of the oven, where was being baked a batch of bread, that from the poorness of the flour had all run together, and when baked had to be cut out with a clean spade.

He sat and ate some of the hard crust, and she gave him to drink some weak gin and water, but after starting his walk for home he became sick and ill, and arrived home at last done up, but a long rest, and home, and mother, put things right, and it was a memory in the long and eventful life of a remarkable Wychwood village man.

ANOTHER MASON'S BOY

A mason and his boy, I was told long ago, were doing some work for a gentleman, and one day, only the boy came on the scene, and on the gentleman asking the lad if he knew when they would finish the job, heard, 'I don't know, Sir, father is gone to see about another job to-day, and if he gets it, we shall finish on Saturday, but if he does not, I don't know when we shall finish.'

CHILDHOOD'S RISKS

One of my early recollections is of a group of boys on the Riding Hill, Finstock, one of whom was in charge of an old flint lock pistol, bird starving. A piece of paper was put up on, or against, the wall as a target, stones were rammed into the pistol — no, we did not any of us get shot, the paper, the wall, or the sky had the charge right enough, when the old sparking flint snicker went off.

Another shooting memory is, creeping along under a hedge behind a lad armed with a double barrelled gun, that would only fire with one barrel, no matter what you put into the other. Shots? Yes, I do not expect Mr. Alderton knew there were any, but I know a blackbird lost his life that day, and the report helped to scare the birds from the wheat, no doubt.

When shooting was on at Wilcote, boys to beat the covers were sent from Finstock school. To my dismay I was never fortunate enough to be selected. A lad got peppered with shot one day, and I could feel shot under his scalp afterwards at school. Meeting him in the street here recently I enquired about it and at once he took off his hat and I felt his head again, as I had done so long ago at school. Mr. Frank Alderton yet carries that which he had as a boy from Mr. Sartoris' gun in Wilcote woods.

One day when I wore petticoats, as small boys did, I fell into a well. The sensation of falling was horrible, and a woman (what I owe to a good woman being at hand in my life!) pulled me out, and I remember starting along to meet my mother all dripping wet, and then, all is a blank. Though I remember the incident, I was too young for the circumstances to be remembered.

Children's games

Children of to-day are said to have lost their games, and it appears that in the larger places, the cinema has taken the place of street games which once had their season in every town and village.

Marbles are still a joy to our Wychwood border places, one is glad to see, but I fear even marbles have had their day where the cinema prevails, and even hereabout many games played most zealously a few years ago have gone out, and are not known.

WHACK-EM

This fine game for a cold day was played by a lad standing against a wall, the 'den.' Clasping his hands together he held them up towards his face, the other lads standing round a distance away whilst he got ready to chase them by saying (with perhaps some variations)

'Whack 'em once, whack 'em twice,

Whack 'em three times over,

Went to buy a sack of wheat

And bought a sack of clover,

If I can't catch, I'll make you run

Blow my finger, and whistle my thumb.

(Pretending to do this and then kicking the wall with his heel)

Kick my den and off I come.'

He then chased, till touching a comrade, they clasped hands, and ran till presently others got linked up, or else became 'Whack-em,' as the boy who started at the 'den' was called, and so the game could go on.

NINE HOLES

This was played by making holes in the turf about the size of tea cups, the players stood round whilst one of the number, either boy or girl, rolled a ball towards the holes, and as the players each had a hole, whosoever's the ball went into, that player had to grasp it, and throw it, trying to strike another, and each triumph was recorded by a bit of 'money,' that is a tiny stone, or other object, being put into the successful player's hole.

'Haul'e Call'e' was throwing a ball against a high wall or building and calling out the name of a player who ran and tried to catch it before it fell, and then threw it to strike another. It kept all on the alert and was a fine healthy game.

PAT BALL BASE, OR ROUNDERS

Standing in a row at the home den, a ball was served to the child at the top, who tried to strike it a pat, with the palm of the hand, and then ran across to a den, a few yards away, in danger of being struck by the ball during the journey from den to den, or getting home from the last. When throwing the ball at a comrade I well remember how to my horror in the excitement of the game, my aim went wide, and the ball struck a man plump on the cheek as he stood sideways, talking to my father, causing his clay pipe suddenly to jump out of his mouth, and as he failed to catch it, get broken in pieces. No, the man took it all right, but I thought, 'Now I am in for it!'

HOCKEY

Pleasant recollections of games played at hockey 'along street' at Finstock are in the mind.

MEG

This was a dangerous game and needed care. A pebble about as big as a hen's egg was placed upon a big firm stone against some wall, and standing a couple of yards or so away, each boy threw in turn a similar pebble, with all his strength, and tried to knock the 'Meg' pebble from its perch.

THE 'P. PUT'

I saw one of these wood squares about $1^1/_2$ inches each way in the Parks Museum at Oxford labelled 'An obsolete Oxfordshire Game.' It was a most hazardous game to play and quite a game of chance, not at all of skill.

A letter was burnt on each side of the 'P. Put.' They were A. P. T. H. O. N. and when it was tossed in the air, the marbles which had been rolled up to it went as indicated by the letter which came uppermost, as follows. 'A,' all, meant take the lot. 'P' put one. 'T' take one. 'H' take half of them. 'O' you are out, done with the game. ' N' none.

LETTER TO A BOY

Charles Kingsley wrote to his son at school:

'My Dearest Boy — There is a matter that gave me much uneasiness when you mentioned it. You said you had put into some lottery for the Derby. Now this is bad, nothing but bad. Of all habits gambling is the one I hate most. Morally it is unchivalrous and un-Christian. Betting is the way of the world, and to the devil it leads.

Your Loving Pater.'

PUNDY

This was a nice game calling for skill and adroitness; girls sometimes were most apt players.

Sitting on a doorstep or other convenient place, five small stones were used (the fossil Rhynchonella did splendidly when a set could be obtained).

The stones were thrown down before the player and, taking up one, it was tossed up about a foot and one by one the other four stones were gathered up into the hand, catching the falling stone each time as it fell, holding the rest of the stones in the hand, this tossing and catching, whilst various things were done with the other four, was most interesting and amusing, I know. One part consisted in reciting during the tossing and catching, of the words:—

'Jacky be nimble, Jacky be quick,
Jacky jumped over the candlestick.'

MORREL

Nine men's 'Morrel.' Oxfordshire.

Nine men's 'Marl.' Wilts.

Nine men's 'Murelle.' France.

Nine men's 'Morris.' Shakespere.

This game that used to be most popular with all ages is quite obsolete, though the lines are yet to be seen scratched on old chaff bin lids in stables or other places. The marks I saw as a lad about Finstock led me to ask my father, I suppose, what it meant and so got to hear about the old game that for centuries was 'all the go.'

It was a great joy to an old man I visited, I remember, some years back that I could play a game of 'Morrel' with him, and the late Miss Pumphrey was, I found, greatly interested and told me in her youth buttons were used to play with.

It could be played out of doors with a 'Morrel' marked in the turf, nine stones and nine pebbles or bits of stick being used as 'men.'

A square or oblong was marked out, another smaller one inside it, and then a smaller one inside that, leaving a centre 'pound,' or space to receive 'men' or 'prisoners' removed as the play went on. Shorter lines were made across the intersections at the corners, and also a line across in the centre at each end or side.

The two players each had nine men, white and black buttons, or sticks and stones, and placed a 'man' on one of the intersections of which there were twenty-four, endeavouring to get three in a row, without passing over the opponents' men, and on the row being completed, a prisoner was taken and put in the pound.

When all were laid down on the lines they were played backwards and forwards, but only from point to point, in any direction, till the winner had taken the other 'men.'

The club

These old clubs or benefit societies were formed as a source of mutual help and brotherhood in the villages, and the day of the annual walk to church and the club dinner was a great event, though drink and shame made it a sad day to very many.

The rules were stringent and sometimes quaint. One club rules stated that 'no member disaffected to His Majesty George III or who has not had the small pox or cow pox shall be a member of this society.' A title page of another gives ten lines of verse:—

'To a good old proverb, listen, pray,
Provide a something for a rainy day,
Age brings infirmity, accidents make lame,
And sickness dire attacks the human frame.
But when disease confines us to our bed
Our Union funds provide our children bread.
Should God be pleased to end our journey here
With fostering hand we dry the widow's tear.'
    'Bear ye one another's burdens.
    And so fulfil the law of Christ.'

Most clubs seem to have had their feast day in May, many on Restoration day. Northleigh on the 4th June. Finstock, Ascension Day. Charlbury old club day was, I believe, 'Shick Shack day,' 29th of May.

A band was engaged to play for the day, costing generally fifty shillings. These performers were led by a man carrying a big flag on a pole, the end resting in a leather pouch slung about his shoulders. The Club stewards each carried a staff about six feet in length, sometimes with an emblem in brass at the top of it (these are sought by collectors) which generally followed the sign of the Inn where the club had its headquarters, as the 'White Hart,' 'The Bell,' 'Salutation,' etc.

There are fine collections to be seen at Taunton Museum and at Bath. Flowers were tied about them and the club went to Church. I remember, as a boy at Finstock, the text one year was, 'There are spots in your feasts of charity,' and this I felt, and keenly too, was very true.

Great preparations were made for the dinner held in my uncle's barn, the wall lined with fir branches, a big branch of chestnut in flower suspended from the beams in the centre. Lord Churchill's club was held at the school, their dishes were carried from the place where they were cooked on a ladder by a man at each end, the dishes reposing in fine style along it.

About 4s. per quarter was paid, which entitled the member to so many weeks' sick pay and a doctor, but the weak point about most of them was that the division of the surplus took place so often that there was no reserve to tide over a time of special sickness, if some epidemic came along, and after paying in for many years, when a man began to fail, his club was broken up and gone.

Lord Churchill's club did not do this, and when the membership died down to some three or four, and was then dissolved, each man had quite a nice bit of money as his share.

The preparation for one club feast at Finstock I shall never forget, as a little lad. I rode in a cart to Charlbury with uncle and his man, and on the return journey was put to sit on a sack on some coal in the cart, a basket of grocery on one side of me, and a hamper of basins and plates on the other. William Gee led the horse, uncle walked behind. Somewhere past Baywell turnpike the horse bolted, I can see Wm. Gee hanging on, away went his hat, and at last he hung both hands to the cart shaft, face upwards, his legs trailing the ground, and then in a moment or so he was gone, and we were over him (the wheel went, I heard afterwards, between his legs), whilst away went Bonnie who had but one eye; away like the wind, towards dear old Finstock. I was too small to try to get out, or reach the reins, and all is a blank as we sped along, safely turning over Fawler bridge, and Bonnie slowed down. Uncle appeared in the distance having run as for his life, losing his hat, he was shouting 'stop him' to old Georgie Brown who was further up the road; he put a broom up to Bonnie's face and our mad race was ended.

The man we ran over recovered, for a great wonder. Why was I preserved all helpless as I was, for a little later Bonnie bolted again, and trying to turn a corner in Finstock threw the cart, and Bill Busby, his mother's only child, died as the result? I remember the sight of his white face as he lay dead, his mother gave me a book of his. I keep it yet.

My father was secretary to the Club for some years and once at the time of the surplus division, for one night we had at our house over £100 in cash, and I thought as a lad many things when I saw father bring his axe in the bedroom, and lay it under his bed.

The Green near 'The Crown' Inn used to be covered with stalls, dancing booths, etc. One year a man brought a table, setting round it various tempting prizes; you picked what you would like, paid your money, and gave the pointer a twirl, and if — yes, 'if' — it rested pointing to your choice, you had it.

I heard him say to a group of women who had failed, 'The money is mine and you have nothing.' At Oxford a little later the police turned the table over and found a bar of wood underneath that could be pressed against the pivot of the spinning arm. The man kept his hand against the table, and so could stop it just where he chose.

As a boy, without a word from anyone, I could see that to follow the path I had resolved upon I had best give club feasts a wide berth, and after these many years I see no cause for regret at the course resolved upon.

Copland, Harris, Ramsden and Charlbury

John Copland, after a furious contest, took captive David Bruce, King of Scots, at Queen Philippa's great victory at Neville's Cross, 1346, and was made a knight banneret (the highest rank of knight) on the field, with ample means to support the dignity.

Robert Copland was an assistant of the famous printer, Wynkyn de Worde, and a legatee under his will. He was a stationer and bookseller at the sign of The Rose Garland, in Fleet Street, 1515-1547(?). The productions of his press are very rarely met with.

William Copland, thought to have been his son or a younger brother, carried on the printing, with the same old type, and though the work is poor, his books are valuable and command good prices. He is credited with over sixty different publications.

Gabriel Copland paid tax 8s. at Enstone in 1641.

George Copland, Gentleman, of Charlbury, bought from the representatives of Richard Butler, of London, and Leonard Bowman, of Oxford, on July 1st, 1699, the residence, and other lands, at Ramsden, now the property of Lord Olivier. This property seems to have been sold off from Wychwood during the Commonwealth, 1649.

Mr. Copland evidently built the house opposite the original house at Ramsden on Crockwell Assarts, 'G.C. 1704,' are upon it.

Part of the Ramsden fields had been enclosed from 'God's fields' (an interesting and beautiful name for common lands used in the deeds).

Leonard Bowman, Mercer of Oxford, was Mayor 1641, also in 1661. His wife died that year and is buried in St. Mary's Church. In 1665 he paid hearth tax iijs. on his house at St. Mary Magdalen, and a house he had with five chimneys was empty, it appears.

From what I have been able to gather about George Copland, Gent., from Lord Olivier's Title Deeds, the memorials here, and other sources, it appears that he lived where Dr. McNeight now resides, in Charlbury; this accounts for the striking doorway, pillars and pediment, to the front entrance. The property extended further back than it does to-day, with an acre of land now absorbed with 'Nine Acres,' and this explains why the field known as Nine Acres, is actually ten.

From Mr. Copland's Will, proved 1748, he left his house, orchard with close at the over end, and one acre in Nine Acres, which is enclosed (planted sanfoin) after his wife, to Anne Dennet.

His Coate property to Elizabeth Cole, Mary Harris, Ruth Harris, Rebecca Harris, Anne Harris and Silvestre, all sisters of Richard Harris, to whom he left his Ramsden property.

Mr. Copland's stone is in the Pudlicote aisle in Charlbury Church, inscribed — 'George Copland died, Oct. 30, 1748. Aged 79 years.'

His coat-of-arms is carved on the stone. A horse's head on a wreath, above a visor in profile, this indicates he was of the rank of esquire. The shield beneath it bears a horse statant (standing) with three ringed moons.

The stone is next in the floor to that of Ruth, the wife of Samuel Harris, Gent., of Chilson, who died Nov. 1730, aged 83 years. The said Samuel Harris' stone in the north transept is dated 1699.

George Copland's arms

Richard Harris rests beneath a ponderous slab of Hornton stone, near to the south Porch, in a row of other stones to the same family, a good altar tomb amongst them that bears at the west end a cartouche, but the arms carved are not now discernible. His son, Samuel, was in business at 'Hanging Ditch,' Manchester, a tasty name for a street!

Richard Harris' Will, proved 1758, shows he left Rev. Thos. Griffiths of Burford and Ralph Rawlins of Walcot to clear up his estate, his son Silvester to have £400.

The woman's name, Silvestre, and the son Silvester, gives the idea that they were connected with the noted Burford family of Sylvester and were not ashamed of the name.

Near to the entrance of Ivy House on the stone to the memory of Fanny Penson Harris, is the whole of the Lord's Prayer — is not this unique as an epitaph?

The corn

The *Illustrated London News*, Sept. 22, 1849 states that a grain of wheat obtained from a mummy at Thebes was planted at Stow-on-the-Wold by Mr. Enoch (see his name on Enoch's Tower at Stow), and it produced fifteen stems with upwards of 1,600 grains of corn. Mummy wheat, it is said, will *not* grow.

'O the golden sheaf, the rustling treasure armful,

O the nut brown tresses nodding interlaced.'

So sings the poet, and truly a field of wheat is a beautiful and cheerful sight, and the joy of harvest is a reality to all country dwellers.

All through the long years what simple implements were used for this the oldest craft of man to win his daily bread! The plough, the reaping hook, the flail, and even now they are not completely driven from the field. If Boaz had looked across his fields where Ruth was gleaning, and had seen a modern reaper and binder at work, he would have been filled with both wonder and alarm, there is no doubt.

The panting hideous tractor has not yet driven the whistling plough boy from the fields, it is pleasant to know.

The fagging hook was in great use before the reaping machine came in, and was a most effective tool in the hand of a strong and skilful man, or woman; yes, some women could 'fag' in days past, as well as reap.

The sickle for reaping was a tool of beautiful shape, with a long snake-like blade, well shaped and balanced, the reaper grasped a handful and with the sickle 'cut it off at knee.' There was danger for beginners to cut badly the little finger which grasped the stalks.

The fagging hook was a heavier, broader-bladed tool, with a longer handle than the sickle, and was swung with force and skill, cutting the corn stalks near the ground as they were held in place by a fagging stick, a stick about two feet in length with a crook about nine inches at the end, then walking backwards the 'fagger' would bring what he had cut by the help of the stick against his left leg, and deposit it on to an open band laid ready by his 'tier up.'

Hard long days of toil were spent at this work by our worthy village fathers, trying to earn a little extra money to help keep the wolf from the door, and though they did nobly many went down in the struggle for bread.

THE FLAIL

'They laid the sheaves upon a floor

And beat them o'er and o'er.'

In barns many men were employed during the winter wielding the flail for many long hours. Here at Charlbury were two men living next door, each had ten children. They walked to Pratt's farm at Spelsbury to thrash for twenty pence a day, beginning work at six in the morning, on sheaves spread on the floor in readiness the night before, and by daylight they were about ready to turn over and thrash the other side.

I heard a story when I was a lad of a man who took a grist of corn to a windmill on his donkey's back, and as the mill was not working the sails were still and the end of one was within reach, so he gave the halter a hitch to the sail and, taking the bag, carried his corn into the mill. Just then the miller put the mill in gear, and the terrified man rushed out to see his poor donkey taking an aerial passage dangling to the mill sail.

Dress

Since the day when, as the fine old Genevan version of the best of Books says:—

'They sewed fig-tree leaves together and made themselves breeches,' clothes and dress has been an intimate, and sometimes an engrossing, subject. A fine flint knife about three inches in length, and a magnificent local flint scraper I have, remind us of far away Wychwood days when

'Daddy went a hunting
To get a little rabbit skin,
To wrap the baby bunting in.'

An old stone spindle whorl into which used to be stuck the bobbin on which the thread was wound as spun by spinster fingers by whirling the stone on the floor, tell us of the time when weaving had come in, and cloth could be used for garments.

The idea as to the Romans finding our forefathers with not much besides blue paint upon them needs to be taken with understanding, for to-day our race strips, when anything strenuous is to be tackled, and tattooing seems to be inborn, for arms and body, as everyone knows. We gather that we had a love for colour and plaids and stripes; this is yet in evidence.

A good lady said, 'People stared so.' She did not realise I think that one could not help seeing a handsome person from a very long way when she was dressed in stripes of contrasting colours about two inches wide.

It is quite easy to see in our nearby village churches, from brasses, effigies, etc., beautiful representations of the garments worn in days past in this district. In Charlbury Church are corbels with contemporary headgear, and the empty matrix in the slab (broken across and reversed at some period) over Lady Bridges' grave, enables us to see the shape of the hat and mantle she wore, when she was the grand lady at Charlbury, and led the way, perhaps in dress as in many other things, hereabouts.

Sir Henry Lee's monument at Spelsbury is a fine study. Visitors will surely notice the beautiful lace collar he is carved as wearing, also the dresses of his lady and her children about her.

At Glympton the Tesdale brass and the figure in the ponderous monument above it show us how these people were attired. The magnificent Fettiplace figures, tier on tier at Swinbrook, are well known. The brass (now on the wall) of the cleric at Kiddington Church should be seen.

In the now almost inaccessible old Church Chancel at Heythrop in what was the Park, 'Ichabod' in thistles and ruts seems written over the place now, brasses and glass depict armour and dress.

A study of the fine series of brasses in Chipping Norton Church is worthwhile. The four 'Pargett' girls with quaint head gear all massed on one small brass is very curious. The fine tomb effigies in the west end corner must be seen.

Carving from an earlier church built into south wall of Heythrop Church

The tall head dresses so exalted and big take us to Great Tew south doorway at the Church. It looks as though the lord of the place said to his wife, 'My dear, why don't you go to church?' 'You see I cannot get in,' she would reply, and glancing at her fashionable head he started off as though light had come. Calling Roger the mason and taking him to the church, pointing to the Norman tympanum over the door, he said, 'Roger, her ladyship cannot get in, can you remove that stone ?' 'Leave it to me, sir.' And forthwith marking some of the forms he was used to cut, he made head room and left us a doorway quite out of the common. Is there another like it ?

At Great Tew if you roll back the carpet in the chancel you will be rewarded with a sight of fine brasses and, to step aside, stand at the foot of Mrs. Boulton's monument and look into the face of the figure if you would see how Chantry could make marble live.

The beautiful figures at Northleigh Church are well placed for study. Lady Wilcot's in S.S. collar shows she favoured the house of Lancaster. Henry IV loved the Speedwell, and had this little flower wrought in precious metals and together with the initial S, originated a striking bit of adornment. Her hair is gathered up into a finely jewelled net on each side of her face, and they say in that day ladies did not shingle but went one further and had the hairs plucked.

Other Churches all round Wychwood have objects of interest such as I have given.

Weaving used to be done in many a home and spinning was done on all hands. Witney for long decades was a centre for this business, an old story illustrates how their rough cloth was used for great coats, so a Witney man could be told by his coat.

A man with more drink than he could carry crept into the pigsty of an inn to sleep it off, not being aware that a man travelling with a dancing bear was staying the night at the house and had chained up his beast to sleep in the sty. When our hero crept in, he found two big strong arms, he thought, hugging too tightly to be comfortable, and feeling the bear's rough coat he began to shout, 'Let go Witney man, let go Witney man.'

An early writer states that 'Wytney standithe by cloth.'

PATCHES

The symbols of virtue, as they have been called, a book and a rosary, gave way in the frivolous years of the Restoration to a mirror and patch box.

Pepys says: 'This day I allowed my wife to wear a patch for the first time, she looked mighty pretty.' The patch was a bit of black cloth, cut diamond or some fancy shape and stuck somewhere on the face. The little boxes with mirror in lid turn up from old domestic stores, I have a specimen.

The farthingale of Elizabeth's day went off to be followed by a period of slim silhouette to reappear near our day as the crinoline. To give balance and steadiness to these things a few of the big Georgian pennies used to be sewn in round the circumference unless the proper leaden weights, of which I have a specimen, were at hand.

STARCH

When starch came in and linen could be folded and pressed into folds and orderly frills various machines and devices were used to do this pressing.

Those too poor for a smoothing iron used to use a big round lump of black glass as a polisher. I have a couple.

The story of the little girl whose home had neither iron or polisher, and yet came out on Sunday morning with her pinafore in the proper folds, is that early in the week it was washed, and when folded put in the seat of father's big chair, under the cushion, so at meal times, and evenings, father's bulk was pressing his little daughter's bit of Sunday finery into wearing condition.

When men starched their beards and dyed them vermilion red, as they did, that was starchy in the extreme.

BREECHES

The sight of padded breeches on monuments and brasses reminds us of the various ways men have covered their legs, all down from the Celtic breeches through the days of 'full slops', 'galligaskins', to 'Oxford Bags', Apple Stealers' and 'Plus Fours.'

GLOVES

The motto of the Company, 'True hearts and warm hands.'

In a case at the stairs-head in the Ashmolean Museum are some gloves of historical interest.

The gloves sent to the Great Exhibition in 1851 were stitched by Mrs. William Boddington at Finstock. A pair given to a religious object there a few years ago by a Miss Holyfield, as she was then, had some 2500 stitches in one glove — she counted them. Fancy making a *pair* by hand (as they were) for 4¹/₂d a few years ago!

HATS

When tall hats were the fashion plough boys wore them. Mr. Henry Hall told me they used to go to plough wearing knee breeches, white stockings and low shoes, and the tall hats being of cheap quality, when it rained, the dye not being fast used to soak out and run down the wearer's neck and face, and they got in a fine pickle; yet were in the fashion.

BUTTONS

That these have figured largely in English dress a glance at the brasses and the corbel heads in Chadlington Church will show. The saying describing one who is not all there as 'not having all his buttons on,' everyone knew in olden days the meaning, seeing what a number it took for a person to be well and completely dressed.

PATTENS

'A round ring, a wooden thing,
Two bits of leather, and a bit of string.'
What is it? Why, a 'patten.'

These useful adjuncts to female dress for so long, went out when high heels came in. For who could walk 'cocketting' on pattens with high heels? Gay speaks of one —

'Safe through the wet on clinking pattens tread.'

Wren's church, St. Margaret Pattens, keeps up the name of the former patten makers' locality in Eastcheap, London

Girls wanted to keep them on their feet in the classes in school; old minutes record this, of Charlbury and Finstock Sunday Schools.

STAYS

'Opens like a barn door, shuts up like a trap,
You may think of many things before you think of that,
And a jewel case at that.'
What is it ? A woman's stays.

These curious things with whale-bone inserted and a big wooden busk making stooping difficult. Some old busks were ornamented with initials, ornaments, or love emblems.

WIGS

The fashion of wearing wigs was so common that mention must be made of them. Most men wore them from the middle of the sixteenth century. The demand for hair to make them was so great that children used to get their hair stolen if they were walking alone. Clergy and laity wore wigs. I have a big lump-ended pair of curling tongs as used to put them in curl, and the pipe clay curlers turn up fairly often.

John Wesley's mother wanted him to have his hair cut and wear a wig, but in this he would not listen to her.

A WIG STORY

The wife of a judge desired to go with her husband on circuit, and at last he consented but only on condition that she had no bonnet boxes with her. As the coach sped on, his lordship stretched out his legs and his feet touched a band box under the opposite seat; at once he reached it out and sent it whirling out of the window and they sped on. At their destination when putting on his robes he asked for his wig. 'That,' said his valet, 'was in the box you threw out of the window as we came along the road.'

THE SMOCK FROCK

There were about half a dozen of these worn at Finstock when I was a young lad. Slops, jackets and coats were generally worn by men and lads.

BONNETS

In Victorian days a tilted cart used to visit the fairs round Wychwood hung all inside with bonnets made at Finstock — certainly a forerunner of the modern motors that one can see on the same errand to-day at markets as at Oxford, etc.

Some articles of attire, as the surplice amongst the Puritans, and colours as blue amongst the Quakers, were avoided formerly; this objection to blue as a dress colour no longer seems to obtain.

With the thought of a 'coat that was without seam' we will stop, though, like the bagpiper's tune, there is no end to our subject, Dress.

An old bill, 1647, in my possession

A bill for wgas gatg his lay out and work dun for MR. EGOMAT MALBOY, 1647.

Making of two wyett wast cooates 2/4.

7 duson of buttons 9d.

Making Mr. Malboy a quillet wastcooat 1/6 and 3d., 2s. 2d.

Making of a sutt and slosl lind with plush 15/-.

Ramint and stilmyo 3/-.

6 duson of buttons 3/-.

Sewing o sliwging o silks 2/-.

Tarotay 3/6.

16 yards of ribin Coligroosd goolas and Eyot 14/-.

3/3 and a nayll of plush and yolem laro 13/9.

A nool button for 2d. and drawing o of cloak and cooff 2/2.

Marlmy o 2 gooseloatt for Mrs. Maboy 5/-. Of wool and sumar Saroputy 5/4 per 13/9.

Silver lat at 4/10—6/-.

4 yards of riban at 8d. and fer silk too peticots 2~8.

Print slov soup to Covor pootsloatt 2/4.

Gerigotiens to Covor mer Cooatt 10d.

Making a sutt wat Droost 7/-.

Camiso and plisninso 3 and for 6 doson of srost butons 7/6.

Silk to Colipooit goold and Eyot and lopp 2/4. Plush, etc., 12/-.

Making your mans Cooatt 2/6.

3 doson of buttons at 6d. loop lat 10d. more buton and silk 3/-.

Making Mrs. Malboys peticoatt 3/6 and—to Conox 6/-.

Yoh and Silver lace to flourloot peticoatt 14/7.

Silk and riban and drawing o ye coullos 1/11.

Curlingo of a sutt Mr. Malboy 2/6.

Making of Mr. Malboys sutt and Cloak and Short Cooatt 16/-.

Canuit and slising 3d. and 12 duson of buttons 15/-

2¹/₂ doson of Cloak buttens 6d. and 9d. of yerh silvour loop 8/9.

Sowing a strivingo Sililo and 1¹/₄ of a noll of laffotay 18³/₄6.

¹/₂ a noll of plush 9/6 and a nosl button p. 2d. and golomeas 11/6.

Drawins o 2j9 Colyoorot and 5/2.

Colerd shag to lyne two brigsb 12/9.

Yurll 9d. and sasingo yernbloatler and 1 duson buttons 12/2.

I asotay to sutt 2/6

Colard Cloat to lyn ye brisgob and making a sut and cloak 11/10.

Carnis and stasingo and drawings 9/-.

1/2 dosan buttons and loops at and Colsar 6d.

Colourd Claot, riban knot of 1 go Criget 3/4.

Coligooevl evoslot and 2 payor of goslodot 2/5.

Sowing and sinpingor Silver 3/3.

Courlingo of a shertt Cooatt 1/6.

Making Mrs. Maltby a silk Calominto gown 12/–.

Vamis and stismigo 3d. p. laso 11/10 Silk 2/6 17/4.

Sustogon to Lyn to Stayol and 4 yards ribon 5/2.

A roult and a buslar 4d. a yard and a quarter of Cloat 14/4.

Buttons and silk 1/3.

2¹/₄ of yards of Cloath to make your man a cooatt 1/2/6.

Golour laso and 5 duson butons and on to ye wast 3/7.

Making a sutat of floavloatt p. Mr. Malboy 4/–.

Sowing a steigmao and ribans 2/3.

A dousan of Caso 5/–.

Riban and yorlodot lingo to wast band 1/8.

Soak lato and lafotoy and a giml Coshon 3/8.

The sum is   19   7   0

BILL OF WORK, 1647

Receaved of ALICE LANGXAM in full of this bill the 24 of feburary 1648 of all recknings by me IP.

The marke of JOHN POWELL.

Dialect and pronunciations

The notes given in *Charlbury and its Nine Hamlets* on Dialect appear to have given interest to many people, so I am giving other words with examples of the use of our words, and local pronunciations.

In our Wychwood forest district, from one parish to another, there may be quite a marked difference in the pronouncing of our dialect and other words, as well as their intonation, or drawl.

These words, and the way they are pronounced, can be heard where village children play, men talk together amongst themselves, and in cottage homes. Generally any attempt on the part of any member of the circle or family to drop the dialect, and use 'grammar' as it is called, is at once the butt of scorn and ridicule. To those born to its use, there is no question as to its being most expressive, as well as understandable, to convey the meaning intended, and in moments of excitement, stress, or ecstasy, comes most readily to the lips, and most easily and fully gives utterance to thoughts and feelings.

A word in the dialect of a village, with the intonation quite unconsciously given, may mean very, very much to one from the same place. A Policeman in London at once, in answer to a question, said, ' I be Oxfordshire, I be, and I can fight.' Only a native can give the old forest intonation, running up at the end of a sentence, and ending with a drawl on a high pitch. Beginning with the bass, and ending with the treble, perhaps only one, or two words, and the slur from a low to a high pitch is there.

The words ending with 'ing' are pronounced 'in ' or 'en,' 'o ' is pronounced as 'a', as in Wesley's Journals, 'Cornbury' is spelt as it is spoken 'Carnbury.'

> 'A whistlin ooman, and a crowin' hen,
> Are neither good, to God nor men.'

is in dialect.

The words 'It is not,' are 'Tis'nt,' or at Finstock, 'Chent,' at Milton 'Chunt.' 'Bayver,' afternoon lunch. 'Burra,' shelter from the wind. 'Brev-et-ing,' searching around. 'Bang-el-ing,' awkward gait. 'Caddle', chatter, gossip. 'Cocksie,' conceited. 'Dabster,' an expert. 'Duckett,' a bill hook with back chopper. 'Fither-e-fo,' a thin frayed thread. 'Gaby,' a silly. 'Gal-ous,' a bad lad. 'Gubbin,' muck. 'Goos-gog,' gooseberry. 'Hoont,' a mole. 'Jessop,' drainings from manure. 'Kim-kam,' disorder. 'Lol-lup,' leaning lazily. 'Lubber-yed,' a stupid. 'Moll-hern,' a heron. 'Nackey,' a fool. 'Niddle Noddle,' nodding repeatedly. 'Pitch pole,' heels over head. 'Plank stones,' flag stones. 'Roffage,' rubbish. 'Rhy-ful,' annoy. 'Slom-ux,' untidy dress. 'Squish,' close, reserved. 'Sly-ver,' a big slice. 'Shuffic,' fork or prong. 'Trang-doms,' fitments, accoutrements. 'Twis-sel,' tangle. 'Un-massy-ful,' great, a lot. 'Wherry,' sour. 'Wisp,' a stye. 'Yaffel,' noise of a pig eating. 'Yel-put,' a young dog's bark. 'I-zed,' big, tremendous.

CONVERSATIONS IN DIALECT

Over the garden wall: 'What bist thee a making that gret box far, then?' 'To put thy silly questins in, if t'ull be big enough to ha'ld em.'

Tossing an empty match box: 'Thur's a box to put thy civil answers in, if tis little enough, when tha can'st keep the her an and give any.'

At the draw-well, failing to bring up a bucket full of water: 'I can't get much in him, but our Poll can bring him up cock yep' (cock heaped). Apples, etc., piled up in a measure are said to be cock heaped or, in dialect, 'Cock yep'pd.'

Over a dead jay pie that has been wrongly fed: 'Our Poll gin him some cheese, and that died en.'

'Wur bist thee a gwaain?'

'Down Studly, to find our donkey. If I can't find en, I'll chop es yhed (head) off.'

To throw stones at an object is to 'Pelt it,' at Finstock, or 'Peggle' at it; at Milton-under-Wychwood it would be to 'Dub it.'

Hair at Finstock is 'Hur,' at Stonesfield and Handborough 'Har.'

'Wur bist a gwa-ain?

To Kraws (Crow's) Castle,

To take a passell,

For our Bet, if her'l et,

If her wunt et, I'll make her.'

'Kal ak e' is 'here look you.' A Yorkshireman used to play this off on to his mates at Witney when they twitted him about his Yorkshire talk.

'What has't got in that baag ?' 'Taters, all the biggest and best be ratten, and the little uns be no gret size much.'

Another reply finished with 'Gret round taters, as long as my arm.'

'Bist coming up to our feaast? We shall have shouder o mutton, an pudden a top.' Or 'Two sarts o mate, out o one pig; mutten an beef.'

I remember a Field town man saying that 'at Finstock you has Fuz (furze) Pie, and spider puden.' He was trying to score one against our saying things about his village.

'What bist doing to that little bwoy? I'll give tha a licker in the yer ole if tha cass'a'nt lev en a be.'

A labourer working with my father said to him, referring to the day after, some village merrymaking he hoped to attend in the near future, and as to the effects of the drink he would consume said, 'If I be alive and well, I shall be three parts dhead' (dead).

An old story is that a recruiting sergeant had got a lad to take the shilling, and his mother began to weep and lament, saying, 'My poor boy'll be starved,' this, over and over, till the sergeant said, 'O bless e missis he'l see plenty o vitt'als wer he's a going.' Then said his mother, wiping her eyes, 'I'll cry na more, fer I knows if ever he can see it, he'l ha some ont.'

Epitaphs, etc.

'And some there be which have no memorial, who are perished as though they had never been.'

Epitaph written in 1744 by a lad eight years of age on a Crow which he had buried in the garden, from MS. I have:—

'Here lies the body of John Crow,

Who once was high and now is low,

Ye brother crows take warning all,

For as you rise, so you will fall.'

Another from the same MS. collection:—

'Here lies General Tully,

Aged 105 fully.

Nine of his wives beside him doth lie,

And the tenth must lie here when she doth die.'

On a neat stone near south entrance at Enstone Church, without name or date, spelt as given:—

'A loving husband

A father dear

A vertious man

Both far and near.

A loving neighbour

A faithful friend

And so he made

His Godly end.'

At Woodstock:—

'Robert Bruce, died Jan. 26, 1732, ordered this tomb in memory of his brothers and sisters, left the rest of his estate to place out the sons of freemen, inhabitants of Woodstock. It is reported in the town that the trustees sold the property and spent the money.'

On the north wall inside Heythrop old Church is a small brass inscribed as follows:—

'Without and near the Opposite Window

Lye's Ursula, wife of

James Martin, Rector of Heythrop.

Her well-bred, pious never ruffled mind

Won for her the love of God, and all mankind

She her own Graces to her Daughter join'd.

Her skill and Pity heald' the ulcer'd Poor

Well did her prospect Stomach-Pangs endure

(Swoon'd to Heavens Vision) but no skill could cure.

Blessed by the poor, will her and SHREWSBURY'S hand

Survive the grave, as good SAMARITANS.

Labascenti muro refigatur

quoeso mi Successor heice Lamina.

Died June 1743. Aged 45.'

An Epitaph on a doctor. I. Letsome:

'When people's ill they comes to I,

I physics, bleeds, and sweats 'em;

Sometimes they lives, sometimes they dies,

What's that to I. I. Letsome.'

Another doctor's epitaph:—

'He survived all his patients.'

At Spelsbury .—

'My life was short
The longest is my rest,
God called me home,
Because it pleased Him best.
    S.I. 1793.'

In the Church porch floor, Chadlington:—

'Sacred to friendship and every amiable virtue.

Here rests from a long series of pain and weakness Borne with equal courage and resignation the mortal part of Elizabeth, wife of John Cartwright of London. A woman Possest of these Virtues rendered her agreeable to herself and friends. She died Sept. 1766, In the 33 year of her age.

Truly lamented by those who recall with a pleasing melancoly her past life.'

At Fulbrook Church, on a large wall Tablet, 1672, occurs the following:—

'If Bloud or Beauty Parts or Grace could Save from the Corruptions of the Comon Grave or without Death conferre Devinitie we might have wondered this Dear St. did dye. But since to Bliss Death must Induction give of need She dy'd that Shee might better live, dy'd, Ah too Early! yet let none Complain This was necessity, That was her Gaine.'

At Hook Norton:—

'He was, but room wont let me tell you what,
Name what a friend should be,
And he was that.'

Fresh teeth at 106

'In Memory of SARAH JARVIS who departed this life 11th day of Dec. 1753 in the 107th year of her age. Sometime before her death she had fresh teeth.'

The above I saw in bold letters on the top of a tomb at Corsham, Wilts. This is how it was discovered that she had fresh teeth: A store of apples was seen to be getting less, and the old lady owned to being the culprit, but, said her friends, 'you cannot eat apples having no teeth,' and so it came out that she had grown fresh ones.

Mother Shipton's epitaph

'Here lyes she who never ly'd
Whose skill often has been try'd,
Her Prophies still survive,
And ever keep her name alive.'

Her predictions, some of them are striking, recorded 1448, British Museum MS:

> 'Around the world thoughts shall fly,
> In the twinkling of an eye.'
> 'Carriages without horses shall go,
> And accidents fill the world with woe.'
> 'Under the water men shall walk,
> Shall ride, shall sleep, shall talk.'
> 'In the air men shall be seen,
> In white, in black, and in green.'

At Crayford in Kent I saw the stone bearing the following remarkable epitaph:—

> 'Here lies the body of Peter Isnell, 30 years clerk of this parish; he lived respected, a pious and mirthful man, and died on his way to Church to assist at a wedding, on the 31st August, 1811, aged 70 years. The inhabitants of Crayford raised this stone to his cheerful memory, and as a tribute to his faithful service.
>
> > The life of this clerk was just three score and ten,
> > During half of which time he had sung out Amen.
> > He married when young like other young men;
> > His wife died one day, so he chanted Amen.
> > A second he took, she departed,—what then ?
> > He married, and buried a third with Amen.
> > Thus his joys and his sorrows were treble, but then
> > His voice was deep bass, as he chanted Amen,
> > On the horn he could blow as well as most men,
> > But his horn was exalted in blowing Amen,
> > He lost all his wind after three score and ten,
> > And here with three wives he waits till again
> > The trumpet shall rouse him to sing out Amen.'

Some years ago I spent many happy busy weeks at Shenley Church, lodging with dear good Mrs. Gregory, gone to the Home beyond long since. There is at this place an epitaph describing a former village worthy:—

> 'Silent in the dust lies mouldering here,
> A Parish clerk of voice most clear.
> None Joseph Rogers could excel
> In laying bricks, or singing well;
> Though snapp'd his line, laid by his rod,
> We build for him our hopes in God.'

At Wilcote:—

'To the memory of Ann, the faithful wife of Wm. Weeks, formerly of Poulton Farm, North Wilts. She departed this life Jan. 17, 1852. Aged 77 years.

Son of man behold I take away from thee the desire of thine eyes with a stroke. Yet neither shalt thou mourn nor weep, Neither shall thy tears run down. Ezek. c. 2. v. 16.'

Also of Wm. Weeks her husband who died Oct. 30, 1872. Aged 88 years.

On a large foot stone is the following:—

'Blessed are ye when men shall revile you and persecute you and shall say all manner of evil against you falsely for my sake. Rejoice, and be exceedingly glad, for great is your reward in heaven, for so persecuted they the prophets which were before you. And every one that hath forsaken houses, or brethren, or sisters, or father or mother or wife or children, or lands for my names sake shall receive an hundred-fold and shall inherit everlasting life.'

When Mr. Weeks died at his daughter's, Mrs. Matthews, at Little Barrington, his coffin was made at Northleigh, from boards kept at his desire for that purpose by the carpenter, Mr. Hicks, from the same tree that had found the wood for his wife's coffin.

'HAM FOR THE FUNERAL'

An old man was very ill and the doctor said, 'Let him have anything he wants,' as he was past human aid, so someone went upstairs and said to him, 'Is there anything you would like to have?' 'Yes,' said the dying man, 'there is a nice smell about, I should like some of that,' and at once he was answered, 'Why, that is a ham cooking for the funeral, you can't have any of that!'

Years ago at Great Rollright the parish clerk was a quaint and unusual man. He was a son of Crispin, by trade, and as though he must sport something special to his calling, always wore boots with yellow tops at a funeral. After 'earth to earth,' he would smite his hands together and then blow his nose loudly, using a big red handkerchief.

A CENTENARIAN

Some years ago I made the acquaintance of Richard Withers at Great Rollright, who was then one hundred and three years old. He had been a shepherd, had married very young, and had a son eighty years of age. He walked up to the Church door to stand there for me to photograph him, asking his housekeeper for his best hat for the occasion. He had never drunk a bottle of medicine in his life. He had buried three wives just inside the churchyard not many feet from his cottage wall, close to the churchyard entrance, where is now a surprising, and, to me, not pleasing, gateway. Mr. Withers was a small man. He lived to be 105.

Knitting sheaths

'She knows how to sing and to knitt,

And she knows how to carry the babe,

While she drives the kye to pasture.'

Men, women and children all used to knit in former days, waggoners as they drove their teams along the roads in some parts, and on winter evenings friends gathered about the fire to knit and talk. One who could read, read aloud, perhaps a book or newspaper.

The end of the needle on which the work was being done used to be put into a sheath fastened to the person. My grandmother, I remember, had one made of a strong quill sewn into some material about four inches square which she used to pin to her side, but many were made of wood, some quite plain, just a straight stick with a hole in the end, twisted into the apron string of the knitter. Some were turned, or notched, or carved, some cut like a fish, a coiled serpent, or other form. Devices or lettering, dates, initials, and mottos were on others, as:—

'I am of box, and brass within,

My place is on your apron string.'

Another:—

'On thy breast my heart doth rest. B.K.'

Ornamented and inscribed sheaths are prized to-day, and are worth collecting.

Light

'Her candle goeth not out by night.'—Solomon.

Our fathers sitting by firelight, with perhaps a burning rush held in a pair of nips, were not so well off for artificial light as we have been the last sixty years or so.

Rushes were gathered, dried, and strips of bark peeled off three sides, then long lengths were soaked in a fat boat, filled with melted fat and beeswax, gradually moved up as they burnt away through the jaws of the rush holder, they gave enough light to see to move about, and to see if you were indoors or out. Wax and tallow candles were better, but more expensive.

Bunyan says:—

'Man's like a candle in a candlestick

Made up of tallow and a little wick,

And as the candle is before it's lighted

Just such be they who are in sin benighted.'

The candle snuffer was anxiously watched in church and chapel as he went his rounds during service, to see if he took a wick too low and so put out the light.

One old man at a service reached a candle out of its socket, snuffing it with his fingers and then holding it near his book so he could see to sing, till presently giving a cough he accidently blew out the candle.

A preacher knocked a candle down on to a bald head just below.

Candlemas day used to have processions carrying lighted candles, in memory it is said of Simeon's words in Luke xi, 35, 'A Light to lighten the Gentiles.'

A grocer's servant in olden days went into the cellar for something, leaving the candle she was carrying alight without a candlestick below. 'Where have you left it?' said her master. 'I stuck it into that bag of seed,' she said. Like a man gone mad, he rushed below; he remembered he had left open a bag of gunpowder, and there he found the lit candle which he safely rescued, breathing more freely, and Mary no doubt got a little good advice when he arrived on the scene again.

When I was a lad my father brought from Abingdon a paraffin lamp one Saturday when he walked home for the week end. He was working at Culham Church. I believe it was the first lamp in a cottage in the 'Bottom,' at Finstock, and was much admired. Before that mother used to sit and sew by hand the long seams of the vast skirts worn in those Victorian days (she was a dressmaker) by candle light. I can see the snuffers as they lay in their tray on the table now.

ELECTRICITY

The wonders of light and power by electricity are coming to our Wychwood district, and the one thing I grieve over is that the hideous poles and cables suspended therefrom help to ruin the beauty of our country-side. The telephone poles and wires were bad enough along our roads, the poor trees having their tops mutilated to let the wires pass, and now this awful fringe of ugliness adds to the shame. Underground out of sight they ought to go, especially in our streets and at the borders of our villages.

The newspaper

Our Wychwood forest district can claim connection with newspaper publication from early newspaper days.

The earliest Oxford newspaper was the *Mercurius Aulicus*, issued Jan. 1st, 1642. A famous Burford man, Peter Heylin, was joint editor with John Birkenhead. Heylin, born at Burford 1599, entered Hart Hall in 1613, the next year became a Demy of Magdalen College. Birkenhead, a servitor of Oriel at 17, became secretary to Archbishop Laud, and was presently made a knight.

It was rather a ticklish business, and editors ran risks of prison, and death, if they did not mind their P's and Q's.

Cromwell proclaimed that 'no person whatever do presume to publish in print any matter of public news or intelligence without leave of the Secretary of State.'

Printers who dared, or blundered, got into hot water, and worse. One printer named Twyn was hanged, drawn, and quartered in 1663. Another newspaper man who was very much to the fore in his day was Marchemont Needam. Born at Burford in Aug. 1620, at 14 he was at All Souls College and a chorister. He appears to have been a smart fellow, but lacking in discretion. He edited three papers all printed in the city, one favouring the Roundheads, the second the Cavaliers, and the third the Commonwealth. He might have thought such an attempt would lead to disaster. He lost the respect of all concerned, and died at London in great poverty in 1678.

The oldest existing newspaper in England is the *London Gazette*, the Government paper which contains all official announcements. First printed at Oxford as the *Oxford Gazette*, issued Nov. 5, 1665 (whilst Charles II had his Court there) by Leonard Lichfield, it was at first half sheet only, printed on one side. It was soon transferred to London and an edition in French issued. It never contained any intelligence the Court did not wish to be known, and a wise and clever man was needed, there is no doubt, to preside and watch the matter before the printer got it in his columns. Charles Perrott, M.A., an accomplished linguist and traveller, did this for five years; he died April 23, 1677 and was buried at Northleigh.

Many sheets were issued at Oxford till in April, 1753, was the first number of a paper that for many years was of great account in all our borders. The first name it bore was *News, Boys, News*; or *The Electioneering Journal*. About the fourth number the name it bore, and that became a household word, was Jackson's Oxford Journal. Mr. Jackson, the printer and proprietor, was an eccentric man. His paper stated: 'Whosoever shall please to send him anything curious, on either side of the question, may depend on the strictest impartiality, as well as the utmost secrecy. From their humble servant W. Jackson.'

In 1712 a tax on newspapers was a crushing blow to many worthless sheets: also a duty of twelve pence had to be paid on every advertisement. Writers hid their names for excellent reasons. England was not yet a country where

'Girt by friends or foes,
A man may speak the thing he will.'

In early 19th-century days when my grandfather had *Jackson's Journal* at Finstock (I believe he was the only person in the village who had it) the cost was sevenpence per copy, plus postage. In later years 'Jackson's' was left out of the name, and now the recent stir in newspaper matters at Oxford has swept out the 'Journal.'

Mention must be made of the articles for long years contributed to the Oxford papers from the pen of an ardent lover of our Wychwood area, the late Mr. Harry Paintin, who earned the regard and gratitude of hosts of readers on all hands.

An early example of illustrated press advertising

ADVERTISEMENTS AND NEWS

1776. James Dent put up a stage at Charlbury and as a Mountebank had some chance game, for plate, and other articles, to the great disturbance of the place and neighbourhood, encouraging Gaming, Idleness, Riot, and Debauchery. The Earl of Litchfield saw to it that James had time for reflection as to his doings at Charlbury, by sending him to Oxford Castle for a period.

'Take Notice—Spring Guns, Man Traps and Spikes for Dogs are set in Cokethorpe Park, Barley Park and Boys Wood. All Persons found getting Nuts in any of the before mentioned Woods will be prosecuted. Walter Strickland, Cokethorpe Park, Sept. 10, 1817.

Jan. 8, 1799. Wanted, a journeyman warming pan maker who may depend upon constant employment.'

July 28, 1817.

ORATORIO. HOOK NORTON.

JOHN PROCTOR begs leave to inform his friends and the public in general, that the Performance of SACRED MUSIC advertised to take place in the Parish Church of Hook Norton, on Tues. July 29th, is POSTPONED until Tues. 12th August, when it will certainly take place.'

Dec. 3, 1819. 'On Sunday se'night four inhabitants of New Woodstock, in good health, attended Divine Service in that parish Church, whose ages together amounted to upwards of 347 years.'

Mistakes in the rush and hurry of newspaper production are pardonable, but in more serious publications are most unfortunate. Printers' errors are sometimes most unhappy. Several notable editions of the Bible got their title from some mistake, as the 'Wicked' Bible, where 'not' is omitted from one of the commandments, but one very striking and lively one was in a Prayer Book, in the lesson to be read at the burial of the dead, when leaving out a 'c' makes it read 'we shall all be hanged in a moment, in the twinkling of an eye.'

Paine's of Fawler Mill

A letter in *The Times*, followed by a talk broadcast from London on Destroying History, by C. A. Barnard, Esq., F.S.A., led to a mass of correspondence being placed in his hands, some of which included 422 old letters from 1782 of the Eden family of Honeybourne, near Evesham.

Articles about them by Mr. Barnard have appeared in the Evesham Journal, which, having read my *Notes on Charlbury*, he was so kind as to bring to my notice.

These letters were about to be handed over to a youth for the watermarks and postage stamps; Mr. Barnard's letter saved them. Many of them were written by Mrs. Eden, the wife of Nathaniel Eden, to her five daughters, all of whom married, some of them twice, the youngest, Sarah, having as her second husband Mr. Jno. Paine of Fawler Mill.

Mr. Paine held the mill on a 99 years' lease which expired in 1864. As a business man, methodist and musician, he filled a worthy place in local life. The letters contain things of interest both general and family.

Mr. Eden visited his daughter in London, a Mrs. Fisher, whose son Eden founded the City firm 'Eden Fisher & Co.,' and the letter which follows describes his journey home on horseback to Forest Hill the first day, and the second stage to Honeybourne on the morrow.

Honeybourne, Jan. 5, 1801.

Dear Sir,

According to my promise I'm going to give an account of my journey home. I left Emanuel's on Monday at half-past six, accompanied by him and Ben Steinmetz. After riding through many hours rain we reached Uxbridge quite wet through. I've often heard tell of the Cockney's disliking the farmer, but thinking myself in pretty good hands I went as cheerfully on as the weather would admit, but enquiring if my guides were to be depended on—as they undertook to pilot me—I found they had brought me full three miles out of the road. We were forced to go back every yard so they gave me a soaking of six miles, clever fellows!

After breakfast on Tuesday morning we took leave of each other and I set off for Forest Hill, where Nancy Smith is married. I never knew worse riding. The snow balled to such a degree that I could hardly get on at all for the first ten or twelve miles, but about six in the evening I reached Mr. Orsbond's, and found him very well, and cheerful and happy. I found myself quite tired, but after a good supper and sincere friendship I began to revive.

I took leave of my friends before eleven, fixing for Mr. and Mrs. Orsbond to lie in bed, and for me to have a candle at six which the girl punctually brought. In two minutes after the girl was gone down stairs Mr. Orsbond came to my bedside in his shirt, desiring me to lie in bed, saying it was a deep snow, and to spend the day with him. But wishing to get home as soon as I could, after thanking him for his kindness, I begged he'd go to bed and tell Mrs. O. I was very much obliged to her for her great care of me.

Setting out at half-past six I rode many miles in deep snow, without the least track, before I reached the great road, but by the help of Providence I arrived safe home a little before seven o'clock, sadly fatigued. I found Mrs. Eden quite brave, and my children well, Dr. Hirons better, and Miss Tomes on the mending hand.

I am much obliged to you and your friends for all favours received. Please to make my love to Mrs. F. and the children. With best respects to your mother, Mr. Stringfield, Mr. and Mrs. Fountains and all friends. I am, dear Sir, with our united best respects.

Yours sincerely,

Nathaniel Eden

His wife was a good woman, her letters show this. In one telling of converts she says of one 'who has left off fiddling for dancers, and has left off drinking.' On a Sunday: 'at six in the morning there is a Prayer Meeting at Mr. Darks, then breakfast, Church at ten, then at Mr. Darks at two o'clock, then tea, at six out preaching.' So she runs on.

A wedding in the family leads her to describe the dinner: 'A rump of beef, a quarter of lamb, a ham, three fowls, apple pie, cheese cake, syllabubs, blancmange, with scarlet beans, potatoes, cabbage. The next day twelve were at dinner, and lawyer Green popped in, made us thirteen, a very unlucky number.' Evidently this was not the Quarterly fast day.

After staying at Fawler Mill she writes how there came a mob five or six hundred strong threatening to pull down the mill. (Bread riots were the order of the day. No bread could be sold that had not been baked twenty-four hours previously). Bread was 6s. the peck loaf.

Mrs. Paine was a woman of deep joyous faith, her letters disclose how fortunate she felt herself in many good friends, especially Mrs. Spendlove of Charlbury. In her last letter written to Mrs. Fisher from Fawler Mill, April 1814, she says how glad she is to hear that her sisters, Mrs. Fisher and Mrs. Bushell of Charlton House, and cousin Betsy, are coming to see her, hope they will have a safe journey. The stage coach 'The Royal Defiance,' reaches Charlbury from London at about seven or eight in the evening.

It appears that Mrs. Paine's grandfather, Thomas Eden, was intimately acquainted with John Wesley and built the chapel at Broad Marston.

On Saturday last, July 13th, 1929, a party of Americans on tour called here, introducing themselves by saying 'we are descendants of Jonathan Paine, of Fawler Mill, and we are all named Paine.' It was very pleasant to see these good people and talk over the family story. They had been to see Waterloo, and had in America a sword that the Paine that fought there brought home from the fateful field, when Napoleon saw his famous Guards fail before Paine of Fawler, Joseph Oliver of Stonesfield and William Poole, and many other Oxfordshire men. When he saw them crumple up, I was told when a lad, that he said 'All is lost,' and galloped madly from the field, presently giving himself up to Captain Maitland on board the *Bellerophon*, later on to be guarded by a Langford of Finstock, at St. Helena. So villagers pass on one to another stories of the happenings in which any of their number have taken a share.

'Thus done the tales to bed they creep,
By whispering winds soon lulled to sleep.'

Napoleon was buried in a coffin without his name or even initials upon it.

We will back to our Fawler friends. One child was drowned in the mill race. A son, Nathaniel Eden Paine, became the master of Truro Grammar School, another, Rev. John Paine, a clergyman, of Dewsbury Moor.

A letter written by Susan Eden, 1798, who is on a visit to Birmingham: 'We have a deal of company, the ladies some of them are dressed so nicely with their long muslin trains. It is beautiful to see them. We had two ladies the other night with muslin petticoats and silk jackets. It looked so smart that I intend to have one for the next assembly. My dimity jacket is very much admired. People told me when I had my new hat it would get me an admirer, but I think if anything, it will be my dimity jacket, but I think the young men at Birmingham are very dull.' Later on she married a Mr. Bushell, and did very well, so the dimity jacket, or something, seems to have been effective. She lived to be an old woman, and in 1840 writes of the chapel at Pebworth being opened: 'the Chapel was crowded … last night.' Collections £31.

Parish registers

Thomas Cromwell, who is said to have been the chief agent in establishing Tudor absolutism, after the Act of Supremacy when Henry VIII took the title of 'on earth the Supreme head of the Church of England' suggested Parish Registers, but so much opposition was offered to it, that for a time the idea fell through, but in 1597 a general plan of registration was adopted.

(The doings of this man are noted and spoken of sometimes, I know, without the use of his Christian name, Thomas, and some set down his doings at the door of the great Protector, Oliver Cromwell, who has much vandalism charged to his account done before he was born. Thomas and Oliver were different men).

The Registers were to be kept on parchment, and parchment copies were to be made of the old registers, which were on paper. The whole of the entries of the previous week were to be read out openly and distinctly on Sunday at the conclusion of either mattins or evensong. A copy of the register was to be sent annually within a month after Easter to the Diocesan Register to be preserved amongst the episcopal archives. I found there are transcripts of Charlbury Parish Registers at the Bodleian Library at Oxford. They are written mostly on long narrow strips of parchment about 2 feet 9 inches long and 5 inches wide. Some unusual names occur, and a few items may be of interest.

In 1740 in Charlbury and its hamlets there were 33 persons baptised. The Marriages are as follows:

John Clark and Judith Hall of Chadlington.
Edward Hughband of Wootten and Ann Lord of Long Coombe by Licence.
Love Grace and Hannah Badger.
Jno. Holyoak and Ann Baty of Chad.
Jno. Hacking of Warwickshire and Elizabeth Tennant.
Rich. Brooks and Mary Scarlett.
Stephen Wallington of Daylesford and Grace Gardner of Chad. by Licence.
Wm. Scuse to Ann Bister.
Rich. Lainchbury and Eliz. Bowerman of Finstock.
James Bates to Ellen Bowls.
Thos. Flaxon to May Hyat.

It appears that J. Arrowsmith, who attests the manuscript as curate of Charlbury, also held at that time the appointment of Master of the Grammar School, as did another curate in 1787, Richard Thorne.

Buried 1740:

Mr. Thomas Osbaldeston of Charlbury.
Wm. Cambden of Finstock

Ann Kench of Fawler.

Jane Hesther of Fawler.

Mary wife of Thos Cox of Fawler.

Mary daughter of Mr. Fairbrother of Fawler.

Mary wife of Wm. Green, Charlbury.

Elizabeth Ward.

Elizabeth daughter of Ben. Clifford.

George son of Geo. Maycock of Finstock.

Charlotte daughter of Jno. Ward. Charl.

Elizabeth daughter of Rich. Harris.

Jno. son of Jeremiah King.

Wm. son of Rich. Claridge of Chilson.

Widow Flaxon.

Mary Hancock, Finstock.

John Read, excise officer, Charlbury.

Mary Alder, Finstock.

Mrs. Elizabith Eyans of Chad.

Sam. Ward of Enstone.

Thos. Edgerley, Charlbury.

Elizabeth Clary

Signed by

J. Arrowsmith, Curate

Nicholas Wurford ⎫

Thomas Cox.   ⎬ Ch. Wardens

In 1741 it is remarkable that there were no marriages, the word 'none' is distinctly written. The Burials were:

John Marten. John Hawten. Wm. Hyett. Thos. Bowerman, Finstock. Mary Green, Chilson. Elizabeth Collins, Ramsden. John Hutt, Finstock. Mary Betts a widow. Ann Bailiss, Finstock. Ann her daughter. Sara Walden. Ann Reeves, Finstock. Simon Birdseye. F. John Hutchins. John Alder. F. John Brookes. Wm. Passon. Elizabeth Day. F. Frances Shepherd. Rebecca Collins. Elizabeth Dipper. F. Rich. Haines, F. Sara Wood. Ann daughter of Wm. Radford, a traveller. Benj. Chapman. Jane Cortice. F. Wm. Moss.

Thos Hayood, Vicar.

Wm. Badger, ⎫

John Williams. ⎬ Ch Wardens

In 1791.

Richard Gardner and Sarah Broom, minor, were married in this Ch. by Licence with the consent of Wm. Broom, father of the said minor, by John

Cobb, Vicar.

Huntley a name at Walcot.

Norgrove at Finstock, also Potter Lane.

Ann Debbin of Ramsden, should be De Bank, they were called Debbin.

Photography

AT CHARLBURY, FINSTOCK AND LEAFIELD

In 1839 Daguerre and Niepce found they could get a picture on a silver plate sensitised with the fumes of iodine when exposed behind a lens in a camera. The next year Fox Talbot, who lived at Laycock Abbey, Wilts. (where I saw his cameras yet preserved as he left them when I went over the place some time since), invented another process, and this was greatly improved by Scott Archer in 1851 and wet-plate work came into being.

Charlbury Market House. Photo by Mr W. Baughan on home-made plates. This ancient building was destroyed in the [eighteen-]seventies. The *shame* of it!

The early photographs in existence of Charlbury old Market House were taken by the late Mr. W. H. Baughan here by this process. Mr. Taylor, the watch-maker, of Leafield, took it up, he was a very clever man in many ways.

Eden Holyfield of Finstock, in early days, did a little at the business, but my recollections of it being carried on was at Tommy Goody's cottage nearly oppo-site the school at Finstock. In one corner of the cottage a dark room was fitted up, and I used to watch Mr. Taylor of Leafield and Tommy Goody coat the plates with collodion, and then sensitise them with silver iodide. They were used at once, wet, being put into a dark slide with silver fittings where the plates rested. The camera was without bellows, but was made of wood, in two parts, which slid, telescope fashion, one into the other. Our Finstock studio was the cottage pantry, which was something of a ruin, there being no roof, but we had rare times there as I watched these earnest men with their plates, dishes, and chemicals. The image was developed by ferrous sulphate, or pyrogallic acid, and fixed with potassium cyanide. The picture was reversed, but we exulted greatly at the results obtained, and my old friend Tommy would hop round like a boy on his crutch, helping and assisting, whilst my joy was great on being allowed to be present, to see it done, this to me was a keen delight and is a most pleasant memory. Now, a camera is held, the shutter snapped, the spool turned, someone is paid to develop and print the pictures, and this is photography; 'You press the button, we do the rest,' then 'Look at the photos I have taken.'

A landscape painter, Litherland, lived and worked at Finstock long ago, so my father told me. 'Litherland's Farm' is to the right hand above the Church, the house is pulled down. Litherland's paintings to-day fetch good prices

Mr. Brook, the miniature painter, lived next door to my grandmother. A portrait by him of my grandfather, mother told me, was just like him, a good likeness.

Punishments, gibbets, whipping, etc.

'Give to me the good old days.' ? ?

The Manor Court had power of 'fossa and furca,' that is the gallows for hanging men and the pit for drowning women. No doubt a good deep hole as 'Devil's corner,' in our Evenlode, was used here, but a pit of water, where there was no stream handy.

Most lords of manors had a gibbet in early days, greater lords and barons a double one. It is probable that the name Staple Hill, or Staple Hall, as at Witney, means the place of the stake or pile, or post, from the Anglo-Saxon 'Stapela,' a post or pile. Death was the penalty for a great number of crimes; any person stealing property to the value of one shilling (which in Henry I's reign was about the value of a heifer) was liable to be hung. Even as late as the 18th century for breaking a fishpond bank, so that the fish could escape, or cutting down a cherry tree, death was the penalty. Poisoners were boiled to death, hanging being too good for them. Richard Rice was boiled to death for this crime.

The gibbet with a man upon it was so common as to seem almost a natural part of the landscape. The hangman's pay was as low as thirteenpence halfpenny, with three half pence extra for the rope.

The last man gibbeted was in 1832, when a bookbinder was hung on a gibbet 33 feet high, and such a disorderly rabble assembled and also on Sundays, just as they did on Capps Lodge Plain to gaze at the two Dunsdens, that it became a scandal and hanging in chains was abolished in 1834.

The Mr. Secker, spoken of in my Charlbury book as the landlord at Capps Lodge, when Harry and Thomas Dunsden were arrested, was not the landlord but the constable who was sent for at the time, and Mr. Secker's grandson tells me he has yet in his possession the five pistols taken from these highwaymen that day when the tapster Marding was shot, one of which was loaded till he discharged it a few years ago. The date and initials cut into the living tree which formed the Dunsden gibbet used to be recut yearly by John World, a stone mason of Fullbrook.

Gibbet irons

It is not known with certainty what became of the third Dunsden, but it is thought that he was the robber who thrust his hand through the hole in the door at Tangly, when it was held fast, and it was cut off from outside so that he could get away, and that through bad surgery he died.

The names of the fields, Gallows Piece here, and at Handborough, and Galley Hill, at Witney, are evidence of those 'law on the spot' days.

When heads were fixed up on poles the hangman, as described by an eye witness, 'Put them in his kettle and par boyled them with Bay Salt and Cummin seed; this to keep them from putrifaction, and thus keep off the birds from seizing of them.'

SMUGGLING

'Five and twenty ponies trotting in the dark,
Brandy for the parson, bacca for the clerk,
Lace for a lady, letters for a spy,
Watch the wall my darling,
Whilst the gentlemen go by.'

Poaching and highway robbery helped to fill jails and make the hangman busy in our district, whilst active smuggling was carried on most extensively round the coast.

I have a forceful little tract Wesley wrote against it, Methodists had difficulty in keeping their hands clean. In fact far away from the coast smuggled spirits and goods could be obtained, and the 'Smuggler's Song' of which a verse is given could be sung. The book *Margaret Catchpole* is worth reading, telling of smuggling days.

CORNERING

Forestalling and regrating, that is buying up corn or wool so as to get a bigger price, was harshly dealt with. Cornering our fathers would not have. Into the stretch-neck, or the stocks, and be pelted with all the town refuse, if not turned out of the place as well.

In November, 1693, there were lively times at Charlbury, the mob rose and took away the corn by force out of the waggons as it was being carried away by an ingrossor, saying they were resolved to put the law into execution since the magistrates did not do it. One can fancy dear old Charlbury that day long ago in its indignant wrath at both magistrates and ingrossor.

ALE TASTERS

In early days there were two official ale tasters in Charlbury Manor to see that ale offered for sale was up to the right standard, also Bread was weighed and tested. Offenders went into the stocks or, if persistent, into Banbury Castle.

PUNISHMENTS

'Any person taken begging, vagrant, wandering or misordering themselves might be ordered to be whipped till their body be bloody.'

Some of our Wychwood district stocks had tall posts, as Charlbury, Stanton Harcourt, with iron straps to hold the poor wretches' hands, man or woman, who had to be thus punished.

Where the stocks had no provision for this, the hands were tied to a cart wheel, or as at Chipping Norton, I think, the last man to be sentenced to this public punishment was tied to a cart tail, and a little before that at Witney the same kind of thing took place.

It must have been a terrible ordeal to undergo. We think of Our Lord and many others who were scourged or whipped. I am able to give a personal description by a man of note, as to his experience of being whipped.

The Quaker, George Whitehead, who married Ann Downer, daughter of a Charlbury vicar, describes how he was whipped; he says:—

'A foolish fellow with a long sharp whip laid on so violently that thereby he cut and wounded both my back and breast with long stripes, tearing the skin and shedding blood till some people present cried out to stop him... Yet by the Lord's power I was enabled cheerfully to bear it all with patience, great comfort, and rejoicing.'

POACHING

In 1292-6 poachers in the forest were caught and dealt with.

William Atte Hoo fine 1/2 mark. Robert de Boscare.

Henry Clarice, Richard Bole de la Felde, Nicholas de Rammesden, John de

Boscare. Robert Tril, one mark. John la Wylde de Crawole, William Salern la Felde, John Daylin, Thos. le White de Wytteneye, Simon Mountford, Richard le Porter, Richard Poghel, Simon de Prews, Great Tew, Parson.

In Edward III's day Wm. Beaucham and Thomas le Hunt with two unknown men came with six greyhounds in Shipton fields to do wrong to the King, but they took nothing but were arrested there.

William, parson of Wilcote, with two others at Coggs wood in the forest, with three dogs took thence a three year old buck.

In 1376 a poacher was prosecuted for entering the forest with bow and arrow, the penalty is not given.

The penalty in old forest days for killing a boar unlawfully was the loss of both eyes.

A WYCHWOOD BUCK

At Ascott-under-Wychwood some years ago when a farmer there paid a man for harvest work he said to him, 'Now if you were to go into the forest and shoot a buck, you would do pretty well I think.' Said the man— 'Just what I thought of doing master.'

Taking his gun at night fall he went, and up Smallstones way on the forest borders, shot a fine buck, and hurried home, telling his wife to come and help him to load it on to a horse's back so that he could take it at once to Banbury where he knew he could sell it. Taking French leave he fetched a horse out of a neighbour's stable, and together they loaded the buck's carcase, first cutting off its head with fine antlers upon it. Said the wife, 'We can pick this,' so she started with the buck's head mounted on her shoulders or head. It so chanced that a youth of the village had resolved to go the same night to try his hand at deer stealing. His mother, trying to deter him, told him if he went, he would surely see the Evil one. He went, gun in hand, and as he walked in the night up towards the forest, he caught sight of the buck's antlers high up on a figure coming towards him, 'Here he is right enough,' he thought, and flinging down his gun he made for home, his fright and terror making him so ill, he could not get up for a fortnight. Mr. White of Ascott told me the above interesting story of old forest border life.

The Game Laws were very severe and led to desperate opposition and many lives were lost. The following anonymous circular letter was received by magistrates and gentlemen of position:—

'TAKE NOTICE.—We have lately heard and seen that there is an act passed, and whatever poacher is caught destroying the game, is to be transported for seven years.—*This is English liberty!*

'NOW, we do swear to each other, that the first of our company that this law is inflicted on, that there shall not one gentleman's seat in our country escape the rage of fire. We are nine in number, and we will burn every gentleman's house of note. The first that impeaches shall be shot. We have sworn not to impeach. You may think it a threat, but they will find it reality. The Game Laws were too severe before. The Lord of all men sent these animals for the peasants as well as for the prince. God will not let his people be oppressed. He will assist us in our undertaking, and we will execute it with caution.'

NIGHT POACHING. DEATH OF A MAN

Seven poachers with the assistance of two dogs, snares and nets, had caught nine hares when they were discovered by a gamekeeper and his helpers who were on the look out for night poachers. At once they were called upon to surrender and give up the nets and game, and as they were outnumbered by armed men, resistance would be useless. A desperate fight ensued in which sticks and bludgeons were freely used, sometimes comrades getting the blow intended for the foe. One of the poachers fell, calling 'murder,' and asking for mercy. Fighting ceased, three poachers bolted, the others were secured, and with the injured man were taken to the keeper's house when he soon died. Several of the men had to lie in bed to recover from their injuries. At the inquest all agreed the confusion was so great that even one of his own mates might have given the fatal blow.

The last man to be transported for deer stealing was one Wilkins of Taynton. He was a very active, tall, and powerful man. His job was to stand on the forest wall, and beat, and bash down the keepers, and so hinder and prevent them getting over, whilst his mates loaded the deer into the cart, and drove off with them, then he jumped down, and ran for his life.

NOTE THIS

April 30th, 1829. 'Judgment of Death was recorded against 66 prisoners at Warwick Assizes, of whom 28 were poachers.'

AT WILCOTE WOODS

Two men went one night to Wilcote Woods, and presently saw the keeper in one of the lights and knew that he saw them. At once they cleared out of the wood and went up the road to the keeper's house, which was then the lodge at the entrance gates, and standing close to the wall, well into and under the ivy, in the shadows, waited. Presently up came the keeper and went in his house. In a little while he came out with his gun under his arm, and as soon as he was gone, away went the two poachers for home.

These men I knew and one of them told my father the above incident.

A document exists, signed, a warrant to the Ranger of Woodstock Parks to kill 'One Brace of Fat Does of this Season' the same to be delivered into his Majesty's larder at Whitehall on Saturday 31 December.

The keepers delivering the Does are to receive 6s. 8d. for each doe from the clerk of the Kitchen, with seal of the Board of Green cloth. *Whitehall, 7 Dec., 1687.*

Sir Stephen Fox. Henry Firebrace. *Clerk of the Kitchen.* John Sparrow.

Another item of earlier date, not poaching. Edward III—

'For repairing the Queen's crown which the King threw into the fire 3s. 6d.' This item has a domestic ring about it.

Is this a tin Pyx?

The Pyx. 'A little rounde box to carry the Sacrament in.'

Henry VI in his will appointed 'to be made forthwith pyxes of silver and gilt … of the value of four pounds … every parish not having a Pyx of silver gilt or ungilded, have of our gift of one of the said pyxes.'

In Oxfordshire inventories mention is made of 'Tynn, latten copper brass' pyxes. Some years ago, an old house being pulled down at Charlbury, the object below was brought to me as found in the chimney. On reading about the Tin Pyx at Cropredy in Mr. Evans's beautiful book, *The Church Plate of Oxfordshire,* I thought at once of my old tin box, and I wonder, is it a Tin Pyx? If not, what is it? No, positively it is *not* a tinder box.

It is four inches across and is bright within, the outside rust-covered.

The railway

Many persons had bitter prejudice against railways in early days. The line from Oxford to Worcester came along the Evenlode valley instead of the Windrush because of the opposition of the great land owners in that direction. Charlbury and district were the gainers whilst Witney and Burford were left to take their chance over the hill.

The Prince Consort rode up and down from London to Windsor many times before Queen Victoria ventured into a train. At first he was very uneasy and would if speed got up say, 'Not quite so fast Mr. Conductor, please!'

Lots of people protested against Queen Victoria travelling by rail at all. Charlbury Station would have been along nearer the Grammar School, and so saved the hard pull up Dyer's Hill, but for opposition to it from the owner of Lee Place.

Some railways would not take third class passengers at all. Other companies fixed seats in open cattle trucks and charged three halfpence per mile. You were shunted about for hours in these bufferless trucks and at your destination saw a notice, 'The Company's servants are strictly ordered not to porter for waggon passengers.'

Newspaper cutting, 1929:—

'A woman travelling from Banbury pulled the communication cord and brought the train to a standstill, and when the guard enquired why she had done this, to his astonishment heard that she had given a boy a sixpence on the platform at Banbury to get her an apple, and had not had her change.'

The rooks

'In the year 1623 Bunyan of Elstow, climbing after rooks' nests in Burywood, found three rooks in a nest all white as milk, and not a black feather on them,' so records Thomas Archer, a naturalist of that day, never dreaming that the son of the tinker who found the white rooks would become a world-famous man.

When as a child I went to Wilcote with my mother to see Mrs. Hazel at Pickering's Farm, the first time, I held her hand very tightly I believe when passing under the lofty elm trees there, for the noisy cawing, wing flapping, and general hub-bub going on in the rookery overhead was, I well remember, very alarming.

Afterwards my father, who was my great authority, consultant and adviser on all matters relating to birds and beasts, told me what he knew about them. Rooks I found had things about them all their own—nesting in some trees and places and not in others. The avenue at Wilcote House for many years they would not use, even though someone had climbed the trees and placed some old nests as though to set them a pattern and entice them to a desirable building site. Then came shooting the young ones after the March hatch, and they appeared in the tree tops about the nests. How cruel it seemed to my young mind! Yes, but I heard 'they say they will not stop unless some are shot year by year.' Very curious, I thought. The vast flocks that seem to fill all the sky at some seasons as they fly to their favoured nesting places, 'going home from school' we used to say as they passed over Finstock, and wondered where ever did they go and spend the night, and so many of them. Very many roost in the season not far from where I write, at Walcote, in our parish, it appears.

Rooks in such numbers must need an enormous amount of food; wherever they find it would seem sometimes a mystery, and when they take to a field of corn, or a rick, they can very soon do great damage.

The 'baptism of fire' they pass through at the shooting in the spring makes them exceeding chary as to the sight of a gun, and the sentinels give the alarm to the rest and away they fly out of gun shot, being very sagacious and able to profit by experience.

Some think them a delicacy. The neck, if not more of the bones, and the skin, to be taken away and not cooked; baked in a pie, with steak, hard boiled eggs with parsley, under a crust, or, as I have very pleasant recollections as a lad, at my uncle's who was a sportsman, boiled in a pudding; the sight of it, and the eating, are a pleasant and happy memory.

Rev. R. S. Hawker was very anxious to get rooks to inhabit a grove near his house, 'to obtain them he went into his church and, kneeling before the altar, besought God to give him a rookery where he wanted.' Rev. S. Baring Gould records this and that rooks took up their abode in the tree tops and the colony was there at the time of writing.

Sheep roast at Charlbury

'THIS IS TO GIVE NOTICE
That there will be a very large Market held at Charlbury on Friday the 2nd July, 1752, for all sorts of cattle and Merchandise, where will be a very large sheep (above 7 foot and a half long and weighing upwards of forty stone), roasted whole in the Market Place, with a variety Diversions and Pastime; Stalls to be had very reasonable, and Toll free for all Sorts of Cattle; and to be continued yearly, on the last Friday in July for the future.'

Jackson's Oxford Journal has the above advertisement, and so we are reminded of the custom our fathers had of roasting an animal whole in the street at any big celebration or event.

Mr. George Harris tells me the roasting place used to be in the widest part of Church Street and those who wished to take a part in the feast, or roast, 'you went with a knife and fork in your pocket, and taking a plate from one of the piles which stood on the tables of the various public houses, for which you paid a penny, carried it to the roast, and bought your portion, six pennyworth or a shilling, what you wanted, then back to the public house, where bread could be bought, and enjoyed yourself.'

William Thornett remembers the last ox roast, which took place near to what was the old Crown gateway about 70 years ago.

A sheep was roasted at Finstock in early Victorian days, my father told me, opposite Mr. Alderton's house at the road side.

The scissors grinder

One event in our village life at Finstock was when the Scissors Grinder and Tinker used to visit the 'Bottom,' and grind the glovers' scissors and repair tin ware, etc. To watch him turn his wheel was fine. Thumb on scissors blade, deftly touching it against the swiftly revolving stone, a flame of sparks responding to each whirring touch, then rivetting or screwing together, testing on a scrap of leather, tapping to adjust, then leaving his barrow to deliver his work and draw his pay.

One man who came had a little forge with bellows, up in his barrow, for heating his soldering iron for tinkering jobs, and this I shall never forget. One day all my companions were engaged elsewhere and I was the solitary lad left to watch and admire this clever man. When he had gone to take a job home, I was filled with a desire to see if I could turn the magic wheel, so I took hold of one of the wires and gave a sharp pull, and, O horrors! up tipped the whole machine on to the front part, and out came tumbling coals from the forge, and I know not what else. Though British born, and Finstock too, I fled, and what was said or done when master Tuffry came back I left the angels to witness. How sorry I was, and if I reach the Land of the shining shore, I hope to tell that tinker how unwittingly I did this, and how sorry I felt!

Tables and trenchers

KNIVES AND FORKS

Early tables had loose tops and could be turned over for different uses. Some had circular depressions cut into them for use as plates or trenchers from which food was eaten, one of these old tops was in this locality not many years ago.

An old man told me how his father working as a lad at a farm at Taston was asked to go into the house to eat his 'nunckin' (dinner). The farmer stuck his knife into the cabbage, and picking up a portion on the blade, plumped it down on to the wooden dresser, without any plate, for him to eat it from the board. Trenchers were in use seventy years from us.

I have a round apple-tree-wood specimen that was in use at Stonesfield, and my grandfather, I was told by my mother, would always have his dinner on his trencher.

Many bundles of trenchers can be seen in the Corporation Cupboards at Abingdon, formerly used at the banquets there.

THE KNIFE

The knife has a much longer pedigree than the fork. Flint knives (such as I have) are found in the soil about us, and one of the earliest of aids to the fingers must have been a sharp stone.

When bronze came into use, the dagger — I have a specimen, also a fine bronze sickle — no doubt were used for all cutting purposes, domestic as well as weapons of attack or defence.

What stories could these early knives tell could they speak!

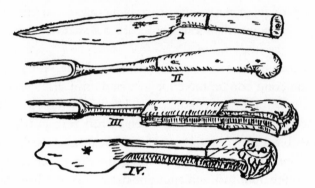

Knives and forks

Early table knives were pointed (see picture). Cardinal Richelieu is responsible for the alteration to round ends. A certain Chancellor dining with the Cardinal used the point of his knife as a tooth pick, and forthwith the mighty Cardinal ordered his Steward to have all the table knives altered to round ends, and this soon became the fashion, as to this day.

A knife is the Emblem of St. Albert, St. Christina, and St. Agatha. Zadkiel in Christian Art bears a knife. At a time when spoons were rare and forks unknown knives were a necessity.

Much skill and ability was put into their making, engraved blades, and elaborate handles. A specimen of mine has an ivory handle, engraved (Fig. iv.)

Carving knives had broad flat blades, for helping the diners by conveying slices to their trenchers; there were no forks.

Sheffield had a name for knives in the 14th century. I have a large clasp knife, when open about 20 inches in length, evidently made by a local smith. This I obtained at Coombe, so most likely it was a hunting knife.

A queer body, the wife of a most excellent man I knew, always stirred her tea with a knife, and never ate any food before her husband.

FORKS

Forks are said to have first mention in 1379, though there is a Saxon example in the British Museum. They were great rarities and not generally used for eating meat till the end of the 16th century.

'The use of silver forks by us, by some of our spruce gallants taken up of late, came from China into Italy and thence into England,' Peter Heylin of Burford fame writes thus in 1652.

Forks were re-introduced to this country in 1601 by a young man, Thomas Coryatt, who was a great traveller. He saw many things, but the greatest discovery he made was the fork. He describes how he observed Italians using a little fork at meals: 'neither doe I think that any other nation of Christendom doth use it.' So pleased was he that he brought one home and used it, finding himself the object of ridicule and abuse. He was satirized on the stage as the fork-carrying traveller. The Pulpit rebuked him, saying it was impious to assume that God's good gifts must not be touched by the fingers. He kept on and won. The fork had come to stay and a great change came to table manners as the result.

Folding forks (I have one, see Fig. iii) were made, and were carried by ladies; many gentlemen at first refused to use a fork at all, and many people even yet use the knife to convey food to the mouth, shovelling it in.

Readers of *Cranford* will remember the difficulty the ladies had with the two-pronged forks and the green peas, at the batchelor's dinner table. Miss Pumphry told me that as a little girl she went by coach, and having dinner at Chipping Norton, green peas and a steel fork to eat them with was a difficulty, till old Mr. Simms the watchmaker said, 'Go and fetch the child a spoon.'

The paper frill about a ham bone was so that the lady carver could grip it with her hand, forks being unknown.

An early silver fork came to light a time ago — just a plain straight flat bar divided at the end into two prongs with hall marks 1632 and silversmith's initials R.C. with engraved crests of Manners and Montagu. It was made no doubt for John Manners, Earl of Rutland, who married Frances Montagu.

'Treasure hid in a field'

'The pot of money' is quite a common expression amongst men engaged in removing ground if the pick should strike a broad flat stone. Many hoards have been found and doubtless there are many yet lie in the earth undiscovered.

In days past it was the safest place to keep valuables, or money or jewels, and if the place was lost or the owner died without revealing his secret the hoard remained till perhaps unexpectedly found.

The glamour and surprise of finding is great. A man I knew was digging a grave in one of our churchyards and he saw a silver coin, and knowing he had some loose silver in his pocket, thought it was one of these slipped out as he worked, till presently, the number he saw in the earth made him realise he had struck a hoard of big silver coins.

Some years ago some rogues worked from abroad a swindle, sending letters to people in this land, telling of buried treasure, and offering a share of the spoils to those who would lend themselves to the discovery, and first send on some pretext an advance of money to the writer in Spain.

No doubt many people were deluded and sent money, as it was carried on for some years and may be yet for aught I know.

The letter which follows I received, and noted that though written in Spain, the envelope bore the *Post mark* 'Moreton in-Marsh,' so the question was, did a confederate here pick the victims and post the letters?

I replied, asking for further particulars, and the second letter came from Spain, together with a military document, all stamped and signed, as though it was all true as the Gospel.

> Copy.
>
> Castle fort of Valence, 29-12-1900.
>
> Mr. John Kibble.
>
> Dear Sir,—The cruel situation which surrounds me, and the sad fate in which lives herself my daughter, 14 years of age, whom I maintain as boarder in a College, are the circumstances which oblige me to direct myself to you, of whom I have the best references of honorability.
>
> Being a Captain treasurer of the 12th of foot soldiers in garrison in the City of Carthagene, to comply with my conscience I joined the rebellion which was to take place in August last, but as we were victims of the greatest treason, I was obliged to emigrate in English ground taking along with me the money which I had to my charges, valued to £15,000, after having resided sometime in this country, I received the sad news my wife had died, leaving my dear daughter in despair and without help.
>
> In this sad situation I found myself in the necessity of coming back to Spain to help my daughter and bring her in my company to England.
>
> Before starting, considering as imprudent to take along with me this sum of money, I decided to hide it in the neighbourhood of Charlbury, taking immediately a plan of the ground with all the marks and measures of the spot.
>
> Then very satisfied that the money was in security, I started for Spain where I was discovered by the police, brought immediately before the military authorities of Carthegene, and condemned to 7 years penal servitude, then the government destined me to undergo my condemn in this Castle.
>
> Thus by return of the Mail let me know if you are willing to lend me your help and protection to recover the money in order that my daughter

and her governess may start for your respected house bringing the plan and all instructions for the discovery.

If you accept my proposal in answer to your next letter I shall tell you the exact conditions to realize plan about which you must keep the most absolute secrecy, at the same time I shall send you a certificate identifying my person and the causes of my captivity.

As I am strictly watched it is dangerous you direct your letters straight to me, for this reason I expect you will put your answer written within two envelopes the one within to my name and the one outside to the name of my servant who has the charge of helping me.

Waiting for your answer, I am your very friend,

ANDRES NIOLA.
Address: Spain,
Mr. Alberto Sorolla, to
Valencia, Spain.

Castle fort of Valence, 29-1-1901.

Mr. John Kibble,

Dear Sir.—I have received your kind letter, and seeing its contents I send you enclosed the certificate which I obtained from the military authority of Carthegene to identify my person and the causes which have been the motives of my imprison ment.

I believe it is a duty of my conscience and my honesty to advice you that your participation and your help in this affair cannot be in anyway prejudicial to you, because according to the international law the authorities of Spain no more than those of your country cannot trouble you for the only fact of lending me your protection.

Then I must tell you that in order to bring this affair to a good end it is necessary you follow exactly my instructions with which and with the plan my daughter will bring to you, there can be no obstacles at the moment of making the discovery.

As you will understand it is necessary that the journey of my daughter is as soon as possible, but as the sad situation in which I am allows me not to make the advance of the money for the journey of my daughter and her governess, because I have been put in jail, and all my properties have been confiscated for these reasons if you accept the conditions I explain below as reward for your sacrifice and trouble which may arise for you from this affair, I secure to you the third part of my entire fortune, money which you will take from the bag which contains it, it is in gold and English bank notes.

1st. That you admit in your house my daughter with her governess.

2nd. That you make the advance of the money for the journey, in order that they start for your respected house.

3rd. That you accept Felisa as your adopted daughter, in the case I should die during the captivity to which I have been condemned in order that with your advice and your protection she may live decently near you. This is to inform you of what can happen on account of my many mental pains.

I will write to my daughter giving her the notice of the contents of your letter. Felisa speaks English.

In her name and in mine receive, my dear Sir, our most sincere salutations.

ANDRES NIOLA.

A request for further information did not get any reply, but about that time the papers reported that police interference was taking place over the business. Mr. Marshall Sturge, with whom I talked over the matter, told me that he knew whoever was conducting the swindle understood several languages from tests that had been made.

Witches and ghosts in life and literature

The witch of Endor in sacred story is a very striking example as told in I. Samuel 28, 7. Well do I remember when I heard at Finstock as a little lad talk about witches, and asked my father what it meant, the day stands out alone in childhood's memories when he found the place and set me to read for myself the story of Samuel, Saul, and the witch.

The word 'witch' and 'wizard' denoted originally someone who 'knows.' Magic and hypnotism no doubt had a part in the practice of wizardry, and superstition and ignorance made it possible.

The Hebrews had stringent laws against its practice, and St. Paul witnessed the burning of the books at Ephesus of those who used 'curious arts.' The wife of Xerxes, who was under the influence of Magic, sacrificed seven children to the god of darkness; and a similar sacrifice was offered to the same god when the Persians were marching into Greece.

A bull was issued against witches by Pope Innocent III.

Some persons burnt at Edinburgh in 1591 confessed to the worship of the evil one.

Sometimes heretics were charged as wizards as an easy way to get them condemned to death and so be rid of them.

I heard a story long ago of a carter, on entering his stable one morning, finding his horses in such a state as he felt sure they had been used for witch steeds during the night. Another story is of a blacksmith who found a long strand or coil of woman's hair on his forge one morning. He set it down to witchcraft and lit his fire and holding the hair in the tongs burnt it.

The story of the Epworth knockings is told in Wesley's life by Southey, and Shakespeare uses the ghost and these uncanny things with effect in his writings, also Sir Walter Scott, and many others.

The story of the Lee's Rest Ghost, as I remember it, was that when challenged by someone with 'In the Name, etc, why troublest thou me?' a hand appeared, pointing to a stone in the wall, and a voice said, 'Take out that stone.' On this being done, a hoard of money was found in the wall.

I know of a cellar in our town where a corner is walled off, and in a barrel of wine within that corner is said to be laid a ghost.

At Chadlington a hare used to be seen that was considered to have been a woman who, as a witch, took that form.

When witches were burnt at Dean Hawk Stone the chain went in the notch at the top, it is said.

The founder of some almshouses in 1679 stipulated that no liars, lunatics, or witches should be admitted.

We smile at these stories and it seems almost unworthy to write about them, but, with all our vaunted enlightenment, are we better than our fathers?

AMULETS, WITCH-BALLS, AND THE EVIL EYE

Amulets or charms to protect the wearer or owner against bad luck generally, or against some particular kind or form of disaster, seem to have been in use from very early days and in every nation under the sun. We hear that in some lands the use and belief is as strong as it was ages ago. Mascots of one kind and another even in our own land which so proudly boasts of its advanced enlightenment,prove that the old superstition is not dead.

Something on the front of the car, or the motor, or airship, or worn on the person, or constantly carried in the pocket, shows this old idea yet persists. There are powers outside us, happenings beyond us, how can we cope with these things and protect ourselves ?

Much of this seems to be connected with the ancient and world-wide belief in the evil eye. A horse shoe nailed on or over the door, a curiously shaped brass on the horse's forehead, a star, a crescent, or other form, a stone, a gem, a medal with a device upon it worn about the neck, or a ring, all may be linked up under the same idea, 'protection against the powers of evil.'

This danger was believed to lie only in the first glance of the Evil Eye, which certain wicked persons were supposed to possess and exercise against their fellows; so if this glance could be diverted from the face to some object worn, then he was safe and could afterwards be looked at without harm resulting.

I have a lump of iron pyrites through which I put a thread, this possibly is an early, very early, amulet, as it could be suspended and worn.

A monkey's foot that a Chinese woman tied on the breast of her weakly boy to make him strong was given me by Dr. Vicars.

THE WITCH BALL

Superstition dies hard and old witch-balls are sought after. They vary in size from three inches upwards and are of different coloured glass. Filled with water, and never dusted, these heavy balls when hanging from the house rafters were better, so it is said, than a horseshoe to ward off evil. As long as any water remained you were safe.

The Psalmist knew of something better than these things, 'The angel of the Lord encampeth round about them that fear Him.'

Is it not time, with all that this age prides itself upon, that we put away childish things? Mascots will not keep evil away or bring luck. This world is not governed on foolish lines. Providence is not chance. Faith in God, like perfect love, casteth out fear. Superstition and fear are not far removed from each other.

'Oh, the road to En-dor is the oldest road
  And the craziest road of all!
Straight it runs to the witch's abode,
  As it did in the days of Saul;
And nothing has changed of the sorrow in store
For such as go down on the road to En-dor!'

When the pig was killed

Killing the pig was a great event in village cottage life in days past, and all the bustle and excitement of a something out of the common was evident about the place. A burden of straw (wheat for preference) had been obtained; a killing stool fetched out of some place where it was carefully kept from one killing to the next, or borrowed from a friendly neighbour; a besom, or a bass broom, together with a 'shuffic' (fork or prong), stood ready at hand. Sundry little boys and girls began to gather, some with chins in a comforter, for the sight of the preparations going on, and the butcher bustling into breakfast (on big rounds of toast with cups of tea) soon made all the children agog with excitement to come out in the cold, early as it was, to see the pig killed. One of the biggest, or two together, might hold the fore leg cord perhaps? Then a nice warm at the fire after the butcher had carefully and lightly covered the pig with straw, holding his face aslant upwards to feel the way of the wind, and lighting the pile accordingly. Then directing skilfully with knowledge and great adroitness portions of the burning straw held on the prong to different parts that might require it, till all was cleanly and evenly burnt, free from bristles. After the brushing, scraping and scrubbing, and the pig is fixed on its back, its legs skywards, the children run for the hoofs as the butcher forces them off with the point of his steel, soon to tire of gnawing them and throwing them away in disgust. With a long slit down the centre, or two cuts if the pig is large, from the neck downwards, a long piece is taken out and all the inside is carefully removed.

Sundry talk goes on with the butcher as to the weight; how many score? It is carried inside and hung up tail downwards to a beam, or stood up against a wall on a pig stick, to get cool and firm by next day when it is cut up into joints, chines, hams and flitches. First the head, then a round chine (the Christening Chine), then the sides separated, the back bone also, if it is to be taken out. Visions of a tasty pie with a glorious crust came up at the mention of it. Next the hams, then the joints, spare rib, griskin and perhaps the short ribs, but not these always.

Many savoury dinners for the home, and others, will be had before all the offal is used up, not like an old man I knew, whose family he found after the pig killing, were up long after he was in bed with the frying pan busy, and on his protesting they said 'There's no end to a fat pig' —but there was. Yet in a small household very many meals can be had before the flitches of bacon are touched.

The chitlings after clearing, washing and soaking, turning inside out back and forth on a 'chidling stick' about 18 inches in length, are well boiled. Some perhaps filled with a mixture of groats, herbs and bits of fat and tied in links, these for 'hog puddens.' These, toasted brown, or carefully fried, make a nice meal. The others are sometimes eaten hot, but most people prefer them to be fried later on, and the dish is fit for princes.

My grandfather was invited to dinner one Sunday in old simple days, and the spread was to be 'boiled chitlings, and green peas' he heard. The liver fried with fat, or pieces of the sweetbread, as the mid rib is called, or cooked in a tin with onions, suits a village boy well. One I knew, I was told, said, 'Mother, I wish our pig was all liver.'

Scratchings or cutlings, left after straining the lard, are nice eating. The pig's leaf in olden days used to be laid on a bench and beaten with a square iron bar till all of a 'pomme' (dialect for squash) before being put into the pot to be melted down for lard, now it is cut into bits or pieces.

In cottage homes others were thought of and the good things of life shared with friends and the feeble, sick and aged. A scrap of meat perhaps, a bit of liver and a taste of fat to fry it with, and some poor body was made glad, who had served her day and generation, and now was getting half a crown and a loaf weekly 'along at the Mans,' as the relieving officer's pay and bread delivery place was called.

I hardly know if I ought to write this, but it gives a picture of the independence of a very poor old woman. I had the great honour, and most responsible job, to carry one of these little packets of fry to an aged woman, when I was a little lad. To my astonishment she went and fetched a big plate with a gaily painted border and putting it into my young hands said, 'Take this plate to thy mother and thank her for the fry.' Grateful for the gift, but out of her poverty must make some kindly return. That plate is not far from my elbow now, and in my time at least, I trust nothing will happen to it.

A big black mark was left after the pig burning at the roadside, so for some time passers-by could see who had killed a pig. This was quite a joke in earlier days, that the Methodist preacher looked out for these and made the house where the black patch was his headquarters for the day. The story is told how a preacher was being invited without success to a place, till the person inviting said, 'We shall be killing the pig and it will be our pig feast.' 'Say no more, brother, I'll be there,' was said to be what he heard.

The Walker Farm pew in Shotteswell Church

Ann Walker provided for Charlbury Grammar School and for Scholarships at Brasenose College, by leaving lands at Cropredy and Shotteswell in the hands of the governors of Brasenose College, Oxford. Amongst the documents preserved in the College archives I saw this quaint old document, which the College authorities kindly allowed me to copy. There is nothing to show who heard this testimony. The farm pew is not in existence now, I believe, about which these good folk could not agree.

Sept. 6, 1684.

'Testimony concerning the Pew in Shotteswell Church belonging to the ffarm now in the tenure or occupacen of ffrancis Petifer and ffrancis West as followeth.

ffirst,

Thomas Bazely doth say that he is between 70 and 80 yeares of age and he doth remember that Mr. Wm. Hall built the said Pew when he lived in the ffarm where ffrancis Petifer and Wm. West doth now dwell.

Hester Miller sayes she is now 80 years of age and doth say that shee do's remember Mr. Wm. Hall paid for building the said pew when he lived in the ffarm where the said ffrancis Petifer and ffrancis West do now dwell and the tenant after him did sitt there w'hout any molestacion.

Rebecca Izards says shee is between 60 and 70 yeares of age. Wm. Hall pd for building the said Pew where now Ric. Crosbee sitteth, and the tenants after him sate there w'hout any molestacion.

Anne Gregory about 60 years of age wife to the new P'isch clerke do's say that shee remembers Mr. Hall did sit in the pew when he lived in the ffarm where the said ff. P. and ff. West do now live after him, Simon Draper and Richard Brasset rented the said ffarm one after another and sate in the said pew w'hout any molestacion.

Manor Farm House, Shotteswell

John ffrancis sayes he is about 80 yeares old and sayes he doth remember Mr. Wm. Hall caused the said pew to be built when he lived in the ffarm … and after Mr. Hall sold the ffarm the tenant sate there till Thomas West turned Quaker.

Mathew Coleman about 50 yeares old sayes he do's remember Simon Draper a tenant sit there and after him Ric. Brasset both tenants of the said ffarm did sit there w'hout any molestacion.

Thomas Barlie says he is about 40 yeares old and says that he did see Ric. Crossbee josstell ffrancis West one Sunday and would not let him sitt in the said pew.

Edward Gregory now P'ish Clerke saith he did see one Sunday Ric. Crossbee josstell ffrancis West and said he should not sit in the said pew.

Thomas Grant now constable of Shotteswell aforesaid saith that he did see Ric. Crossbee and his mother hold the pew doore and told ffrancis West he should not come there.

John Abbotts says he is 59 yeares old and he do's say that Mr. Wm. Hall caused the said pew to be built when he owned the ffarm and sat there himself and after him Simon Draper and after him Ric. Brassett sate in the pew w'hout molestacion.

Samuell West says he is about 60 yeares old and does say that he doth remember that Mr. Walker bought the said ffarm of Mr. Hall and Mr. Walker sat in the pew after he bought the said ffarm.'

Wychwood cottages

'The cottage homes of England!
By thousands on her plains
They are smiling o'er her silvery brooks,
And round the hamlet fanes.'

The cottage homes about Wychwood, stone built, either thatched, or else slated with stone, are not only of picturesque appearance, but many of them are quite all right in which to be born, to live and to die.

The materials, stone and slate, prevail all round our forest, save Stanton Harcourt way, bricks, but mostly timber work, and plaster from early times were used there. Freestone about doors and windows were used on the north and western side of the forest where our stone, famous for centuries, was dug; used in all the noble buildings hereabouts, and even as far as London.

Our masons had for centuries more than a local reputation for ability and skill, Sir Christopher Wren and others employing them at St. Paul's and other notable buildings in the land. The late Mr. Harry Paintin pointed this out in his articles which used to appear (an outstanding feature) in the *Oxford Journal* for so long, and to whom I am indebted for much encouragement.

Stephen Danbury's Cottage at Finstock with sundial on chimney

Christopher Kempster had quarries at Burford, and with the Strongs of Taynton was employed on the most important buildings of the day. There were four generations of Strongs. Valentine Strong is buried at Fairford; his epitaph:—

'Here's one that was an able workman long,
Who divers houses built both fair and strong.'

They were employed amongst them building the Church of St. Benet, Paul's Wharf; St. Stephen's, Walbrook; Cornbury; Kensington, and other places.

Edward Strong's epitaph says.—

'Whose Masterly Abilities and skill in his Profession, The Many Publick Structures He was Employed in Raising will most Justly manifest to late Posterity, In erecting the edifices of St. Paul's, several years of his Life were spent, even from the Foundation to His laying of the last Stone.'

Thomas Strong, a brother of his, of whom Sir John Belcher, R A., said 'Thomas Strong, a great name in all matters of masonry,' was Sir Christopher Wren's right hand man, he was master mason over the building of St. Paul's from start to finish — 22 years. The Clarendon wing at Cornbury was carried out by him under Hugh May, Architect.

Important work, it is pleasant to know, has continued to be in the hands of our local Wychwood men.

Our late King Edward VII (then Prince of Wales), at the opening of Holborn Viaduct, shook hands with the foreman, Mr. Samson Groves, who hailed from Milton-under-Wychwood. Our King George V, at the opening ceremony at the completion of seven years' painstaking labour and care under-pinning Winchester Cathedral, a work of national importance, shook hands with the Clerk of Works, the late Mr. Edwin Long, of Handborough, a mason, who for so many years was one of Sir Thomas Graham Jackson's right hand men.

In early days houses were without chimneys, and after they had begun to be built someone seems to have imposed a tax of a farthing a chimney or hearth and 'smoke farthings' were paid. Stonesfield paid 4½d.

A COTTAGE BUILT FOR TWENTY SHILLINGS

A cottage built by Queen's College, Oxford, in 1306, cost twenty shillings; the carpenter's work cost 5s. 8d.

Our building materials were used extensively over a wide area.

In 1414 Richard Bradwell was paid 17s. for carting wood from Wychwood to Adderbury Church, whilst John Scott had £3. 10s. for 'carting 28 loads of stone from Teynton.' 6d. was allowed for a man to go to select the stone. Robert at the Green of Walcot paid £1. 14s. 6d. for carting 17 loads of timber from the forest at 2s. per load plus 6d. The best masons then had 6d. a day, others 5d.

There were deposits of stone at Heythrop, Sarsden, Milton, Northleigh, Taynton, and Cornbury stone from the forest.

For scaffolding flake hurdles were used. These were made from hazel twigs, woven basket-work fashion, about 6ft. by 3ft., and till quite recent times were the accepted usual scaffold. Holes were formed right through the walls and putlogs inserted to carry the flakes laid upon them both inside and outside the wall being erected. Thomas Hyckes and Wm. Mylyn of Stonesfield supplied these hurdles when Merton College Bell Tower was built in 1447-50. Deal planks, and foreign poles, were not at hand those days, and hurdles were in use for scaffolding in quite recent times.

WATTLE AND DAUB

Flake hurdles were used in cottage building for partitions and ceilings, being fastened in position and then plastered, or the twigs were interlaced instead of using laths and plastered over.

The faulty, poorly built cottages were not the work of our craftsmen in stone and wood but were erected by men of no skilled training.

A bit of land from the waste, stones collected, the prospective occupier with his own hands building in some fashion the walls. Round poles from hedge or coppice were used as timber, just high enough to give head room, so they sprang up, presently to be a ruin, or to be re-built as the years have gone past. Many cottages were stone slated, and this is a splendid roofing material, on good timbers, put on by a slater craftsman, and the roof is a pleasure to look at and to dwell beneath, snug and warm in winter and cool in summer. Great quantities were formerly dug at Stonesfield.

Mr. Henry Ford's son, having seen our stone slates, imported enough to cover his house at Detroit, and a slater from Stow-on the-Wold has been over and used them.

Sixteenth century house at Charlbury

Chipping Norton

The Ceteosarus

It is remarkable that the first notice of this mighty lizard is said to have been that sent from Chipping Norton to the London Geographical Society in 1825, by Mr. John Kingdon, who told of the finding of vertebrae and other bones at Chapel House. These huge bones can be seen at the University Museum at Oxford.

Traces of early man abound in the near neighbourhood, flint objects, standing stones, burial mounds, and at the Bratch quarry just out of the parish early cup graves have been found.

Roman influence was sure to be felt here.

When Diuma, the Saxon Missionary, was winning converts to the Cross in all this district, and then being laid in his grave just over the hill at Charlbury, surely the influence of Him Who said, 'I, if I be lifted up, will draw all men unto Me,' was felt at Norton.

Domesday 1081. Nortone

William granted lands in Chipping Norton to Ernulf de Hesdin, who appears to have been, from the little that can be gathered about him, a baron above the average. He was a skilful farmer, and remembered the poor.

When charged with sharing an attempt in 1095 to dethrone Rufus, as a Norman trial by Ordeal of Battle was his right, and he was victorious against William of Eu. But not knowing how Rufus' hatred might work, even yet, though 'the stars in their courses' had seemed in his favour, he joined the first crusade and left England for the Holy Land, and his fate is unknown.

'They ben lyke to children sittynge in the chepping.' Luke vii, 32. *Wycliff's Bible*.

The Saxon word 'ceping', a market, was not used in early records. Now, 'Chippy' is used alone in common speech without Norton, to denote the ancient market town.

William Fitzallan of Clun is granted by King John a yearly fair. The town did not like fairs, all traders had to close their shops while they lasted. The lord pocketed the tolls, and fees, whilst all the riff-raff gathered from far and wide, and hub-bub was the order of the day.

Three mills yielded 72 pence a year; these paid the lord very well.

The lord of the manor is granted the right to kill game in 1253, so some of our venison no doubt soon was in his larder.

Oxford City Documents record that a culprit from Chipping Norton in 1285, on a charge of parricide (murder of a parent), when near St. Mary's Church escaped, most likely saw his chance and took Sanctuary within the Church, and no one could touch him, Chipping Norton was to be prosecuted.

When a man took sanctuary, gripped the Sanctuary door handle, or knocker (one can be seen on the vestry door in the chancel at Handborough Church), he was safe. He took an oath to quit the realm, and, carrying a cross, to a port he went 'un-gut, un-shod, bare-headed, and in his bare shirt.'

In 1302-5 the town sent two members to Parliament.

An extensive common was given to the town by Lord Arundel in 1377. The enclosure award was July, 1770.

CHIPPING NORTON AND CORNBURY PARK

In 1381 William Pepyr was to put a hedge and ditch about Cornbury Park and a little earlier than this is to sell wood to pay for work. In 1383 Philip Rose and William Riche were to get masons to build a wall about Queen Anne's Park at Cornbury. She brought side-saddles (Burford saddlers soon mastered the mystery of making them no doubt), also she introduced a remarkable cap for ladies. Though times were bad and she brought expensive tastes and ways, yet not only did King Richard think worlds of her, but she is spoken of with the greatest respect. 'Whitney, Bloxham, Combe, Stonfield, Hanberg and Chepyng Norton,' all bought wood, so helping to fence and care for the Queen's beautiful park at Cornbury.

In 1346 Edward III sent a writ to 'Chepyng Norton' demanding 'iii armed men.' These helped to form the army that all men know did wonders at Crecy.

Again in 1350 came another writ, this time only asking for one man, 'of the bravest and best of the inhabitants, to be well and decently furnished, with proper arms.'

THE MONASTERY

Some early masonry in the town is considered to have belonged to a monastery.

THE CROSS AND MARKET PLACE

The base stone of the roadside cross lies at the corner near the Police Station. When this was in position with shaft and steps, the old circular butter market, and then the towering elm tree with rooks, the market place; before desecrating hands had swept these away, must have had a most striking and picturesque appearance.

'An Elm of growth sublime, its age unknown,
Shades and adorns the centre of the town
Vast is its trunk, and large its spreading arms,
High rise its branches, and its foliage charms.

Oft have the traveller and the stranger-guest
Their admiration of the scene exprest;
A circumstance, elsewhere perhaps unknown,
A copious rookery in a market town.'

THE WARS OF THE ROSES

'John de Clapham that fierce Esquire,
A valiant man, and a man of dread
In the ruthless wars of the White and Red;
Who dragged Earl Pembroke from Banbury Church,
And smote off his head on the stones of the porch.'

In those terrible days between 1455 and 1471, when twelve battles were fought in our land, thousands lost their lives on the field, whilst prisoners of note and rank were beheaded, as was the Earl of Pembroke in Banbury Church porch after the battle fought near to Oxfordshire soil at Edgcot, near Banbury. Chipping Norton figured as on the side of Lancaster, and after the battle of Barnet, John, Earl of Oxford, lost it, and Chipping Norton was given by the King to his brother Richard, Duke of Gloucester, John himself being condemned to death. So gory and awful a thing is war.

THE WOOL TRADE

'Commons to close and kepe;
Poor folk for bred to cry and wepe;
Towns pulled down to pastur shepe;
    This ys the new gyse!'
'Ambicious suttletie brought VI farms to one.'

The Black Death carried off the workers, one man could see to many sheep. Wool meant money, and so Chipping Norton had its share of thriving wool men.

A fine brass in the Church:—

'By the grace of God, here lyeth John Yonge, some tyme Wolman of this towne, whiche dyed in the year of our Lord 1451. And Isabel, wyfe & their children. On whose souls God have mercy.'

John Yonge is depicted standing on a wool pack.

In 1530 Sir Thomas Pargiter, a native of Chipping Norton, was Lord Mayor of London.

The borough

The first Bailiffs were William Diston and William Hunt, 1607.

Chipping Norton had its Bellman and Beadle 'to keep nightly watch,' and see that order was kept and regulations carried out regarding the management and good order of the place.

A few items recorded show how this was done.

'1757. Thos. Crutch was presented for milking his cows in the Public Market Place, morning and evening, a great nuisance and very offensive to His Majesty's leige subjects.'

Thomas Robinson presented for forestalling the market by buying three fowls near one hour before the market bell rang.

The Guard of the Mail Coach for wilfully and repeatedly throwing down the Commons wall.

In 1815 the Jury had great concern at persons at the corner of New Street and Church Street on Sabbath days 'lewd and base' and wish the magistrates to consider this matter.

A man was flogged at the cart tail as a thief in 1820.

Barley bread

In 1630, the year the *Mayflower* sailed, a time of great poverty, and discontent prevailed. Barley was the poor man's bread corn, so malting was restrained. The bailiffs of Chipping Norton were practical, sensible men, and complained that one Simon Hathaway had bought corn to make malt, so the justices took it up, and there is no doubt bread won, against beer, thanks to Chipping Norton wide-awake bailiffs.

Ship Money and the Civil War

In 1636 Chipping Norton was assessed at £30. This hated tax John Hampden thrilled the country by refusing to pay. Some paid a part, and so the thing rankled in the life of the nation, till civil war was in the land. Troops were marched, 1642, to Chapel House to intercept the Cavaliers from Oxford, and the county as they came from Banbury rose with them some 300 strong. They only captured a few scouts, so not much came of this.

In 1643 the Lord General passed through Chipping Norton on the way to Stow-on-the-Wold. The King was to have met Lord Artley at Chipping Norton with 1,500 horse from Oxford, but this did not come off. So the town seemed to be spared the direct stir and horror of war above many places. A good kindly providence seemed to be over the ancient market town in those terrible days.

William Diston and Henry Cornish were taken prisoners by the Royalists, and had to pay dearly, and in Cromwell's day, 1655, the Council paid Diston £250 to assist him under his losses.

THE BOROUGH MACE

The Mace was a weapon of iron used in the Middle Ages to smash an opponent's armour and to unhorse him. When ecclesiastics took the field, as in dim days past they did, this was their weapon, considering the sword was forbidden them by our Lord's words to Peter, 'Put up again thy sword into his place, for all that take the sword shall perish with the sword.'

It came to be recognised as a symbol of authority, and was made later of the precious metals. In our forest borders they are rare, so the interesting specimen possessed by Chipping Norton is to be highly prized, and all the boys and girls of the district would do well to know something about it, and go and see it.

If the King visited Chipping Norton the mayor himself would go before him carrying the mace. I think, since Richard II's day, no sergeant of any town is allowed to carry his mace out of his own liberty or township.

The Charter of Incorporation states, James I 1606, 'two officers … called Sergeants at Mace in the borough afore said' … shall carry and bear maces gilded with gold or silver and engraved and ornamented with the sign of arms of us, our heirs and successors.'

These symbols of authority were provided, for the Council ordered, March 11th, 1754, 'That the two maces be repaired and reguilded.'

About 1875 one mace went into private hands, the other was sold and, like the poor boy's eye, 'is clean gone.'

I saw the existing Mace at the Ashmolean Museum at Oxford some time ago with questioning in my mind as to its being there, and on the Museum authorities being approached by Chipping Norton, it was willingly returned to its proper home.

The shaft is of James I period, the head of Commonwealth pattern, the acorn badge substituted for the original head. The whole surmounted by a crown-like canopy, with orb and the remains of a cross. It is well worth seeing. It is of silver gilt, 31 inches in length, and has had a veritable 'vicar of Bray' existence. Altered at the Commonwealth period, in 1660 was altered again; and a Puritan legend upon it erased.

Crowns were added to Maces in 1660. Upon the flat surface of the head beneath the arches the arms are engraved and initials C.R.

It may have been in use as a cup, with a cover, as possibly it has been, rather big and clumsy screws fasten it together now. It is richly ornamented, but no trace as to who made it could I discover, but marks or name may have been lost during its many alterations and adventures since April 20, 1653, when Oliver Cromwell stamped his foot at the sight of the mace in the House of Commons and said, 'Take away that bauble.' (Even Chipping Norton mace presently felt the effects of what that stamp and those words represented).

About 250 years ago a writer says, 'A large but straggling town, yet compact about the market place. It is a town corporate governed by two bailiffs and other officers.' These have been superseded by a Mayor and Town Council.

Joseph Higgins, a character, who died Oct. 2, 1832, wrote re-electing the Bailiffs:—

'Empowered as justices of peace to act,
Search out and punish every guilty fact;
And by their Town Clerk, learned in the law,
Protect the good, and keep the bad in awe.'

THE CASTLE

'There is
No Chronicle of all its martial state
To testify what once it was.'

At what period was first erected a castle here there seems at present to be no certain clue, and, as there is no mention of it in Domesday, the popular tradition that in Stephen's day the castle was built, may be correct.

The situation it occupied is plainly indicated by earthworks, 'The Mount,' to the north of the church. An idea of its strength and extent can be easily conceived. Here probably a majestic keep once stood in massive strength, battlements, gateway, etc. (see the 'Borough Arms'). An old entry 1566 says, 'Sometime a Castell standing, but now an old barn only.'

Tradition says it was the quarry, near at hand, that provided stones used to build the church, which is more than likely.

THE CHURCH

'How rose thy Tower serene and bright
To greet the dawning day?'

The Church of St. Mary takes an honoured place amongst the stately and beautiful churches in our Wychwood district. It stands on the site of an earlier building existing in the 13th century.

Its position, low down the hill, is against its appearance, but a near view and close examination are worth while. Mixed styles of architecture are to be seen. Chancel, nave, north and south aisles, embattled tower, sanctus bell, sexangular (6 sided) porch, beautiful entrance doorway, all have a message for those who can take it. The interior, though scraped, restored, and tessellated, gives evidence chiefly of the energy and genius of the builders of the Perpendicular period, the impression of the nave so lofty and so light is not easily forgotten. The tower, rebuilt 1825, replaced that mentioned in 1549, when 'Henry Joyce the Vicar of Chipping Norton to be hanged upon the steple there, a traitorous person.' It is not known if this horrible sentence was carried out. Let us hope it was not. There is no west window to the nave, but a blank wall. The massive old Altar slab stands edge-wise against the wall in the S.W. corner, centre of conflicting ideas, we think of the words:

'Christ was the word that spake it,
He took the bread and brake it,
And what that word did make it,
That I believe and take it.'

Memorial, or sacrifice, which?

Many wall tablets have been put round a corner, many sky'd. Use a glass to read the upper ones.

The names of those who fell in the Great War are remembered on a Tablet in the south aisle.

When the floor was torn up the brasses were stored in the parvise, over the porch, those not lost are on slabs, against the north wall, note these.

The stones with arms and inscriptions from the floor are, I believe, those laid at the west end outside. A pity.

Stone coffin in north part of Churchyard. Ought to be within the Church.

One memorial near by, recording the loss of a wife, ends with 'Glory be to God.'

Another records: 'Wm. Eaton, gent. A learned and an honest lawyer, 1721.'

On a Headstone near the path:

'Here lieth the body of Phillis wife of John Humphrys, Rat Catcher Who has Lodged in many a Town and travelled far, and near by age and death Shee is struck down To her last lodging here.

Who died June 11th, 1763. Aged 58.'

Eynsham Abbey records show, that about 1406, there was a proposal to exchange the Church at Tilbury for the Church at Chipping Norton, but the 'swop' did not take place.

The Rev. P. H. Ditchfield records:—

'Until the year 1856 the churchyard of Chipping Norton was let to a butcher for grazing sheep probably by the vicar, and for this reason was assessed to the poor rate in the revaluation of the borough. An old lady told an aged correspondent 'that she never purchased meat from old — the butcher as she thought that sheep grazing in the churchyard gave the mutton such a deathly taste.'

The Friends

A large Meeting House with burial ground in New Street was re-built in 1804. Such extensive premises mean that in those days numbers must have gathered to worship there.

Once when the late Mr. John Albright was on his way there from Charlbury a lightning flash struck off a branch from a tree under which he was passing, but neither he nor his horse met any harm.

William Jones records in his Journal, 1787, 'Went to C. Norton on Albright's horse and brought Hannah Albright home behind me.'

Thomas Wagstaff, a noted horologist and Quaker, ended his days at Chipping Norton. Born at Banbury, he was in business at 33 Gracechurch Street, London, for many years. He made a bracket clock playing four tunes at the hour. In the Hilton Price collection is a repeating watch in silver pierced cases, the thumb piece or opener of the outer case being a diamond. A number of long cased clocks by him are in America. He was a noted Quaker, and when Friends from America visited London they were used to lodge at Wagstaff's house, and on their return often took one of his famous clocks with them.

He was married at Milton-under-Wychwood meeting. He was an author and wrote parts 8th and 9th of 'Piety Promoted.'

Died at Chipping Norton in 1802.

A clock story

An old rhyme runs something as follows:—
    'There was a man named Andrew Mears
    Who daily wound his clock for forty years,
    But when an eight day clock it proved to be
    Andrew Mears was very wild as any one could see.'

The Baptist Church

The act of uniformity of 1662, which the Bishop of Hereford said 'was one of the greatest misfortunes that had befallen the Church of England,' was felt in this neighbourhood. Men who felt they could not assent to its demands had to turn out of the livings they held and in some cases suffer bitter persecution.

Two ministers were ejected at Chipping Norton at the same time, Mr. Clark, and Stephen Ford, and I am able to give a few particulars of interest about the latter.

He appears to have been a remarkable man, and was educated at Oxford. On his appointment at Chipping Norton he said, 'At the time I became your minister I had three places offered me, one worth near twenty times as much as this poor Vicarage. But I found my heart inclined more towards you than any of the said places, and through grace I refused them all for your sakes.'

His labours were crowned with eminent success. He says 'the saints in this place are many.' After ejection he continued to preach but was sadly harassed, and later his life was threatened, so he retired to London, where he held classes for young men, and later on when liberty was granted, a Meeting House was built in Miles Lane, near Cannon Street, of which he became minister.

He printed a discourse on regeneration. The Baptist Church at Chipping Norton was formed as the result of his labours, and the present fine building is on the site of the earlier building in which he ministered.

Some years ago a man named Mason with his good wife who lived at Ramsden Heath, I have heard, were members, and used to walk to Chipping Norton and back to worship on Ordinance Sunday.

Under the Conventicle Act, in 1664, Jas. Wilmot of Hook Norton, the Baptist Minister, was fined £20 and put in prison. Sir Thomas Pennystone who committed him said, 'He shall rot in gaol.' All his goods were seized and brought to Chipping Norton where they were offered for sale, but no one would buy them, so they were carted away to be bought later by one of his friends, and restored to him.

The Puritans of the Commonwealth were not such 'kill joys' as some people make out. Charles Lamb tells us that apprentices and other young people were given every alternate Thursday as an entire holiday for sport and games.

TELL ME A STORY?

A clergyman tells the story of a very young curate who was christening his first baby in the parish church, and was so nervous that he let the tiny bundle slip through his hands into the font, thereby giving it 'total immersion.'

It is said if several babies are to be christened together, it is best to leave the girls till last, else they will develop beards when they grow up.

METHODISM

'You know what Wesley did, how a whole movement of spiritual life began which moved England.' — Dr. Gore.

I cannot find that Wesley preached at Chipping Norton, but the general movement, stir, and awakening reached it, and a 'cause' was established, a chapel being built in 1792 in Diston's Lane, which later, after the new Chapel in the main street was built, became the Primitive Methodist Chapel. It may be news to some, that it has been said that since Wesley's death, Chapels at the rate of two a day have been built around the world somewhere. Chipping Norton was in Witney Circuit, till, in 1813, it was made a separate Circuit. James Sydserff and Thomas Hayes were the first ministers.

There is a record of Thomas Atkins, an early member, that he was a regular and attentive hearer for more than 50 years, and a member over 40. He appears to have been a most Godly man. He attained the age of 92 years.

Many villages had a 'cause,' together with Stow-on-the-Wold. Wesley's Journal records:— 'Friday, Aug. 28, 1767. I preached at Stow-in-the-Wold, about ten, to a very dull quiet congregation, and in the evening to almost such another at Gloucester.'

A faithful old soul, 'Old Nelly' she is called, who walked many a mile to hear the Methodist preaching, figures in days past in the district.

THE ROMAN CATHOLICS

The Catholic Church at Rock Hill with graveyard, is evidence of the faith as held by that communion being amongst us. The altar from the Church formerly in Heythrop Park is preserved here. Some time ago I saw graves and memorials at the site of the dismantled Church at Heythrop Park inside a plantation of trees there.

THE SALVATION ARMY

The Army have opened again their Hall after being closed for some time.

When General William Booth was walking along Chipping Norton street, with the Mayor and the rest, when on one of his tours, I saw him do a gracious thing I thought by standing still, letting the procession pass on, so that a boy with a camera could get a photograph of him.

EDUCATION

From early times Christianity has had a share in education in this land. This is evident at Chipping Norton from the certificate of Edward VI.

'The Trynyte Guild. Certeyn landes and tenements gyven by Dyvers and soundre persons unknown to the said Guilde to Fynde a morrow prest, a Scole Master.' 'Sir William Bryan of 60 yeres, yerely £6.'

The Grammar School was from this origin. The old building was pulled down in 1852. An advertisement of 1799 says, 'Founded by King Edward the Sixth.'

'J. Handley, with sentiments of Gratitude and Respect acquaints his Friends and the Public that his Boarding School will be opened again on Monday the 21st instant.'

There were several private schools.

Charles Stewart Parnell, the Irish political leader, was at school at Chipping Norton.

Mrs. Bulley's school, started in 1785, continued for many years. Her prospectus states, 'C.N. is pleasantly and healthfully situated on the Turnpike Road from London to Worcester, and Coaches to and from both Places pass through it every day.'

Mrs. Russell's terms at her Seminary were: 'Board, English Grammar, History, Geography with the use of the Globes, and plain and fancy needlework £18 18s. 0d. French £3 3s. Drawing £3 3s. Writing and Arithmetic, £2 2s. Washing £2 10s. Tea £1.'

The charge for tea is noticeable, did Adam's Ale take its place to those that did not pay the £1?

The National and British Schools have had a part in dealing with the young life of the town, and mention must be made of a late master, Mr. John Roles, appointed 1866, who is remembered with esteem and gratitude by many far and near. He founded the Band of Hope, which has helped to set many feet in safe paths.

CHIPPING NORTON COUNTY SCHOOL
SECONDARY SCHOOL FOR BOYS AND GIRLS
Headmaster: B. C. ORME, M.A.

The newly erected County Schools, an imposing building, are a centre to which the young life of promise in our district is taken, attired in green and gold, by motor bus. Surely any glint of genius in a boy or girl will have a chance to shine in these days.

THE NATIONAL CHILDREN'S HOME

Mention must be made of the great work done for cripple children at the Chipping Norton branch, surely our Lord who said, 'Suffer little children to come unto me' favours this work done in His name. All honour to those who give their lives to this as did Sister Lydia Woolcock, who now 'rests from her labours' in that bright home beyond the river.

CAUGHT BY THE PRESS GANG

There came into my possession from Diston's Lane, Chipping Norton, a Journal, kept by William Collins, who had been caught by the press gang, and had to serve on board H.M. Ship *Sceptre*, from July 17th 1806 to June 1808. His notes give a picture of life before the mast, as to the French ships they captured, the short allowance of bread, rice, flour, etc., served out, pretty often it appears; working at the pumps, when they sprung a leak, and, at last, putting a sail underneath the ship, after heaving overboard ten of the lower deck guns:— 'it pleased the Lord to stop the leak at half past 4 o'clock in the afternoon. The same evening splicing the main beam with a gill of brandy.'

The captain of a French tug they took, ransomed his ship for 4000 Spanish Dollars. The ship *Princess Charlotte*, captured two days later, was ransomed for 1000 Dollars He writes in a most casual way of what they did, as though taking French ships was as easy as taking one's dinner.

Captain Joseph Bingham seems to have understood his business, and one wonders what he did, or what became of him after his pressed man, William Collins, made his last entry in the little book he kept:— 'Came to an anchor in the Downs, June 20th, 1808.'

THE OFFICIAL TOBACCO DESTROYER AT CHIPPING NORTON, 1668

King James I issued his 'Counterblaste' forbidding the cultivation of tobacco in this country, and the odious Court of the Star Chamber imposed a tax of 6s. 10d. per 1lb. Charles II in 1660 passed an act stating:—

'It is found by experience that the Tobaccos planted in these parts are not so good and wholesome for the Takers thereof, and that by the planting thereof Your Majesty is deprived of a considerable part of your Revenue arising by Customs upon imported Tobacco…' The latter no doubt being the real reason of the prohibition. All crops were destroyed, trampled down by horse troops, or in other ways.

Mr. John Cuttleford, the official sent to this district, charges in his expenses as follows, 1668, August.

> 'Wed. 5:— To Chipping Norton wheare Sir Compton Reade and Will Walder summoned in the Constables of Chadlington hundred to be at Chipping Norton the Munday following.
>
> Tues. 6:— Went to Enson (Enstone) to Ascott to Minsterlovell soe back to Chippinge Norton.
>
> Friday 7:— To Whitford to Bourm to Dickley, to Wilcot, to Chipping Norton fell sick, of an Ague at Chippinghorten 9s.
>
> Monday 10:— The Justices met and the hundred of Chadlington brought in their retourne but there was noe Tobacco but a small quantatie at Chadlington and a few plants in Chippinghornten as the retourns will shew which I delivered to Mr Morgan but I was soe sicke the Munday that I could not take the retourns but gott one of the Gent. of the Guard that was with me to doe it for me. I was at Chipping Norton 6 dayes and nights 4 men and 2 horses ,£5 2s. 3d.'

The cost of physic for 21 days was £1 15s., the doctor's fee £3, accommodation at the inn 18s. 6d. Evidently that innkeeper did not overcharge.

COLD, OR 'FRIGIDE' NORTON

Away on the hill was the Priory of the order of St. Augustine, founded in the reign of Henry II. A deed speaks of 'Frigide Nortune' 1269. 'Henrico Medico' attested another deed about that date.

The Prior granted some of the property for a quaint rent 'a clove of gilly flower yearly,' not much benefit to his monastery, such a rent as that.

In the reign of Edward III a petition was sent to the Bishop of Lincoln stating: the priory being in a barren place, adjoining two of the king's highways, intolerable crowds of wayfarers called for hospitality, storms destroyed the buildings, there were no funds to repair them, and no labourers to till the land owing to war and pestilence, the Canons would have themselves to take to the road unless help could be given. In 1377 he presented the Priory with the Rectory of Steeple Aston to help the funds.

The martyrdom of St. Paul.
Embroidered picture from early cope, formerly at Steeple Aston Church.

There is a suggestion that the Steeple Aston cope, famed for its great beauty, originally belonged to Cold Norton priory. It appears to have no history, but is a most beautiful example of embroidery of the middle ages. It is now at South Kensington Museum.

A deed of 13th century exists relating to a grant of land in 'Stockwellestreete' at Chipping Norton by Richard Winn to the Priory.

John Wootten, the prior, died about 1496 and presently the Priory became part of the endowment of Brasenose College, Oxford.

CHIPPING NORTON SILVER CRUCIFIX

In Samuel Lewis' *Topographical Dictionary of England*, 5th Edition (1844), it is recorded that 'on the road to Birmingham, half a mile distant (from Chipping Norton), was an ancient chapel, the site of which is now occupied by a posting-house and hotel called Chapel House. On digging for the purpose of enlarging this building, stone coffins were found containing human bones, among which were beads and a silver crucifix; and three urns were also discovered in a vault, with some fragments of masonry and painted glass.'

What became of these things?

Dr. Johnson stayed at the Chapel House posting house, 'Shakespeare's Head,' in his day, as did our late Queen Victoria as a girl with her mother.

THE CHIPPING NORTON HIGHWAYMAN

Capt. Hinde the highwayman, found himself hard up, near Wantage, and seeing an elderly man on a donkey, accosted him, and finding he was poor with a family of ten children, Hinde, telling him who he was, persuaded him to hand over the small sum of money wherewith he was just going to Wantage market to buy a cow, assuring him that he would meet him at a given time and day and repay him double. This was faithfully done, with twenty shillings extra so he might have the best in the market.

Hinde was hanged for his crimes at Worcester, his head parboiled and put on a pole on the bridge there.

The concluding verse of a poem written at the time:—

'Tis the same vi'lance, says Anselm,

To rob a house, or waste a realm.

Be henceforth then, for ever join'd

The names of Caesar and of Hinde,

In fortune different, one in mind.'

THE CHARITIES

The Charities, showing much kindly thought for the poor, are very numerous, and of variety, from that row of eight almshouses by Henry Cornish in 1649, right through a list, flour, sermons, bread, groats, coats, gowns, shoes, cash, premiums, and help in many ways to be given to needy people, and Henry Cornish, worthy man, left £2 to be spent on a dinner for the Bailiffs and Burgesses. So his memory should be kept green for certain.

Advertisement in *Oxford Journal*, Feb., 1773.

'To be sold by auction on Wed. 24 Feb., 1773, in the White Hart Inn in Chipping Norton — all the Right Title and Interest of a Charter for holding two Fairs in the said Town yearly one on the last Friday in May and one on the last Friday in November for ever. The Tolls of the said Fairs amount to about £13 yearly.'

This did not mature.

RACE MEETING AT CHIPPING NORTON

Lord Clarendon's Diary at Cornbury, March 28, 1689. 'Mr. Mayott (of Fawler) came to me from the race at Chipping Norton.'

A GOOD INN AND DINNER

Mrs. Delany, friend of Swift, writing Oct. 30, 1746. 'to Chipping Norton … there we had a good inn and dinner.'

Chipping Norton tweed

This world renowned material, the invention of the late Mr. Bliss, had its beginnings through a small weaving factory being established in 1758. A fire destroyed the lower mill in 1873; the present factory is considered to be one of the best appointed establishments in the kingdom.

The hail storm of 1843

On Wednesday, August 9th, 1843, a terrific hailstorm, accompanied by lightning and thunder, passed over the north and northwest parts of Oxfordshire, by which a considerable district from Churchill to Souldern was more or less injured — the losses were some £35,000 chiefly in glass and growing corn.

Chipping Norton suffered much from the effects of this terrible storm, damage to windows and roofs exceeded £1000. Slates were broken and pounded to pieces, lead looked as though marked with the small pox. Flowers and vegetables were cut to pieces. At Great Tew corn crops were not only thrashed out as they grew but the stalks were beaten down and driven into the soil by the force of the hailstones. The smaller animals and birds were killed in large numbers — hares, crows, pheasants, and partridges.

The average size of the hailstones measured by the Rev. J. Jordan at Enstone, was six inches in circumference.

A subscription, headed by £100 from Queen Victoria and £50 from the Prince Consort, was organised by Rev. John Jordan, which realized the sum of about £4,400 for the relief of sufferers through this terrible visitation.

Those who witnessed it always spoke of it with awe and bated breath, and here at Charlbury neighbours went into a Godly woman's house and she read and prayed to comfort these terrified women. The thunder started about three o'clock one day and seemed to roll without stopping overhead till three o'clock the next.

A riot

'RIOT. Great excitement prevailed in this town on Wed. last owing to the committal to gaol of 16 women from Ascott for intimidation ... a large crowd, composed to a considerable extent of the Labourers' Union wearing their distinctive badge, a blue riband, congregated about the Police Station.

It was evident that they expected that the prisoners would be sent off to Oxford by rail, and it was equally manifest that it was their intention to effect a rescue.

As evening came on their numbers were increased by frequent arrivals from the neighbouring villages, and they were received with cheers and

shouts of 'Stick to the Union,' 'Fetch out the women,' etc. As night still further set in an attack was made on the Station, stones being thrown and most of the windows in Supt. Lakin's house were smashed and a few in the Station, also the street lamps.

A telegram in the meantime was sent to Oxford for a van to take the prisoners direct from the Station, and for further assistance.

The Mayor urged the well disposed to go, and announced that unless the crowd dispersed he should be obliged to read the Riot Act. Ultimately most of them went away, and by one o'clock the road was nearly or quite clear. About two a brake arrived from Oxford with a reinforcement of Police, and the prisoners being placed therein, started under a strong guard for gaol, a number of additional men being left should their services be required. All is quiet at the time of writing (Thursday morning) and it is expected that the ringleaders who are known will soon be in custody. In justice to the Union men it is but fair to say that the ringleaders in this affair did not wear their distinctive badge, but consisted of roughs who took advantage of the opportunity of gratifying their malice.'

— *Jackson's Oxford Journal*, May, 1873.

'Ascott-under-Wychwood. On Friday, the 20th, the sixteen women who were recently sent to gaol for intimidation were presented with £5 each the result of a subscription got up for them.

Mr. Arch and Rev. M. Attenborough arrived from Leamington in the afternoon, and were received at the station by the sixteen women and a crowd of people who cheered them on alighting from the train.

After having tea at the Swan, an open air meeting was held ... Mr. Attenborough and Mr. Arch addressed the meeting at some length, and the money was given to the women by the former amid loud cheers.'

— *Jackson's Oxford Journal*, June 28, 1873.

The explanation is the sixteen women had met two men from another village who were on their way to work at Ascott on a farm when the men of the village were on strike, standing round the field gate and telling them to go back. They were summoned for obstruction, etc., and committed by two clergymen to gaol, some for ten days, others for seven, with hard labour, hence the riot, and a thrill was felt far beyond our district.

It was in transition days and things at such times get done in haste and precipitately, that sober thought and reflection consider unwise, so we must be gentle in our judgments, and as we 'cast a stone.'

It turned out to be a splendid advertisement as to the condition of farm workers and the Union.

SEVENTEENTH-CENTURY TRADERS' TOKENS

Mr. Evetts, of Tackley, in a recent issue of the *Oxford Times*, stated that he has some Oxford tokens, and readers may be interested in some facts about what has been called this 'illegal money of necessity' so largely and widely used in the seventeenth century.

In quite early times (1378, it is said) the King was asked for permission to issue local coins of small value to pay for, say, bread and ale; when the best ale was only 1^1/$_2$d. a gallon some coin which would pay for a smaller quantity than that was necessary for most ordinary drinkers. Tokens, as they were called, thus came into use. They were made of metal, and even leather, cut and stamped with letters or some special device.

Those minted in the seventeenth century are pretty much in a class by themselves, and Oxfordshire is represented by many specimens, some of special note and interest. The denominations are pennies, halfpennies and farthings generally of copper, some of brass, and at one place in our county of more precious metal. The shape was generally round, but square, diamond, heart and octagonal shapes are to be found. Sometimes the inscription contains a punning allusion to the issuer's name or business, and his wife's initials sometimes figure upon them. Thomas Appleby, of Oxford, had the words 'Mallia Cadreen' upon his token, leaving a mystery which seems never to have been solved. What does it mean?

According to Williamson's edition of Boyne's *Tokens*, there were issued in the county 254 varieties, the number of places issuing being 31. Town pieces were issued at Burford, Henley-on-Thames and Oxford. Northleigh gives us one issued by William and Ann Mason, trade partners as well as man and wife. Finstock has a token but, strange to say, the descendants of E. Gardner, the issuer, do not know what was the business of their ancestor.

The City of Oxford and its traders issued 188, and if Mr. Evetts' specimen, 'Sarah Wood, Thames Street,' is from Oxford, that is another to add to the list. Four of the Oxford issuers were women — Ann Turton, Ann Pierson, Alice Lant and Olive Hind. In Oxford tokens were issued at the 'Pestle and Mortar,' the 'Cock,' the 'Gilt Looking Glass,' the 'Bush,' the 'Sugar Loaf,' the 'Racket and Ball,' the 'Three Kings,' the 'Three Salmons,' the 'Fox and Goose,' the 'Mermaid,' the 'Three Blackbirds,' the 'Golden Key,' the 'Crown,' the 'Salmon,' the 'Angel,' the 'Bird in Hand' and the 'Spectacles,' all these signs being named.

The following trades are represented: apothecary, chandler, cutler, clothier, clockmaker, draper and clothier, rug-maker, vintner, watch-maker, milliner, mercer and silk-weaver. Reference is made on the tokens to North Gate, Turle Gate and East Gate.

A token of Chipping Norton and one of Henley-on-Thames bear the arms of Oxford, but the reason is not known. A carrier of Duns Tew, Thomas Barrett, had his basket panniers depicted on his tokens. It was very rare for a carrier to issue a token. The unique position in the whole series of seventeenth-century tokens is occupied by one issued by Richard Hearne, of Thame, in 1669, for it was struck in gold, weighing 23 grains. An interesting collection of Oxfordshire tokens can be seen at the Ashmolean Museum.

There are sixteen 17th century tokens recorded as issued at Chipping Norton by the following; John Cornish, Michail Cornish, Joseph Davis, William Diston, David Dix, Samuel Farmer, Henry Fawler, Mathias Prout, Richard Groves, Edmond Rowbright, Philip Wisdome, and one has initials only without name.

The Town Clerk, F. W. Morris, Esq., has several of the series, and would like to complete the set with a view to presenting them to the Council if any reader can assist who may have one or more.

A token is before me:

'ROBERT BROOKES OF CHALBVRY, 1665.'

Though there is no recorded token as issued here, yet as Robert Brookes signed the petition to Brasenose College concerning our Grammar School, and though the letter R is not in Charlbury (spelling was free in those happy days) it looks as if this is a Charlbury specimen. The Brookes family residence is now the home of Dr. Scott, 'The Willows,' Charlbury.

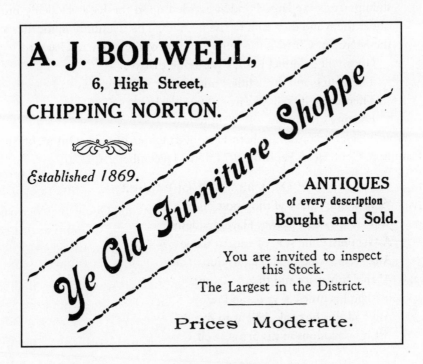

Churchill

Domesday CERCELLE.

Earl Harold had held it.

The Vicarage ordained, it is said, in 1340.

The old Church (with some of the village) appears to have been moved from below, to the hill top in 1828, when a new church with an imposing tower, a replica reduced of Magdalen College Tower, Oxford, was built. The chancel of the old church was left standing, and the church yard enlarged as a cemetery, the splendid cedar tree standing there used to be in the Vicarage garden, whilst over the wall the depression in the field was the fishpond. The base stone of the font can be seen in the turf. The old entrance gateway is charming.

The five bells cast in 1630 still ring in the present tower.

ON A HEADSTONE AT CHURCHILL

'Sacred to the memory of James Joiner and Charles Pugh, the one aged 16 and the other 15 years. On the 26th December, 1822, as they were sliding across the large Pond at Sarsden upon the Ice it suddenly broke under them and they sank to rise no more. Their youthful innocence and the Mercy of Christ is the only Comfort of their afflicted Parents.

　　Gods will be done! but if t'was done that ye,
　　The young and thoughtless might your warning see,
　　Then mark it well; you live in fragile clay,
　　Eternity's beneath:— Repent to-day.'

A wall tablet records: Elizabeth Diston, daughter of Giles Diston, of Short Hampton, Gent. Born Feb. 6th, 1674. Died December 1st, 1720.

ON A BRASS AT CHURCHILL

'Stay gentle reader yf thou dost enquire
Who Mr. Gostwick was Have thy desire.
A Gentleman he was, of antient name
And welbeloved of all that to him came.
At th. University and then at Court
He had his times of study and resort.
After all this he took delight to dwell,
Att his devotions in his private cell.

Happy old man w'ch so his youth could spend
That he was happy at his latter end.
Obt Anno Dm'i 1618. Feb. X.
Aetat 75.
Sir John Walter and other lords of Sarsden were buried at Churchill.

THE SCHOOL

Provision for a school at Churchill was made in 1705 by Anne Walker's legacy of £600. A school was provided, with a mistress, girls were taught the three R's, gowns and bonnets were provided for them, and Bibles and Prayer-books on leaving school.

1819

'J. Laskey's School for Boarders. At Churchill, on Dr. Bell's (improved system of Education). His plan, beginning with the principles of the Christian Religion, as professed by the Established Church, comprises Reading, Writing, Arithmetic in all its branches.

English Grammar, Mensuration and Geography on the following terms, viz.:—

	£	s	d
Board and Tuition, *per annum*	16	0	0
Washing	1	10	0
Entrance		10	6

J.L. trusts, with premises in every respect calculated for a School, and unremitting attention to the moral and religious duties of his Pupils, to merit the public patronage.'

TWO FAMOUS MEN

Churchill was the birth place of two famous men, Warren Hastings, of Indian fame, and William Smith, the father of English Geology. A big stone obelisk, with tablet, to the memory of the latter, stands in the village; and not far away, a tablet on a wall records the fact that Warren Hastings was born there, in 1731. The manor had been in the Hastings family in Henry II's reign. John Hastings was vicar of Charlbury in 1364. Warren's grandfather was Rector of Daylesford, but poverty had come, and Warren, in some notes he left, says, speaking of the brook that flows in the valley:—

'To lie beside the margin of that stream was one of my favourite recreations, and there one bright summer's day when I was scarce 7 years old, I well remember that I formed the determination to purchase Daylesford. I was then dependent upon those whose condition scarcely raised them above the pressure of absolute want: yet somehow or other, the child's dream, as it did not appear reasonable at the moment, so in after years, never faded away.'

All the world knows at what a cost he won through and realised his dream.

In 1788 he was tried for his conduct of Indian affairs, great names were against him, but he was acquitted, after spending £70,000 on a seven years' trial.

Bells rang, cellars opened their doors, when the news of his acquittal was made known.

Stories of his ivory chair, his golden bedstead, linger yet about us. His terra cotta, urn-topped memorial, with 'Warren Hastings August 1828' upon it, at Daylesford, recalls the sulphurous heat of the day of his burial as told of by aged village men, and we are reminded that:—

'The boast of heraldry, the pomp of power,
And all that beauty, all that wealth e'er gave,
Await alike the inevitable hour
The paths of glory lead but to the grave.'

I have an autograph letter by Warren Hastings but do not know to whom it was sent.

COPY

Daylesford House, 23 Sept, 1801.

Dear Sir,

I am much obliged by the credit which you are pleased to allow to my opinion, and have read with much attention, and with much pain, the papers which you have done me the honor to send me for my perusal; and I now return them according to your desire.

Upon the subjects which have involved you in a disagreement with your colleagues in the direction, I have not sufficient materials to qualify me to form a decided judgment.

I regret exceedingly, as every friend of the East India Company must do, the necessity which has compelled you to relinquish the important office in the Direction, which you have so long and so ably filled: but that necessity you have demonstrated most clearly in your correspondence, and particularly in your letter announcing that intention to the Court of Directors.

Most sincerely wishing that the result of these unhappy divisions may be such as to restore to the Company the same benefit of your zeal and abilities, I have the honor to be with the greatest esteem,

Dear Sir,
Your much obliged
and faithful servant,
WARREN HASTINGS.

William Smith, born 1769, as a lad was the opposite to Warren Hastings, in that he was idle, and wandering; so the little schooling he had in the village did not benefit him as it might have done.

His father dying, his mother married again, and he was taken in charge by an uncle who, though not pleased at his wandering habits, and collections of stones picked up and brought home, yet procured him books on geometry and land surveying, and with these, and learning to draw, he qualified himself to be so proficient as to be able to take a place as assistant to a professional land surveyor, with whom he worked over this and other counties. His observations led him to make a notable discovery, and at the age of 23 he thought of an idea to make a model of the strata of the earth.

As he went further afield the idea of the stratification of the earth's surface possessed him, and as he talked constantly about it he was called 'Strata Smith.' Everything his observant eye saw his alert mind grasped, his discovery had been made, but not till 1814, after sacrificing all he possessed and then having to accept help from friends, did this brave self-taught man of science give to the world the result of 20 years' incessant thought and work: 'Wm. Smith's Map of the Strata of England and Wales.'

In 1831 the Geological Society of London gave him its medal.

In his simple way he gained for himself a name that will never be forgotten, by making one of the greatest discoveries as to the surface of the earth upon which we live. He died a poor man, that is, if to give all you possess to science, and then work at your business and earn your daily bread to the end is to be poor. The wandering, idle Churchill boy, by his genius and self denial, made good, and has left his

'Footprints on the sands of time.'

HACKER'S HOUSE

The name Hacker occurs in this district, and we think of the fateful days when 'Collonell ffrancis Hacker' conducted the execution of King Charles, for which he was executed in other days, as a traitor. Some have thought he lived at Churchill, but his home was at Colston Bassett.

In 1645 Ann Hacker, of Churchill, married Ralph Marshall, of Little Tew.

'Here lieth the body of Thomas Hacker of Kingham Gent., who died 15th Jan., 1733, in the 41st year of his age,' is one of the names on an altar tomb near the porch at Ascott-under-Wychwood.

When a very large flat stone near this tomb was lifted some years ago a skeleton lay prone beneath it, evidently a secret burial of some one to be quickly put out of the way. Who? When?

METHODISM

The Primitive Methodists worshipped for years in a tiny chapel in a lane; now a smart chapel has been erected on the Kingham road, where can worship those who prefer a simple service without elaborate ritual, which does not appeal to all.

1914—1918

The Memorial to those who fell in the Great War is of local stone.

Kingham. Konigs Ham

King's Home. Possibly the home of some petty prince in far away days.

Early relics of former residents have been found and Geoffrey de Mandeville has mention, 1086.

The Mill was worth 44 pence, so good trade was done.

Later the Beauchamp family, whose arms were formerly in the chancel window, possessed it.

> 'Many fledden from place to place because of the pestilence, but they were enfecte and myght not escape the dethe … When this pestilence was seased and ended as God wold, unnethe X part of the people were left on lyfe.'

So the old record states how the Black Death swept the land, and as at Kingham 'there was no one to buy, or sell, cattle, goods or chattles'; it looks as though its awful ravages were felt here.

WILLIAM DE WYKEHAM AND KINGHAM

'The King he sealed the charters, and Wykeham traced the plan,
And God, who gave him wisdom, prospered the lowly man.'

Born 1324 to John Long, and Sibill his wife, he took the name of his birth-place, Wykeham, as many did in that day. He seems to have made the best of the chances he had, and at twenty or about is in the service of the King, in whose long reign of 50 years he played a varied part, and though he had bitter enemies, yet he seems to have been a general blessing to his country. The benefit of his fellows, his great endeavour. He founded New College, Oxford, and it is interesting to remember that land belonging to that foundation at Kingham, was acquired by William de Wykeham all these years ago, and New College Governors are Lords of the Manor still,

Under his direction and fostering care seems to have been established what has been called the 'Truly English style of architecture, the Perpendicular.' His mason, William Winford, at New College, Oxford, produced what has been said to be possibly some of the finest Perpendicular work to be seen anywhere. When one sees in many of our churches in this district specimens of this beautiful style — the upper story of our Charlbury tower, the fine celestory [sic] at Chipping Norton, the tower at Kingham, the chancel at Adderbury — though perhaps some of it executed after he was gone to his reward, one feels the debt we owe to his genius, and the splendid masons about him, leaving as a legacy, all over our Wychwood district, of simple lines in stone, that, whilst most effective as to construction, give an idea of repose, strength, and beauty, to all beholders.

THE STOCKS

In 1376 Stocks were ordered to be set up, and though the village stocks have gone, the name persists in 'The Stocks Trees,' and 'The Stocks Well,' at the village green, and in thought we go back to the days of branding, whipping and confinement for those who deserted their masters or demanded more wages, having 'proud and covetous desires,' or misordered themselves in any way. William Fermour (to whom Henry VII granted part of the forfeited estates of Lord Lovell) in his will made Sept., 1552, refers to property he had at Kingham, Idbury, Foscote, Bold, Puddlehill, etc.

His monument at Somerton bears the following inscription:

'Here lyeth buried Mr. William Fermour, Esq., whyche was lord of this towne and patrone of this churche and also clarke of ye Crowne in ye King's Bench by King Henry ye 7th and King Henry ye 8th dayes whyche dyed ye 29th day of 7ber (September) in ye year of our lord god MCCCCCLII (1552), and also here lyeth Mestres Ellsabeth Fermour his last wyffe which was ye daughter of Sr. Wllm. Norrysse Kt., upon whose and all Christen soules Jhu have mercy.'

THE CHURCH

The Church of St. Andrew has features of interest, Perpendicular, and work of later periods greet you, earlier work seems to have been lost.

A church has mention in Stephen's day 1136. A Rector in 1260. Leonard Bawden, 1555.

The stone bench ends are unusual, and were cut by the Jackson family in the village in Victorian days. The chancel window in Spelsbury Church was cut and fixed by the same men, John Jackson, parish clerk, and stone cutter, with his sons, Frederick and Alfred.

A brass dated 1536 can be seen.

A man who did not wish to be buried in the ground was accommodated, the story goes, by being put into the wall in Kingham Church.

The Tower has pinnacles, a clock, and six bells.

Some years ago I saw a man cutting the ivy on the tower walls, standing in a tub, slung by ropes from the battlements, how he got out, and down, and shifted his tub, I did not see, but I looked at him in his novel perch with much interest.

A round lump of stone at the tower stairs' foot to prop the door open, has in days past been carried up to the top by lads, and then thrown down, no joke to have met it as it came thumping and banging down the winding stone steps.

The school

The Schoolroom, tithe barn formerly, I believe, used to stand close to the Church, and I have pleasant memories of attending full meetings, old and young, on winter nights some years ago for lectures on English History by the late Rector, and one on Henry VIII by Mr. Phillips.

The Methodists

The Wesleyan Chapel, the centre of much religious life and interest. Men and women found blessing and grace as they gathered in His Name. I recall Mr. Eaton, Mr. Belcher, Mr. Dennis Rose, Mr. George Keen, and think with pleasure of time spent in their company.

'With the morn those angel faces smile,
Which we have loved long since, and lost awhile.'

Kingham homes

These homes for boys built in no niggard style, but buildings of worth and quality, away on the hill, by the late Charles Edward Baring Young, Esquire, of Daylesford House, must have special mention. A big debt of gratitude is owing to this gentleman, who devoted a fortune to the building and maintaining. and endowing of this splendid institution, with school, workshops, masters, and chaplain, to help needy lads to a start in life. I wonder how many hundreds have, in the years, been set on their feet on this 'Delectable Hill?' We think of Him who said:— 'Inasmuch as ye have done it unto one of the least … ye have done it unto Me.'

A village of a thousand

Kingham has had prosperity at its doors beyond many a village. The presence of good class people residing there, the nurseries, the Engineering works, the Waggon works, the Building operations at Kingham Homes, all meant life, movement and money in circulation.

A native expressed his preference for the place by saying he would 'rather be hanged in Kingham than die a natural death at Churchill.'

Odds and Ends

Worms in teeth

When I was a lad a man told me, in all seriousness, that toothache was sometimes caused by maggots, or worms in the teeth, and these could be got out by
putting some henbane seed in a basin, and pouring boiling water over it, and
then wrapping your head and the basin in a cloth so the steam would go into
your mouth and the troublesome maggots would then crawl out. I believe he
told me he had done it. [Mr. Raymond Alden explains this Cotswold myth by
telling me that heat causes the seeds to explode and the contents are exactly like
whitish, tiny maggots.]

An old farm sale catalogue

'A Catalogue of all the Capital, Live and Dead Stock, and Farming
Utensils, of Mr. JOHN FARBROTHER, of Blandford Park, Farmer, near
Charlbury, in the County of Oxford deceased. Which will be sold by
Auction (without Reserve) by JOHN CHURCHILL and Son. On
Tuesday and Wednesday, the 7th and 8th of February, 1792, on the
Premises.'

Then follows particulars of 145 lots, including several rick staddles, a cyder
press complete, a malt mill, six dozen of twig hurdles, etc., etc. The above catalogue is yet preserved by a descendant, Mr. Thomas Fairbrother, Antiquary, of
Marcham, Berks.

Charlbury Archdeaconry papers give John Fairbrother as of Finstock in
1742, also 1789. The spelling was easy in former days, you spelt as you pleased
in those happy times.

Copy of will 1767

In the name of God Amen the twenty sixth day of March in the year of
our Lord 1767. I, Elizabeth Berisford of Charlbury in the County of
Oxford Spinster being very sick and weak in Body but of perfect Mind
and Memory thanks be given to Almighty God for this same, therefore
calling to Mind and Mortality of my Body and knowing that it is
appointed for all persons once to die do make and ordain this my last Will
and Testament in manner and form following that is to say Principally and

first of all I give and recommend my Soul into the hands of God that gave it, and for my Body I recommend to the earth to be buried in a Christian-like and decent manner at ye descretion of my Executer and all my just Debts and funeral charges shall be paid and discharged. Item I give to my well-beloved Son William Berisford one Messuage or Tennement with the appurtenances thereunto belonging situated lying and being in the town of Charlbury at a certain place called or known by the Name of Pound Hill butted and bounded by John Williams on ye South and the Road lyeing to Spelsbury on the North, to the use and behoof of William Berisford and his heirs for ever whom I likewise constitute make and ordain my only and sole Executor of this my last will and testament.

In witness whereof I have hereunto set my hand and Seal ye day and year above written Elizabeth Berisford's X mark. Elizabeth Berisford sined sealed published pronounced and declared in ye presence of us William Harwood H Edward Claydon H Edward Neal.

A DEED OF GIFT 1797

'To all people to whom these presents shall come I Mary Parker do send greeting know ye that i the said mary parker of the parrish of Nauntin In the County of gloster for and in Consideration of the Love and good will and afection which i have and do bear towards my loving husbon William parker of the same parrish and County Have given and granted and by these presents do freely give and grant unto the Said William Parker his heir, Executers or Administraters all and Singular my too housen and barn out housis gardins Leying or being in the parish of Lower Swell and in posseson of William Brooks and the other Locate in the posseson of John Sale with the barn or out housen gardins or what-ever belongs to the Same of which these presents i have delivered to he the said William Parker. Signed with mine own Hand bearing even date to have and to hould all the Said to housen barn and gardens out houses to he the Said William Parker his heirs from henceforth as his and their proper housen etc. in witness whereof i have hereunto set my hand and Seal this tenth Day of Jan. 1797. Signed in the presents of us. William Rowlands.'

Conclusion

If any serf, villein, or slave in days of yore could escape and live unmolested for a year and a day here, he was free, we are told. How proud and thankful we should be of the name Charlbury, and what it denotes—

'THE HOME OF THE FREE MEN'

Freedom to work, to worship, to play any part of which one is capable, and in a most delightful bit of countryside about whose story I have tried to write. I am glad our Lord was a villager. How natural and homely is the Gospel story, village life, ways and people.

> 'And so the shadows fall apart,
> And so the west winds play,
> And all the windows of my heart
> I'd open to the day.'

FAREWELL, GENTLE READER.

Rediscovering Kibble

Among the joys of re-publishing John Kibble's books have been the phone calls and visits from people who still remember Kibble today.

Among historians he cuts a frustrating figure, always writing about documents he has perused or artefacts in his possession, yet leaving no clue where these things may be found now. But people who knew him have fond memories.

Roy Townsend, who wrote the Foreword to our edition of *Wychwood Forest and its Border Places*, recalled childhood memories of a man fascinated by anything historical and eager to infect children with his curiosity. It can be coincidence that Roy later founded the Finstock Local History Society.

Christine Henman phoned to say her father was a friend of Kibble, who gave him a stone carving for a house he was building himself in New Road, Woodstock. Kibble made punts and people took them on

Kibble re-used this carving by inserting it (face down) in the floor of his house.

the mill stream. But no punting on Sundays…

Blanche Wright (who is 86 this year, and whose grandfather, William James Wright, was a Baptist preacher) clearly remembers him preaching in the Baptist chapel in Shipton-under-Wychwood when she was a little girl. She even remembers the topic of his sermon: he preached against racial prejudice, saying that white people and coloured people couldn't do without one another.

A dragon? Another carving that never found its way out of the carver's garden.

Marjorie Currie recalls John Kibble walking from the chapel after a service, tilting his head so that he would not catch sight of The Bull as he went past.

And Jack Baston came up trumps with the photo of John and Florence Kibble that is reproduced in the front of this book. Kibble ('a real gentleman', says Jack) gave him one of his books not long before he died, and stuck this tiny photograph of himself and his wife in the front of it.

Jon Carpenter

Janet Biggs writes:

John Kibble moved from Finstock to Charlbury in the early part of the century. He continued his work as a stonemason and worked on the estates at Blenheim, Ditchley and Cornbury. An elderly resident of Charlbury, who knew him, told me that he was interested in many things, from his punting business (he hired out punts on the mill stream in Charlbury), to his nineteen garden sheds, some thatched, some tin-roofed, in which he kept a variety of animals — goats, donkeys, hens and ducks. She says he was also known to have acquired a horse-box from the GWR, which housed his various collections and in which he sometimes slept. Groups of children from the school would come to see his collection of fossils, and there he also made a telescope.

John Kibble was a Methodist, and as a child the lady I talked to attended the Methodist Chapel as often as she attended St. Mary's. She tells of Kibble requiring her, as a member of the Band of Hope, to 'sign the Pledge' at a very young age. He preached frequently in the area. A story is told of how, when he preached in Chilson, his congregation, composed primarily of exhausted agricultural workers, would doze off during his sermons until a thunderous

This statue of Queen Victoria was found in two pieces in Kibble's garden after his death. The shoulders were missing, but were improvised by someone else so that Her Majesty could stand in full dignity again!

exhortation to 'REPENT' shook them awake again. He would then observe that failure to obey would bring similar shocks.

Kibble appears to have been held in some awe in later life, partly no doubt because of his appearance, as he had a long grey beard in the 1940s. This was uncommon in that clean-shaven age and must have given him the air of belonging to a much earlier time. But he was known, too, as a gentle and friendly person; the old lady who shared her memories with me recalled how her small daughter expressed a wish that he could be her third 'Grampy'.

A plaster model for a carving of a Cotswold sheep.

The Wychwood Press

The Wychwood Press publishes books of local interest, particularly those of relevance to the area of West Oxfordshire within the medieval royal forest of Wychwood. This area is loosely bounded by Witney, Eynsham, Woodstock, Chipping Norton and Burford, and includes Charlbury and neighbouring villages.

All our books are illustrated, and all are available post free.

We have already published new editions of
John Kibble's **Wychwood Forest and its Border Places** (£7.50), and
Beryl Schumer's **Wychwood: The Evolution of a Wooded Landscape** (£7.50).

Forthcoming titles will include:

• **The Salt of the Earth**, a true and moving account by Dorothy Calcutt of a year in the life of a poor Woodstock family at the turn of the last century. [September 1999] £7.50

• '**Walk Humble, My Son**', Eric Moss's memories of growing up in Ascott under Wychwood between 1918-1939, an authentic description of a way of life that few people can now remember. Together with **My Personal Memories** by Doris Warner. [September 1999] £8

• **The Land of Catavacus**, an account by archaeologist Tim Copeland of life in Wychwood before, during and after the Roman occupation, including a gazeteer of places where you can see Iron Age and Roman remains.

• **The Ascott Martyrs** by Ralph Mann; the definitive story of the 'riots' and imprisonment in 1873, the historical context and the political and social consequences. [March 2000]

• **Discovering Wychwood**, published in association with The Wychwood Project: including contributions by Beryl Schumer, Kate Tiller, Alan Spicer, Mary Webb and Belinda Flitter. Royalties to The Wychwood Project.

• **The History of Charlbury** by Lois Hey, very thoroughly researched.

• Writings and talks by **W.D. ('Bill') Campbell**, edited by Mary Jackson, with many of his Guardian articles.

• An updated and abridged edition of Vernon Watney's rare work, **Cornbury and the Forest of Wychwood**, undertaken by Charles Tyzack.

This is a substantial and time-consuming local history project. Your help, particularly with the recording of oral history, getting documents onto computer or research in libraries, could be invaluable. Ideas for future books or authors are also very welcome. Please contact:

Jon Carpenter, The Wychwood Press, 2 The Spendlove Centre, Charlbury OX7 3PQ • Tel / fax 01608 811969